LOST Identity
The Characters of LOST

By Pearson Moore

LOST
Identity

The Characters of LOST

Pearson Moore

LOST Identity
The Characters of LOST

Cover concept by Pearson Moore 2011
Cover art by Robin Ludwig, Robin Ludwig Design Inc. 2011

Printed by Inukshuk Press

ISBN 978-0615508290

To the fans of LOST

Table of Contents

The Young Woman (The inspector's guide)

"This show is about people who are metaphorically lost in their lives, who get on an airplane, and crash on an island, and become physically lost on the planet Earth. And once they are able to metaphorically find themselves in their lives again, they will be able to physically find themselves in the world again. When you look at the entire show, that's what it will look like. That's what it's always been about."

—Damon Lindelof, interview with IGN, January, 2007

"It's all about the characters."

The anxious-looking inspector stopped on the jungle path, peered into the young woman's face, and frowned. "Wait a minute!" The man's eyes bulged out and he anchored his hands at his hips. "You told me two months ago it's not about the characters. So which is it?"

She shook her head. "That's not what I said. I told you it was all about relationships." She dropped her rifle to the ground and massaged her shoulder.

"Relationships?" The inspector's mouth hung open.

"Yes," the young woman said, dropping down to a crouch, "relationships. She glanced up at him. "Didn't you already send in your report?"

The inspector nodded. "Two months ago. I recommended 'LOST Humanity.' I told 'em it was all about the mythology."

"No." The young woman shook her head. "The mythology is all about relationships. Everything on the Island is about the characters." She adjusted the strap on her rifle.

A voice from the jungle: "It's not about guns, that's for sure."

The inspector, surprised by the familiar voice, pivoted on his foot. The older woman approaching them wore a pleasant smile on her face and an orchid on her blouse. Her hair was beginning to grey, but she was otherwise exactly the same as she had been during the first six years.

"Hey," the young woman said, rising to her feet, "where's Bernard?"

The older woman laughed. "He and Vincent are out 'fishing'—that's what he calls it, anyway. He never catches anything, but it's not for lack of trying. I didn't know you were back on the Island. Aren't you staying with Aaron and Claire?"

"Aaron's on summer vacation," the young woman said. "Claire told me to take a break."

The older woman nodded. "Who's your friend?"

The young woman replaced the rifle on her shoulder. "He's an inspector." She glanced at him. "University of Michigan, right?"

"Yeah," the inspector said, wiping the sweat from his brow. "Ann Arbor campus."

The young woman adjusted the rifle strap to a more comfortable position. "He came here a couple of months ago, doing research for a book. It was good."

"You read it?" the inspector asked.

She nodded. "Every page."

"Oh," the older woman said, "'LOST Humanity.' The one you loaned me last month. Bernard and I loved it." She turned to the inspector. "You wrote it?"

The inspector shook his head.

The young woman pulled a water bottle from her belt. "Some pharmaceutical scientist wrote it. He confirmed everything I believe about the Island."

The older woman smiled knowingly and nodded. "It's all about the characters."

"What?" the inspector shouted.

The two women looked at him with shocked expressions.

"Have you both lost your minds?" He glared at the older woman. "How can you say 'LOST Humanity' was all about the characters? The book focussed on the mythology of the show. It had nothing to do with the characters!"

The older woman shifted her gaze to the jungle brush and frowned. She seemed deep in thought for a moment, but then she pushed back her shoulders and looked over at the inspector, her face taut and resolute. "Follow me." The older woman strode past the instructor, heading toward the beach.

The young woman choked on her water but managed to replace the bottle on her belt in a single motion. She took fast strides to catch up with the older woman and the inspector followed.

"Where—" the inspector struggled to catch his breath "—where are we going?"

"There." The older woman pointed through the clearing to a couple of figures sitting on the sand close to the trees. She glanced down at the young woman's belt. "Knife," she said, pointing to the sheathed hunting blade at the young woman's side.

The young woman quickly unbuckled the knife case, dropped it to the dirt, and looked up at the inspector. "You need to remove all your knives and leave them here."

"Why?"

"Trust me," she said, "it's just easier."

The older woman already stood by the side of the two men sitting near the tree and seemed to be in animated discussion with the long-haired man. The young woman led the way. The inspector tried his best to keep up with her but he lost ground with every effortless step she took across the hot sand.

The men on the beach faced each other across a familiar brown board. The inspector recognised the millionaire Protector of the Island and his one-time nemesis, now assistant—the person the Protector called "Number Two."

By the time he reached the sand the women were already at the side of the men playing backgammon and the inspector had to run to catch up. Just as he approached the four of them, the Protector waved to him and gave a big grin.

"Welcome back, dude," the Protector said. "I thought you were done with your report?"

"Thank you, sir. I am done, but I had to come back. Apparently the University is considering a second LOST book for their curriculum. They asked me to conduct more research, sir."

"Aw, you don't have to 'sir' me, dude. Just 'Hurley' is fine."

"But," Number Two said, peering at the inspector with stern eyes, "please keep your knife sheathed."

The inspector peered at the young woman with a quizzical expression. "What's the problem with knives?"

The young woman lifted the rifle off her shoulder and dropped the butt to the ground. "Ben doesn't allow drawn knives in Hurley's presence. The last guy who tried it just wanted to cut rope. Ben had him sprawled on the dirt before he could get the knife out."

The inspector frowned. "But he allows guns?"

The young woman grabbed the rifle, rammed the butt against her shoulder, aimed it at the Protector, and wrapped her finger around the trigger. The inspector gasped.

The Protector laughed and looked over at Number Two. "Hey, dude, it's your turn."

Number Two rolled the dice. "You can shoot the Protector all you like," he said, not bothering to look up. He moved two of the white pieces on the board.

"Believe me," the older woman said, "Kate has personal experience in this matter."

The young woman laughed and lowered the gun back down to her side. "Save your bullets, a guy told me once."

"The Man in Black," the inspector said.

The Protector and the young woman frowned and looked away.

The older woman took a couple of steps toward the inspector and leaned in close. "Around here," she whispered, "we don't mention Him Who Shall Not Be Named. It's because of him that Kate's a widow."

"A widow?" the inspector asked. "But they never got—"

The older woman's angry glare stopped the inspector from completing his sentence.

The young woman peered down at Number Two. "Why do you even play him, Ben? You never win."

"It's not whether you win or lose," Number Two said, "it's how—"

"It's how the *Protector* plays the game," the older woman said, finishing Number Two's sentence.

Number Two looked up at the older woman and gave a half smile. "Exactly."

The Protector rolled the dice and two fours came up.

Number Two's eyes grew big. "Eight, Hugo!"

The Protector jumped to his feet, took a step forward, a step back, gyrated his hips, and danced around the board. The two women laughed. The inspector stared, dumbfounded.

The young woman peered into the inspector's face. "It's Hurley's number, remember?"

"Aha." The inspector turned to the Protector, who had resumed his place and was moving black pieces on the board. "So the numbers *are* important?"

"Naw," the Protector said. "Ben just gets a kick out of it when I do the Eight Dance."

The inspector frowned. "But what about the Valenzetti Equation? The Dharma Initiative? Preventing the end of the world?"

The Protector turned around and glared at the inspector. "Dude, the numbers don't mean anything. The Dharma people, they were wacked out. They had that Valenzetti thing 'cause they didn't know any better." His expression softened. "Anyway, you make your own luck. Didn't you see 'Tricia Tanaka Is Dead'?"

"Yes, but—"

"What Hugo's trying to say," Number Two said, "is that human volition transcends laws of science. Even the Valenzetti Equation, well researched as it may be, cannot account for the variability of human response to a given situation."

"Yeah," the Protector said, shifting his eyes around. "What he said."

"So," the inspector asked, directing his gaze at Number Two, "you're saying the entire mythology of this Island has no meaning?"

"No, not at all. Every last bit of the mythology has meaning. In fact, the Island has so much meaning it determines the limits of life and death. Number One and I are still learning. Not even Jacob understood everything. Jack Shephard was the only one who ever put all the pieces together, and he saved the Island—he saved all of us. He told Desmond, 'There are no shortcuts, no do-overs. What happened, happened. Trust me, I know. All of this matters.' Number One and I live by those words, every day." Number Two turned his attention back to the game.

"But..." the inspector couldn't find words to express his thought. He turned to the young woman. "If it all comes down to the characters, how could anything on the Island matter?"

The young woman frowned and gazed down at the two players. She stared at them for several moments then turned to face the inspector. Her eyes were intense. "Hurley and Ben are playing backgammon, right?"

"Yeah."

"So," she said, "what if the Island makes it rain here?"

"I suppose they'd put up a tarp, or go play inside."

"But they're still having to change what they're doing because of the Island, right?"

"Yeah, but it's just common sense."

"Okay, but suppose now it's not Hurley and Ben playing, but it's Claire and Thomas."

The inspector frowned. "Who's Thomas?"

"Claire's boyfriend, back in Australia, remember?"

The inspector slapped his hand to his forehead and smiled. "Right."

"Okay, now suppose they're not playing backgammon, but they're playing 'let's make a baby', and they're on the Island before Jack fixed everything."

"Then I'd say Claire's in deep trouble."

"She'll die, right?"

"Unless Juliet's drug can prevent the effects high-field electromagnetism."

"Right. Now, is that 'just common sense', too?"

"I see what you're saying. The Island affected everything."

The young woman raised her eyebrows. "The Island had its own personality."

Number Two looked up from his game. "An extraordinary personality. And because of that, our actions and what we believed about the Island and about each other took on tremendous importance."

"And," the young woman said, "our relationships with each other."

The older woman nodded. "It's all about the relationships."

The inspector gazed at the older woman. "You're talking about the Constant Relationship, the Strange Attractor Relationship, the—"

She shook her head. "We don't call it that. You think I call Bernard my 'Constant'?"

The Protector looked up at them. "Yeah, and that 'Strange Attractor' stuff? Dude, that's so twisted. The argument wasn't over truth and lies. Ben doesn't lie anymore."

The older woman crossed her arms. "It wasn't for lack of trying."

The Protector stood up and faced the older woman. "Yeah, but I mean, it wasn't about telling the truth or telling lies. It was about thinking things through. See, Ben thinks about things, then he figures out what to do. I need that 'cause, well... I don't always think about things before I do something."

Number Two chimed in. "Hugo doesn't need to think things through, Rose. He has a built-in sense of right and wrong—something I wish I had more of. He knows instinctively what to do."

"Yeah," the Protector said, shifting his focus to Number Two, "maybe. But you explain stuff to me, dude. That helps."

Number Two looked down and smiled. "That's my job, Hugo."

"Wait a minute," the inspector said, frowning at the Protector, "You're saying 'LOST Humanity' got it all wrong?"

"No, I'm not sayin' that. I'm just, well..."

Number Two placed the dice on the board and looked up at the inspector. "You have to consider the person who wrote 'LOST Humanity.' He's a scientist."

"Pharmaceutical chemist," the young woman said.

"Yes," Number Two said, rising to his feet. "He invoked aspects of chaos theory, and especially the notion of strange attractors, as a model for understanding human interaction between characters. He wasn't trying to say 'this is how it is.' He was proposing a model, that's all. It was just a way of looking at things intended to help us understand."

"Some characters more than others," the young woman said, frowning. "He never wrote about Libby."

The Protector looked down at the sand and shrugged. "Some characters are more important than others."

"She was important to you," the young woman said. "Therefore she was important."

"Yeah," the Protector said. "But if I was writin' about the characters, I'd do it right."

"What do you mean?" the inspector asked.

"I mean, I'd start from the very beginning, with the very first character."

"Jack?" the older woman asked.

"No," Number Two said, "I think he means—"

"No!" The older woman's jaw dropped. "You can't seriously mean you'd devote an entire chapter to a—"

"Look," the Protector said, "It's not just that he was the first character. He appeared in more episodes than Jacob, Christian Shephard, and Eloise Hawking *combined*."

The older woman stared at him in disbelief. "You **are** serious?"

The Protector nodded. "I am." He turned to the inspector. "You wanna write another book about the Island? You gotta start with the first character, the most loyal character."

The inspector frowned. "But I'm not—"

"Kate," the Protector said, glancing at the young woman, "you like writing: Tell him how to start his new book."

"Okay," the young woman said. Her knitted brow revealed deep concentration. "I think I'd try to set the mood. It has to be done right, because he was the only major character who never uttered a word. Maybe passive voice, even though it's usually weaker. Hmmm... Maybe I'd begin with something like, 'The very first episode was told from his point of view...'"

The Agent

CHAPTER 1: THE AGENT

Vincent is...a dog who seems to know something more about the island.

—Thunderfyre, Book References on LOST,
community.comcast.net, June 2, 2007

The very first episode was told from his point of view. He appeared in more episodes than Jacob, Christian Shephard, and Eloise Hawking *combined.* He was the only character to appear in both the opening scene and the closing scene of LOST—and live to tell the tale.

Loyal to the survivors, devoted to their safety, Vincent displayed a keen sense of purpose and an unfailing faculty for belonging. The thesis of LOST, first expressed in Episode 1.05 ("White Rabbit") was a constant touchstone for him. He was dedicated sentinel, faithful guardian, constant companion. Most of all, he gave final and truest expression to LOST's core philosophy.

The creative forces behind LOST could have chosen to begin and end the series in any way they wished. They chose to reveal their world to us through the eyes of a dog, and made him final witness to the closing chapter of their work. They must have had a reason for making this choice. Indeed. This is Vincent's story.

The Mobisodes

The thirteen "Mobisodes" (Lost Missing Pieces, first released on Verizon Wireless mobile phones from November 2007 to January 2008) are not unnecessary "extras." They are short but essential vignettes and fully a part of the greater series. They were produced with the same actors, directors and production crew as the larger, multi-scene episodes, and are an indelible part of the LOST canon. They not only provided additional and essential information, but in at least four cases they were intended to radically change our understanding of specific, key characters and events.

Mobisode #1, "The Watch", provides critical information on the relationship between Christian and Jack. In this brief scene, Christian gives Jack his own father's watch as a present on the eve of Jack's wedding to Sarah. With the watch come these game-changing words from Christian: "Would you do me a favor? If you and Sarah ever have a kid, try to treat him a little better than I treated you." This is a strong and quite reliable indicator of a previously-unrevealed part of Christian's character. As apparently mean and insensitive as he was toward his son, he genuinely loved Jack.

Mobisode #6, "Room 23", is crucial to LOST's end game. In this 80-second-long episode, we learn critical information about Walter Lloyd, the ten-year-old who scared the wits out of Benjamin Linus. Juliet reports, "He [Walter] has done it again." She and the Others want to give the boy back to his father, but Ben insists they keep him. "Jacob wanted him here. He's important. He's special," Ben says. In light of developments several years later, we now understand Jacob's summons of the boy: Walter Lloyd would eventually be called back, possibly to take Jacob's place as Protector of the Island.

As revealing as these earlier mobisodes were, the final one, Mobisode #13, stands alone.

So It Begins

The episode opens with the character rushing erratically through tall grass, looking about, moving one way, changing direction, trotting forward. We hear the rustling of the grass and a constant rhythm of panting. Whenever something interesting appears in the frame we hear loud sniffing. All of this is occurring half a metre above the ground.

These are the opening seconds of LOST, told not from the point of view of woman or man, but from the perspective of a four-legged canine rushing through the tropical forest. This was no cutesy one-off by a back-bench crew member, reaching for some artistic second take on LOST's opening moments. The episode was directed by Jack Bender, the executive producer who assumed directorial command over only the most important episodes. This two-minute episode, then, was crucial to the story.

The audacity of this was stunning. I was disoriented by the mobisode to the point that I had to view it several times before finally making some sense of the strong imagery. Why would the creative leadership behind a billion-dollar entertainment franchise choose a dog to relate the pivotal first moments of the story?

Vincent had something important to tell us, and it was essential that we understood whatever this thing was from his perspective. This was the hypothesis I began to formulate after several viewings of the mind-warping final mobisode. Jack Bender needed to communicate something at least meaningful, and he chose to do so from the dog's perspective.

When Vincent heard Christian's summoning whistle the episode became not just interesting but compelling. Christian grabbed Vincent by the jowls and gave him a curious set of instructions.

A Dog On A Mission

"I need you to go find my son," Christian told Vincent. "He's over there in that bamboo forest, unconscious. I need you to go wake him up. Okay? Go on. He has work to do."

Christian does not point to Jack's location. He does not lead Vincent there. He provides verbal instruction only. He somehow expects Vincent to understand what a bamboo forest is, that a man is unconscious in that forest, and that it is his job to wake the man.

What is Christian's basis for believing this dog, as disoriented as anyone else after falling ten thousand metres from the sky, could understand and obey a complex set of verbal instructions? How many dogs in this world understand anything more complicated than Sit, Stay, Roll Over, and Shake Hands? In fact, don't dog trainers tell us that these simple commands are more a matter of intonation than anything else? I would imagine dogs understand human speech as well as they read our books and newspapers. Perhaps Christian caught Vincent reading a few pages of *War and Peace* during his sojourn in the on-board doggie kennel.

I suppose we cannot hope to understand the full ramifications of Vincent's assignment without understanding something of Christian's mission. Christian has an agenda. "He has work to do," Christian says of his son, Jack. Christian's task is to prepare Jack for the great three-year mission.

The prevailing theory regarding Christian is that his form, even in this opening scene of LOST, was inhabited by the Smoke Monster. While circumstantial support for this theory is strong, I believe the theory is weak, and cannot explain many events, such as Christian's appearance on the freighter in the moments before it exploded.

Of the more than sixty LOST essays I have penned, the most widely read is "White Rabbit: The Cultural and Symbolic Importance of Christian Shephard" (http://pearsonmoore-gets-lost.com/WhiteRabbit.aspx), in which I dispel the idea that Christian's form was ever taken by the Man in Black. When we see Christian in LOST, we are seeing Jack's father, not the Smoke Monster. If you have not already done so, you may wish to read "White Rabbit" and consider the argument. For the remainder of this essay, I will assume Christian's form is occupied by Christian and no one else.

On the Road to Emmaus

Christian was dead. Darleton referred to him as one of the Island's "undead". He was an apparition, but a very special type of apparition. Some apparitions were simple, such as the forms occupied by the Smoke Monster. Smokey went into people's minds, found the image of a loved one, and took on that form. He did this with Eko's brother, Yemi, and with Richard's wife, Isabella, for example.

Christian's post-death apparitions were more complex than those perpetrated by the Man in Black. He had not only form, but substance and character, too. He was pronounced dead in Sydney, but no one ever saw him in the coffin, even in the sideways world. On the two occasions that Jack investigated, he found an empty tomb.

Something caused Christian to become "undead." But much more occurred to change Christian, to make him something more than the person he had been before his death. He had no tasks in mind for his son prior to his death. But on the Island, his agenda was clear. He articulated instructions to Vincent in precise, fluid language without hesitation in a tone meant to convey gravitas and immediacy.

He could not have conceived of any such agenda prior to his arrival on the Island. The Others lived on the far side of the Island and did not interact with Christian. Jacob did not talk with dead people. The Smoke Monster was not responsible for Christian's reanimation, nor did he suggest any mission to Jack's father. The only reasonable possibility is obvious: Christian received his marching orders from the only remaining entity that could have provided him with a purpose: the Island.

Christian Shephard, in his Island apparitions, acted as agent and representative of the Island (see *LOST Humanity*, Chapter 18 for a more complete discussion of this idea).

In like manner, Vincent could never have understood complex human speech prior to his arrival on the Island. The Island worked its strange magic on the dog, too. Vincent became Christian's first lieutenant, a canine agent in service to the Island.

Focus on the Mission

This was not the last time we would receive essential information from a dog's perspective. In the first hour of the pilot episode a similar event occurred, and it conveyed no less meaning than the beginning of Vincent's mission only hours before.

KATE: [to Jack] Have you ever heard of Drive Shaft?
CHARLIE: [singing] You all everybody... You all every...body.
JACK: [shakes his head] We've got to keep moving.
KATE: They were good.
CHARLIE: They are good. We're still together. In the middle of a comeback.
[Kate and Charlie follow Jack into the jungle]
[Camera pans down to reveal Vincent watching them from behind a bush]

The scene is rich with visual cues, to the point that the dialogue is essentially inconsequential. In fact, in light of the way this scene was shot, I believe only a single line of dialogue in the entire sequence had relevance to the character through whom we experienced the scene.

The scene was given entirely from Vincent's point of view, as was revealed at the end of the sequence. We saw Kate, Charlie, and Jack in close-up, but it was always from the high end of the field containing the tall grass and bushes from which Vincent took in the proceedings. As the scene ended, the camera pulled away from the human characters and then back behind a leafy bush, revealing the back of Vincent's head as he watched the three survivors walk into the jungle, toward the front end of the plane.

The next shot was revealing and downright chilling. Vincent did not take in the scene as disinterested bystander. He was not there in that spot at that time by coincidence, as future events of this type clearly revealed. He was there perhaps out of canine choice, but he was almost certainly there primarily in his capacity as agent on a mission.

His eyes revealed the truth. His eyes were not disinterested, but alert, focussing on the humans, and tracking their every move. The intense interest in his eyes indicated an absorption in the event as it unfolded. He had a stake in what was transpiring. This was nothing less than a continuation of the commission he had received from Christian. "I need you to go find my son," Christian said. "He has work to do." Vincent was there, behind the bushes, continuing the mission, keeping tabs on Jack, who had work to do. Jack was about to come face to face with one of the Island's greatest mysteries, and he could not back down from it or become distracted.

Only five words prevented Vincent from running toward the humans and directing them toward the plane. "We've got to keep moving," Jack said. The expression on Jack's face, the way he shook his head after Kate asked about Drive Shaft, and finally those critical five words, communicated everything Vincent needed to see and hear. Jack was focussed on the mission. Vincent did not need to step in and redirect him. Things were going as planned.

The first few times I saw this scene, I thought Jack was indicating his indifference to Drive Shaft, that he had probably never heard of the group. But in light of Vincent's keen interest and unbroken concentration throughout the scene, I have to believe the scene was oriented around Jack's reaction to Kate's question, and that the real importance, the fundamental concept the director wished us to extract, was that both Jack and Vincent were driven by their new sense of responsibility.

Jack, though he didn't know it, was already in league with a young boy's dog, the somehow resurrected image of his dead father, and an Island that had reached out for him across an ocean, through the agency of its ancient Protector. Today, reviewing the scene again, I realised it was possible Jack not only knew of Drive Shaft, but for all it mattered, he could have been Drive Shaft's biggest fan at St. Sebastian's. Maybe he papered his office with Drive Shaft posters. It didn't matter. The only thing that mattered to Jack was finding the front end of the plane, locating the transceiver, and radioing for help. The only thing that mattered to Vincent was that Jack stay on the path of discovery, confrontation, growth, and enlightenment.

Perhaps other seeds were planted by Vincent. Charlie would recover from the airplane lavatory the bag holding his greatest temptation—the temptation he would have to confront and overcome to achieve his own redemption and martyrdom. Kate, likewise, would have to confront the most terrifying evil, the entity that above any other would seem to justify a life based on running away. Wouldn't anyone be justified in running away from a formless, unstoppable evil? But she would, of course, learn to hold her ground, stand up to evil, and eventually overcome fear and the worst evil, which for her was not the Smoke Monster, but the unbridled need to run away.

Vincent's Allegiance

When important events were underway, Vincent was often dispatched to ensure the participation of critical players. In Episode 2.01, Shannon had just lost Vincent, who ran away into the jungle. Walt asked her to take care of the dog, and with the ache inside she felt over the death of her half-brother, Boone, she needed Vincent more than ever.

As she and Sayid searched the jungle, Vincent barked so they could locate him, and then they saw him. As soon as he was sure they saw him, he ran and Shannon followed. She needed to hear Walt's words, which sounded garbled, but when run backwards, were easily distinguished: "Don't press the button. Button bad."

A relatively good case can be made that Walt's apparition was in some way under the control of the Smoke Monster, even though Walt was not dead. The LOST Podcast of March 21, 2008, includes this discussion between Damon Lindelof and Carlton Cuse concerning apparitions:

Carlton Cuse: Walt.
[Both laughing]
Damon Lindelof: Walt the *person* is a person.
Carlton Cuse: Right.
Damon Lindelof: But there are, there are *apparitions* of Walt that may not be Walt.
Carlton Cuse: Ok.
Damon Lindelof: And also Monster-related.
Carlton Cuse: [chuckling] Excellent.

Darlton tended to mix jokes with serious communication of information to such an extent that it has often been impossible to determine when they were being serious. The above exchange is as close as we will ever come to determining the Monster's participation in Walt's apparitions. Even Lostpedia, which tends to believe the Smoke Monster is responsible for essentially every apparition on the Island, could not definitively assign this apparition of Walt to the Smoke Monster, choosing to say "it is not clear" that the Monster was involved.

If the Monster was responsible for Walt's words to Shannon, we must consider the possibility that Vincent, by association, was in league with the Man in Black. However, I believe a relatively strong case can be made that Vincent was the agent of an entirely separate entity.

Agent of Redemption

In Episode 2.22 ("Three Minutes"), Vincent runs from the beach up to Eko's church, where Charlie is working. The dog is carrying one of the Virgin Mary statues in his teeth, and he drops the statue at Charlie's feet. Charlie looks at the statue and says, "Are you kidding me?" Vincent picks up the statue, tosses his head around, and releases the statue, as if trying to throw it at Charlie. The very clear meaning of Vincent's action is "No, I'm not kidding you." Charlie still can't believe it. He has sworn off drugs, but here is this dog, forcing him to confront his worst temptation yet again. "Did someone put you up to this?" Charlie asks, picking up the statue. In response, Vincent turns around in the direction from which he came, and Charlie follows.

When Vincent leads Charlie to the full stash of statues in Sawyer's dug-out hiding place, Charlie makes the most mature decision of his life. He throws every one of the statues out to sea, believing Vincent is his only witness. The importance of this is that he is entirely his own man, not beholden to drugs, not answerable to anyone. He has truly given up drugs this time, forever. He requires no human sounding board anymore to convince himself or others of a half-truth he wishes to believe is the full reality of his inner self. For the first time in his life, outer actions match inner state without deviation. He is a complete, uncompromised human being.

When he looks to his left to see Locke sitting on the sand, it is as if Locke is putting the seal on Vincent's work and Charlie's conversion. At this point in the series Locke is still the father figure, the mysterious man who answers only to the Island. By looking on, almost indifferently, Locke is the stand-in for the Island itself. The Island knows what Charlie has done. He is now ready for the final stage in his inexorable march toward martyrdom.

Vincent is the agent of Charlie's growth into responsible adulthood and his eventual attainment of the high degree of maturity that will be required to embrace his final destiny. It is Charlie who sets in motion the cascade of events that leads to the installation of Jack as the Protector of the Island. I find it difficult, indeed, to see the hand of the Man in Black as having had any part in Charlie's development. The Man in Black was all about instilling fear and promoting addictions; witness his fear-mongering intervention in Richard's life, for example. That Charlie became sober, without fears and addictions, is a state entirely opposed to the disposition the Smoke Monster sought for those under his control. The Man in Black was not responsible for Charlie's growth. By association, it seems unlikely that Vincent could have been the Smoke Monster's agent.

The Halls of Shambala

Only a few episodes later, Vincent again came prancing toward a survivor, this time with a skeletal arm in his teeth. But not just any human arm: the arm carried a rabbit-foot keychain, and attached to it, a single tarnished, weathered key. It was too much for an auto mechanic to resist. When Hurley crouched down, trying to entice Vincent toward him so he could grab the key, Vincent instead pivoted, lunged, and ran back into the jungle. The dog allowed Hurley to catch up, dropped the bait at the man's feet, and ran further into the jungle. Hurley was fascinated enough by the key that he forgot about Vincent for a few seconds, but the dog was one of the more insistent of the Island's agents, and he started barking again as soon as it was clear Hurley was no longer following him to the great prize. When Hurley finally responded to Vincent's entreaties, what he saw was beyond anyone's imagination.

A van with a battery thirty years dead is a bit more of a challenge to start than a souped-up Camaro that needs only a new carburetor. But it was the perfect vehicle to test the theory that Hurley was cursed.

Curses instill a species of fear surpassing the worst kind of terror. A curse is a severe limitation imposed from outside. It is something over which the one cursed has no control. A curse exudes an aura of inevitability. Somehow, a curse has the power to bend the laws of the universe in such a way that the accursed must bear whatever catastrophes, hardships, and unforeseen horrors the curse decides to impose.

Curses are the most potent tool of someone like the Man in Black. He would have endeavoured at all costs to prevent Hurley from ever questioning or testing the dangerous assertion that he was not cursed, that he could make his own luck. The curse hanging over Hurley's head was one of the strongest cards in the Man in Black's hand, and one he would have been loath to give up. As long as Hurley believe he was cursed, he would suffer under the traumatic emotional bonds that would inhibit him from attempting anything innovative—anything that might disturb the predictable backdrop the Man in Black required to advance his plan.

If the Island was to regain its correct bearings, something would have to be done to thwart the Man in Black. The most effective move, since the two principal players were stalemated in a millennia-old duel, was to shift the balance of power among the less important pieces on the grand senet board.

Thanks to the agency of Vincent, Hurley not only broke free of the cursed shackles that had prevented his emotional and spiritual growth, he literally used the vehicle of his new-found freedom to physically mow down and kill the men who had imprisoned his friends (Episode 3.23). The van became the badge not only of Hurley's liberation from spiritual slavery, but the potent symbol of his new power. Hurley's destiny was no longer controlled by fear, but by Jacob's Progress, which was itself the result of the Island's influence over Jacob.

There could be no greater proof of the source of Vincent's agency. The Man in Black, quite simply, would never have allowed Hurley to gain mastery over his fears and irrational neuroses, since curses and fears and emotional paralysis were the most potent weapons in the Smoke Monster's battle with Jacob. Vincent was, in ways we may never fully understand, the agent of the Island.

Because of Vincent, Hurley became Protector of the portal allowing passage to the halls of Shambala. He was the instrument through which Jack Shephard, the greatest hero in the Island's history, overcame his intellectual ties to the destructive scepticism we call science, and embraced his spiritual bonds to the eternal optimism we know as faith. Thanks to Vincent, Jack, too, was able to walk the halls of Shambala.

Constant Companion

Vincent's mission never changed, and he never wavered in his commitment, even to the very end. Just as he stood by Jack in the first seconds of his mission, he was there in the closing minutes, too, giving comfort to the one he had sworn to guide through the most treacherous obstacles a human being could ever be expected to face. "Live together, die alone," Jack said. At the end of the story, there was sadness for Jack's passing, but the tears that streaked our faces, more than anything, were tears of joy, for a man whose legacy would live forever, for an Island that had become an abode of peace, and for a dog who would not allow a great man to die without another's love.

The most faithful, optimistic, and human face of the Island came to us as our best friend, Vincent, the one who opened the halls of Shambala.

The Believer

> Doctor, my husband is not dead.
> —Rose Nadler

Her wisdom was not our wisdom.

Rose's wisdom was greater than Jack's, for she possessed it prior to his enlightenment. Greater even than Locke's, because it guided her actions before fate brought her to the Island.

Our wisdom is logical. It tells us Rose had cancer, the Island cured her cancer, therefore Rose must stay on the Island. Rose's wisdom was not confined by anything as crude as logic. Her wisdom told her violent people have a disease worse than cancer, violent people inhabited the Island, therefore Rose had to leave the Island.

Rose followed Jack but she did not follow him off the Island. She stayed. Of the seventy-one who survived Oceanic Flight 815, in fact, only two individuals never left the Island: Rose and Bernard Nadler.

She wanted to go, but decided to stay. She rejected Locke, yet no one was closer to him in the end. Her wisdom was not of the Island, yet she was soul of the Island. She was a bundle of contradictions—if we understand her through our wisdom. The most fascinating story of LOST is reduced to this strange truth: There are no contradictions. Rose Nadler never wavered.

Faith Not Hope

Rose never hoped that Bernard was alive.

She loved Bernard. She had faith in him. In terms we might understand, she *knew* Bernard was alive. But this knowledge did not come from statistical probabilities or anything seen or heard. Her knowledge derived of a much more reliable source. Rose knew Bernard was alive, but not in the same way she knew the sun would rise the next day; the knowledge was more certain than the continuity of our star. She had a *spiritual* connection to her husband. She didn't hope. She believed.

JACK: Rose, after the sun goes down, we're going to burn the fuselage. It's just something that we have to do. There's going to be a memorial service back at the camp for those... who didn't make it. For everyone to say goodbye.

ROSE: I'd like to be there for that.

JACK: Okay. Maybe if you'd like to say something, you know, about your husband.

ROSE: What?

JACK: I'm just saying if you wanted to say goodbye to Bernard.

ROSE: Doctor, my husband is not dead.

JACK: Rose, he was in the tail section of the plane. It broke off in mid-flight. I'm sorry, but everyone who was in the rear of the plane's gone.

ROSE: They're probably thinking the same thing about us.

We were given three images of human action in the opening hours of LOST: Jack running, Locke rising, and Rose sitting. Jack ran because... well, because he was confused, at every level of his being. Everything he was experiencing was beyond his ability to cope. Locke rose because he could, not only because his legs worked, but because everything about him that had been a hindrance in California was now a virtue on the Island. He rose above everyone else, because there was work to do, because the Island called.

Rose sat. She sat alone, like an island Buddha, grasping the gold ring on her necklace, staring out into the blue. She was not frightened, lonely, or upset. Her words were calm. She shed no tears, had no regrets, expressed neither pain nor bitterness nor fear.

I can't say I understand with certainty her need to sit alone. Perhaps it was not so much need as inevitability. She had the deepest possible connection with her Constant, and that Constant was on the other side of the Island. Jack as yet had no Constant, Locke was only just discovering his, and Jin and Sun were only a few shouting words removed from divorce.

In retrospect we can certainly understand the image of Rose sitting at the edge of the water as very much in keeping with Buddhist tradition, and at the same time revelatory of Rose's inner state. A countenance unperturbed by any earthly event is the signature image of the Buddha. Rose, virtually alone among the survivors, perfectly adopted the Buddha's calm, both inside and out.

Perhaps I do not read too much into the situation to make this claim: Rose was our teacher. She accepted things as they were, not as she wished they might be. She knew herself and the world around her—something that would become increasingly evident as the survivors' time on the Island turned into weeks and then years.

Rose was confident in herself and in her understanding of the world. She knew Bernard was alive, and she knew it with greater certainty than anything Jack had ever gleaned from a medical text. This was not arrogance. There was never any arrogance in her words, least of all when she pronounced, with unshaken certainty, that Bernard was alive. Her words were those of a person certain of her place in a larger scheme. She was a woman *dans sa peau.*

Rose was the first and most important teacher of the concept of the Constant. The Constant was the title of the most beloved hour of LOST. It was the idea that held together the sideways world and made clear that world's significance to the larger series. Rose retained her sanity for the forty-eight days she endured without Bernard only because she concentrated on him, held his ring in her fingers, and maintained the proper orientation of thoughts in her mind. That is to say, she remembered her Constant.

When Charlie's constant disappeared, Rose knew what to do. Her husband missing and assumed dead, Charlie didn't understand her calm. Rose had no explanation. "It's a fine line between denial and faith. It's much better on my side," she said. Rose had no answers for him, but she and Charlie shared a source of strength few others on the Island knew was available. When the pain was too great and Charlie cried out in anguish, Rose was there. She took Charlie's hand in hers, consoling him, giving strength to the one who would eventually die for her and Jack and the other survivors. Together, they prayed.

Destiny Not Fate

Isaac of Uluru was an unusual healer, able to channel the unique energy of Australia's most prominent geological feature into psychic health and biological repair. He did not perform miracles, could not see the future, made no claims of his abilities. He channeled, and sometimes those in his presence were healed.

Isaac should not be confused with Richard Malkin, the psychic seer. While Richard was likely a fraud (see Lindelof and Cuse, Time Talks, NYT, May 21, 2010; also see http://pearsonmoore-gets-lost.com/TheAaronConspiracy.aspx), Isaac was the genuine article. The fake seer was motivated by greed. Isaac of Uluru was motivated by desire to help, and his abilities were real.

Bernard loved Rose more than anyone, more than anything. A ten thousand dollar donation to Isaac was nothing to Bernard if it meant he might be able to heal her.

Rose, of course, wanted nothing to do with Isaac. "I didn't ask for this! This is... Bernard, I have made my peace with what is happening to me." Peace. Calm. Again we see the attributes that most defined Rose Nadler. Regardless of the situation, whether circumstance favoured her or not, she was at peace with the lot she had been given.

Rose's reaction to Isaac was the most important lesson of her and Bernard's only centric episode, "S.O.S." (Lost 2.19), but the most interesting was Isaac's advice on Rose's condition.

ISAAC: I'm sorry. I can't do anything for you, Rose.
ROSE: I didn't expect you to.
ISAAC: It's not that you can't be healed. Like I said, there's different energies. This is not the right place for you.

ROSE: Where is the right place?
ISAAC: I wish I knew.

No one told her the location of "the right place" that could heal her. But sitting on the sandy shore of the Island, she knew she had found the place Isaac said would help her. When Locke's leg was severely injured by the blast door, he told Rose Jack had said recovery would require four weeks. "But, honey," she said, "you and I both know it's not going to take that long."

Rose's destiny was to find and enjoy paradise on Earth. She had no knowledge of this, and she would have accepted any place on the planet as her paradise. As long as Bernard was at her side, she was where she belonged.

Rose never spoke of destiny because no journey was necessary, at least not in a sense others could understand. Wherever she was, she had already arrived. No effort was required to make do with whatever circumstance had delivered to her.

Destiny for Rose was not a location or a physical condition or a higher place to which one aspired. More than anything, for Rose, destiny was a state of being. She rarely exercised an option to make a decision. When the world forced a choice, she opted for the less irksome set of conditions. Life was not about the number of days but the quality of those days. All of her decisions must be seen in light of her need to maintain equilibrium in her life. When she was obliged to choose between staying on the Island with Locke or leaving with Jack, she chose to leave, even though it meant her death.

BERNARD: (To Rose) You said you'd never leave the Island, if you wanna go with Locke, I'll be right behind you.
ROSE: I'm not going anywhere with that man.

Locke, with his knives and guns, was the antithesis of Rose. He strove for things that required no effort. Peace of mind, the ability to live within one's circumstance, the assurance of one's integrity, dignity, and worth—all of these truths were available to everyone as foundations to the life well led. Locke's obsession with "destiny" was causing greater disruption than anything the most malevolent of Widmore's mercenaries could perpetrate against them. How many had died at Locke's hands, or from his knives and guns? How many had suffered or died because Locke pouted and decided Day 57 was a good time to destroy the Swan Station computer, discharging enough electromagnetic energy to power Manhattan for 1200 years? If these things were necessary to Locke's destiny, he could have it, but Rose would take no part in it.

We are well accustomed to thinking of John Locke as the paramount example of faith. He was the "man of faith" pitted against his "man of science" nemesis, Jack. But neither Locke nor Jack was steady in his convictions. The journey's the thing, because story is born in conflict, and conflict in faith requires doubt and hopelessness and apostasy. Both Locke and Jack suffered all of these deviations from the true path of faith. They travelled the path of enlightenment, not the path of faith. They journeyed *toward* faith, *toward* acceptance, *toward* Shambala. The Buddha was already there, and had been all the time.

Equilibrium Not Enlightenment

The Buddha does not know she is "enlightened", and she sees no need for posturing toward any such claim. What she understands is the simplicity of life and the fact that to draw breath is to count on the equilibrium of self within the world.

When Jack was struck down with appendicitis, it did not mean he had succumbed to genetic pre-disposition or physiological chance. Something more important was transpiring: Jack was not in equilibrium.

BERNARD: Honey, I am sure Jack's gonna be okay. An appendectomy is just about the most common kind of surgery there is.
ROSE: That's not what I was thinking about. I was thinking, "Why did he get sick?"
BERNARD: Why? It's... just bad luck.
ROSE: The day before we're all supposed to be rescued, the person that we count on the most suddenly comes down with a life-threatening condition, and you're chalking it up to bad luck?
BERNARD: Well, what are you saying, that—that Jack did something to offend the gods? People get sick, Rose.
ROSE: Not here. Here, they get better.

Rose alone knew that Jack's illness was the sign of a change in condition carrying immense significance. He had to be so far out of alignment that not even the Island could help him. This was the Island that had immediately cured Rose of terminal cancer. It was the Island that had given Locke legs to walk and a clear vision of something bright and beautiful. This same Island could help Jack if he allowed it—if he could only rise like Locke, or better, sit like Rose.

Island Gothic

In 1977 the Island's inhabitants were facing the most difficult set of circumstances in decades. The balance of power would not shift this radically again until the Purge of 1992. Dozens of lives were on the line. Rose and Bernard must have had some inkling of the principalities and powers moving in those days, but they maintained their placid demeanour.

KATE: Jack has a bomb.
ROSE: Who cares?
KATE: Excuse me?
ROSE: It's always something with you people. Now you say Jack's got a bomb. And what, you guys are all gonna try to stop him, right?
JULIET: Yeah, that's right.
ROSE: We traveled back 30 years in time, and you're still trying to find ways to shoot each other?
JULIET: Rose, we just need to know which way the DHARMA Barracks are from here so we can stop Jack, or you're gonna be dead. We all will.
BERNARD: So we die. We just care about being together. That's all that matters in the end.

It's not that Kate's struggle was not important to Rose and Bernard. It's not that they were withdrawing from society, that they were retired (even though Bernard used this very word), or that they were afraid of engagement. There was no fear in Rose's face. They didn't withdraw from civilisation, they were preserving it. And if Rose was "retired" she was behaving no differently than she had before her retirement.

In fact, nothing in Rose's philosophy or bearing had changed at all. She grew peace, stability, and equilibrium in her garden, as she always had, even before she found herself on the Island. The biggest change was that now Bernard was completely at her side, accepting whatever bumps were thrown in their way but always enjoying each other and the life they had made with Vincent in a little hut in the jungle.

Letting Go

"You can let go now," she told Jack on the sideways flight of Oceanic 815.

Who was this woman of calm voice and steady heart, whose counsels informed the wise, whose courage sustained the strong?

Rose Nadler was the soul of the Island. Her wisdom did not obtain from any seeking after destiny or enlightenment or hopes and dreams. Her wisdom was of the most elementary variety, the type to which we fancy ourselves subscribers, but in reality we have not the slightest clue how to practice. She lived and preached the truths of human existence inscribed on the Cork Stone, those precepts of humanity that define us as civilised people, the categories of thought and attitude that guide behaviour and reason in people of good will. In this wisdom, Rose never wavered. She was our teacher, Jack's teacher, and the Island's most dedicated resident. Rose Henderson Nadler was the only person in six years and 121 episodes who was never Lost.

This chapter is dedicated to my better half, Kim, who survived cancer not once but twice, and whose patience with me is even more enduring than Rose's patience with Bernard, whose love for me is undeserved but always savoured. Rose is my wife's favourite LOST character.

The Candidate

"However, there's also this lighthouse, where... the names seem to correspond with angles or degrees on this rotating mirror. So, is it possible that we know that in the lighthouse Jacob seemed to be watching these people as candidates but he was also writing their names down in a cave? *Why would he do it in both places?* Is it possible, Carlton, that maybe he wanted his nemesis to find the cave and that there's a little bit of misdirection going on here? That maybe he crossed off Kate's name in the cave [but not in the lighthouse] to throw the Monster off his scent? Is...it possible, Carlton?"

—Damon Lindelof, Official LOST audio podcast, March 11, 2010.

She was seeking something. We saw her run, thinking she ran from an undesired reality. But in fact, she was running toward a long-sought goal.

She ran. She ran from the law, from her lover, from her family. She ran from Sawyer, from Jack, from anyone who sought her heart. She murdered. Not once, but many times. She burned a house to the ground, assaulted federal agents, left her husband, robbed a bank, used a dozen aliases, endangered others' lives. She took advantage of a physically handicapped old man, then almost killed him.

Perhaps someone like this woman does not deserve a second chance. But the Island gave her a clean slate. "It doesn't matter," Jack told her, "who we were - what we did... before the crash.... Three days ago we all died. We should all be able to start over."

She found her objective in love. Not the love of strong men who yearned for her affection, but the love of a helpless infant who needed her care. Her life's goal was to devote herself, not to a man's embrace, but to a mother's rehabilitation.

She is midwife, surgeon, healer, nurse. She is daughter, mother, friend, and wife. "I have always been with you," she told Jack in his darkest hour. She has the inexhaustible perseverance and spiritual fortitude required to reach the objective of a lifetime.

She is devotion. She is courage. She is strength. She is Kate Austen.

The Douglas DC-3

Kate held two dozen hostages and shot three men to retrieve a toy airplane from a bank in Ruidoso, New Mexico.

Ed Mars, the federal marshall who tracked Kate over several years, must have thought this important bit of evidence would be safe in a location so far from Kate's normal haunts. Did he know the plane once belonged to her childhood sweetheart, Tom Brennan, who died trying to aid Kate's escape?

Kate hired three men and engineered and executed an elaborate bank robbery, not to steal money, but to recover the small plastic toy from Safe Deposit Box 815. The plane had been Tom's contribution to the "time capsule" they buried in 1989, when they were twelve years old. Thirteen years later, Tom was a doctor. He had a wife and a son. Kate, as usual, was on the run, this time for the murder of her father, Wayne Janssen. The two of them dug up the New Kids on the Block lunchbox and listened to the cassette tape they made in their youth.

TOM: It'll be totally cool when we dig it up in like twenty years.
KATE: How do you know we'll be together?
TOM: Because we'll be married and you'll be a mom and we'll have nine kids.
KATE: I don't think so. As soon as I get my license we should just get in a car and drive. You know, run away.
TOM: You always want to run away, Katie.

Even at twelve years old they couldn't agree on their future. Both of them were correct in their predictions, though. Tom was happy, married, and well on his way to having the nine children he dreamed of. Kate by then had much experience with a life centred on getting in a car and driving, to "you know, run away."

The DC-3 in the stolen lunchbox represented the stable life she could have had with Tom, the commitment he envisioned. It represented normalcy.

A Normal Life

Wayne Janssen was almost all Kate understood of "normal", but as she grew into a woman, she knew something was not quite right about her father's relationship with her mother. Diane's face not infrequently bore the signs of struggle: bruises, scratches, a black eye, a bloodied nose. She knew Wayne was responsible, and she intended to give her mother the gift of a normal life without her abusive husband.

When Kate brought her mother the happy news, Diane was horrified. Ed Mars summed up the situation well, with all the sensitivity of his profession. "White trash mom divorces dad, starts up with some guy who's a drinker. Then he knocks her around a little bit, she marries him, because, you know, that's what happens. And then this drunk, this Wayne, he moves into your house, and you get to lay there every night and listen to him doing your mom right there in your daddy's old bedroom. And even that wouldn't be so bad if he didn't beat her up all the time. But she loves him. She defends him."

Incomprehensible as it was to Kate, Diane loved Wayne, wished to spend her life with him, got pregnant by him. The result of Diane's infatuation was the birth of Kate in 1977. Wayne was the father, but he was not the husband. Diane was married to an absentee husband, off fighting a war that should have ended twenty years before.

These, then, were the circumstances of Kate's "normal" childhood. But they are not the complete circumstances. Just as Kate's mother "made her bed" in choosing Wayne, Kate made her own adult decisions about the acceptable range of normal human life. In the sufferings she endured sharing a house with an abusive father, we might be tempted to feel pitty for Kate. But she had greater examples than Wayne. Almost all of us, even those who suffered the most oppressive of childhoods, become acquainted with examples of lives well lived. In that regard, Kate was more fortunate than many of us.

Sergeant Major Sam Austen

Sam Austen was serving in Korea when Kate was born. He knew of his wife's indiscretion, but he never spoke of the matter with his beloved daughter, choosing to allow her to believe that he was her father. In fact, he was her father in all ways that might have any relevance to a girl growing up in a very bewildering world. He was Kate's anchor, the person who most truly and completely loved her, in every sense her Constant.

Sam provided the correct example at every turn. He taught his daughter to track and hunt game through the forests of Iowa. He stayed with his wife, despite her infidelity. When Kate was on the run, she knew the United States Army employed one man of deep integrity to whom she might turn in a time of great need.

Perhaps if he had explained to her the great value of steering a clean course through life she might have been spared the horrendous rollercoaster ride of so many years on the run. But he was the best father a child could ever hope to have. His life could have served as perfect template for Kate, but rather than cultivating Sam's sense of balance for her own life, she chose instead to impose her understanding of a normal order on her mother's life. But not everyone can be Sergeant Major Sam Austen. Kate's mother made her own choices in life, poorly conceived as they sometimes were. She never lived up to the good example of her first husband, and she could never summon the discipline to order her life according to his rules.

In murdering Wayne, Kate was failing most egregiously to live by Sam's example. She had never chosen to follow his lead. But Sam would become Kate's sure example in her own darkest hour, when the fate of the Island, and the world, rested on her decision.

Kate's World 2003

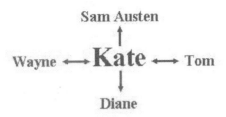

We need to understand Kate's range of choices prior to her life on the Island if we hope to make sense of her final disposition at the time of the Island's greatest crisis. Kate grew up with four life examples: Wayne Janssen's, Tom Brennan's, her mother's, and her father's.

Diane's example was a life in the gutter. Take what you can when you can get it. When life gives you a good man, like Sam Austen, it ends up taking him away for years at a time so he can point his gun toward a demilitarised zone that should have been cleared twenty years ago during their fathers' war in Korea. You can't count on life being fair or even worth living, so take what you can get.

Wayne's example was to live life for the moment: eat, drink, and be merry. If it happens that someone else's wife is there to be merry with you, so much the better. While Diane had scruples, Wayne had none. His was a wild life, lived from one night to another, one bar to another, one woman to another. Instant enjoyment and survival were the only aspects of life he ever contemplated.

Tom offered Kate an ordinary life, a life committed to each other, a life worth sharing. This was a life of equals, of two people who truly respected and loved each other. A mortgage, a car, and nine children. Though with nine children, it would have to be a very big mortgage, and maybe a couple of large vans rather than a car. But all in all, an ordinary life of marriage, work, and family.

Sam called Kate to something higher, to a way of life that would not deviate, no matter the obstacle or condition. Sam did not request from life a woman destined to be unfaithful to him, but this is what he received. He followed the course he knew to be correct regardless of the poor choices everyone around him made. He lived a life of integrity, dedicated to ideals for which he was willing to sacrifice even his personal happiness. One does not extract vengeance, regardless of the crime. A man takes care of his family, no matter the cost. His example was the sure sign of the endurance of a set of principles always available to each one of us. Sam Austen was for Kate, and is for us, an example of our highest humanity.

Kate's Destiny

Kate chose the wild side, the darker, more exciting angels of her nature. One man understood her, knew the kind of woman she was, was happy in the knowledge he would catch her. Kate telephoned him, always on Roman Catholic Holy Days.

MARS: [Picking up the telephone] Agent Mars.
KATE: It's me.
MARS: Well, I'm glad. I realized this morning that it was the Feast of the Assumption and I was feeling bad. How many holy days have come and gone since you last called? I thought you and I were friends?
KATE: I don't want to run anymore.
MARS: What's his name? ....
KATE: Edward, please. I know you don't want to spend the rest of your life chasing me. Please, I love this guy. Just let me go.
MARS: I'll tell you what. If you can really stay put? Really settle down? Then I'll stop chasing you. But you and I both know that's not gonna happen.

Short days later, Mars' prediction proved to be on the money. When Kate missed a menstrual cycle, her first thought was pregnancy. Her second thought was the impossibility of that condition. Pregnancy meant stability, it meant responsibility. It meant commitment. Even if she was married to a man much like Tom Brennan, a responsible, decent man, she couldn't live like him.

KATE: Whatcha workin' on?
KEVIN: Just finishing some IRs, and that fugitive recovery in Tampa. Being a cop is just endless paperwork....
KATE: What if I told you I was a fugitive? What if I told you I was on the run for blowing up my father, and it was only a matter of time before you found out?
KEVIN: This isn't funny.
KATE: [Crying] It's not a joke. I almost had a baby, Kevin. Me, a baby! I can't do this! Taco night?! I don't do taco night!
KEVIN: Okay, calm down, Monica...
KATE: My name's not Monica! I love you. But I can't stay.

If Agent Mars could have heard this conversation he would have been laughing in glee. He would catch her, because the foul droppings of her misguided life would lead her straight to him, and him to her. Working on opposite sides of the law, nevertheless they shared an outlook on life, and their view took in only the seamy side, the dark side, the side they both inhabited.

Ed Mars was right. Kate would fall into any trap he chose to set—it was going to be that easy. More importantly, Kate's future was full of sad hours and dark days, and once in the "sideways" world her soul would never know peace, never feel the warm presence of any Constant.

But then Flight 815 crashed.

A Higher Calling

Kate was the midwife. Always Jack's second, here she was filling in for the surgeon, who had his hands full trying to "fix" Boone. Only Locke understood that Boone was the "sacrifice the Island demanded", but that is a topic for another chapter. For our purposes in these early pages of *LOST Identity*, it is enough to say simply that Aaron's birth was a necessary evolution in Claire's life, the life of the Island, and most importantly, Kate's growth from the darkness of Wayne's world into the light and happiness of life with Jack. With Boone's death came the first successful birth since the days of the Dharma Initiative, when Amy Goodspeed delivered the boy she decided to call Ethan.

Life was no less confusing on the Island than it had been growing up in Iowa and living as "Monica" in Florida. Life was supposed to be a con, a deception, like the life she had started with Officer Callis in Dade County. Life was drunken Wayne and abused Diane. Was it any wonder she became attracted to the man who promised her "afternoon delight"?

She was attracted to Sawyer, and to her mind the attraction was normal and probably inevitable. But she felt something for another man, too. Jack confessed his love for her, and then he did something entirely beyond Kate's experience. Ben was under Jack's knife in the Hydra surgery. Guns were pointed at Jack. When the situation was tense, when lives were on the line, Jack sacrificed his love and risked his own life, not for any hope of being with her, but so that she might escape with her lover, Sawyer. Jack was subsuming his love to Kate's desire, foregoing his own happiness so that Kate might find fulfillment.

Here was a love triangle worthy of prime time. Kate had experienced this depth of love only once, though she didn't know it, didn't understand what Sam Austen had sacrificed to love her in precisely the way Jack was now demonstrating his love for Kate.

The Island was a new world for Kate.

Kate's Island World

Kate had before her a bewildering array of choices. Should she follow Sawyer for "afternoon delight"? Should she try to re-establish romance with that rock of a man, Jack? The decision was inevitable, even if she didn't understand the rationale. In the meantime, there were adventures. Kate volunteered for more expeditions than anyone else on the Island. If there was a dangerous trek planned to a newly-discovered Dharma station or 140-year-old shipwreck, Kate was first in line, shoulder pack ready, gun cleaned and chamber full.

Kate's World 2004

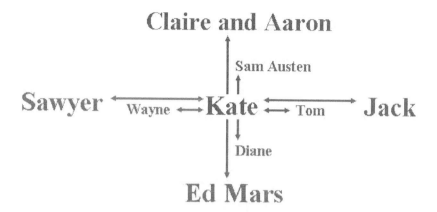

Claire and Aaron

Sam Austen

Sawyer ⟷ Wayne ⟷ Kate ⟷ Tom ⟶ Jack

Diane

Ed Mars

Jacob tried to point her in the right direction in Mr. Springer's General Store, paying for the lunchbox she stole, but Kate was a tough cookie, and hewed close to her chosen life of take-it-and-run-and-to-hell-with-the-consequences. Jacob must have believed his trip important. Probably he had prepared years in advance to meet up with his beloved Number 51. Hers was not one of the Valenzetti Numbers; was she Jacob's "Variable", the person who would introduce the new existence coefficient that would upset the inevitable outcome of Valenzetti? She was important, then, truly essential to the future of the Island, and the world. But for all Jacob's planning and hard work, Kate was undeterred from her rollercoaster life.

When they left the Island she knew she would have to make a life with Jack. He was the kindest, most considerate man she had ever known. She really, truly loved him. Learning that he was Aaron's uncle only confirmed the wisdom of her choice. When Jack proposed, she felt the deepest emotion that had ever filled her soul, and through her tears she said, "Yes!"

Weeks later their engagement was off, their romance in ruins. The apparent cause was Jack's drinking and his jealousy over Kate's feelings for Sawyer. But these were not the real causes. Jack had long known of Kate's attraction to Sawyer, and had even been willing to let go his own feelings for Kate. His nature was not possessive and jealous. The real cause was Jack's gut-wrenching transition from an existence based on science to a life grounded in faith, and that, too, is a topic worthy of its own chapter. For now, it is sufficient to note that Kate never gave up on Jack, never felt the slightest decrease in her feelings for this man. "I have always been with you," she told him. She meant those words more than any that had ever passed her lips.

Kate was confused. The man she loved seemed possessed by the same forces she was now trying to escape. Her life seemed to be coming together, but now it was falling apart again. She was acting as mother to Aaron, but even here she felt something was not quite right.

Jacob could not help her find a way to her true destiny. Jack was stoned on booze and Schedule II opiates, virtually incapable of holding a conversation, let alone dispensing wisdom or providing concrete assistance. Her mother hated her, wished to see her rot in prison. Her father couldn't help her. But she was not alone. Help would come from a source she never could have imagined:

The Island.

To Highest Mountain, To Deepest Sea

Claire had to raise Aaron. It was a ruling somewhere etched in stone, an inviolate law of the universe. But Claire in her own way was as obstinate as Kate. No visit from Jacob would have deterred her from giving up Aaron for adoption. Two visits with the psychic, Richard Malkin, could not dissuade Claire from her decision, and his numerous late-night calls only made her angry. But the Island had more endurance than Claire. During her last visit with Malkin, he produced a one-way ticket for Oceanic Flight 815. It had to be that flight, and it had to be the next day. Malkin said he had arranged for Claire's baby to be adopted in Los Angeles. Of course, he had arranged nothing. But he knew the Island had arranged something: a crash that would instantly kill three hundred of her fellow passengers but would miraculously save her life.

She was not among Jacob's Candidates. Probably Jacob didn't even know her, her name, the enormous role she would play in the Island's endgame. But the Island knew. Claire and Aaron were essential, because Kate was essential. Without Aaron, Kate would never be persuaded to return to the Island after she left as one of the Oceanic Six. But the Island, in the form of Christian Shephard, ensured her return.

Christian—the resurrected Christian Shephard—came to his daughter and asked to be allowed to care for his grandson. We don't know what he told her. He may have told the truth, or he may have concocted a bold, elaborate deception. But he knew the outcome. He would take the infant, put Claire in the hands of the Man in Black and have her escorted far away. Then, when his daughter was out of sight and too distant to hear even the pleading cries of her own flesh and blood, he would place the infant on the path he knew Kate or Sawyer would walk only short minutes later.

Sawyer, finding the baby, became the temporary and quite flustered guardian. Kate, deprived of a real mother in her own childhood, could not bear the thought of any child being forced to grow up without a loving mother. Now, before her very eyes, was the baby she had helped Claire bring into the world. Had Claire abandoned him? Could she not face the responsibilities of motherhood? Kate knew all about irresponsible mothers. She wouldn't allow Aaron to face the kind of childhood she had been forced to endure.

There was no time to decide whether she was acting in haste, no time to locate Claire. She had to leave the Island, and leave now, or she would never be free. With the Smoke Monster looming, with the atmosphere of death that permeated everything on the Island, staying behind was not an option.

Three years later, when Aaron was old enough to laugh at jokes and question the authenticity of children's cartoons, Kate had second thoughts. She was not Aaron's mother. Regardless of her implacable commitment to the toddler, she was no substitute for Claire. And what of Claire? If she was alive, she had to be enduring the worst possible torments that any human being can face, knowing only that her son was gone, was nowhere to be found anywhere on the Island. Was he alive? Dead? Suffering? In the hands of one of the Island's horrible creatures? Was he being tortured? Starved to death? Kate had inflicted on Claire an existence worse than the most painful and unrelenting death.

Losing Aaron in the grocery story, she realised the horror of her action. She had felt enormous, almost unbearable pain in the few seconds that Aaron was missing. Her anguish was relieved in less than a minute. Claire had been enduring the same torment—not for thirty-six seconds, but for thirty-six months. Day after day, year after year, incessant, horrible, mind-altering emotional terror.

Kate felt Claire's pain. And in that empathy was Kate's redemption. In Claire and Aaron she found a cause worthy of lifelong commitment. Kate would give everything—her own happiness, even her own life—to bring Claire back to Aaron. Whether she realised it or not, Kate had finally found Sam Austen's footsteps, and she was firmly planting her own feet in them. She discovered in herself a reservoir of unconditional love, and now she was harnessing that love to serve a mother and a child. This was the objective she herself had never understood. It was the driving force behind a life of running.

Kate had to go back. No mountain was high enough to stand in her way. No sea was deep enough to keep her away. Kate would overcome any obstacle to return to the Island, find Claire, and reunite mother and son.

Devotion. Courage. Strength.

ArtGUS' masterful illustration at the beginning of this chapter captures the Kate I know from LOST: Scarred and wounded but strong. Unsure but resolute. Muscular yet feminine. Fearful yet courageous.

It is a portrait I know most others—even those who consider themselves unwavering fans of LOST—neither appreciate nor understand. "Ugh, it's another Kate episode tonight," many fans said. Whenever I learned the episode centricity was Kate, I was beaming, looking forward with great anticipation.

Kate and Locke were my favourite characters, and I always had a special place in my heart for Kate's character and the actress who played her. Evangeline Lilly bears an uncanny, unearthly resemblance to the protagonist of my first novel (http://pearsonmoore.com/trinity2045.aspx). Whenever Lilly was called on to carry an action sequence, she owned the scene. Her talents were terribly under-utilised during the six years, and I feel this was one of LOST's greatest weaknesses. She was the female lead, outstanding in action sequences, unequalled in emotional scenes, but the writers chose to use Kate mostly as love object to Sawyer and Jack. Darlton, you created the most amazing series I've ever seen, but by relegating Evangeline Lilly to essentially soap opera roles, you fell short. Whether she continues as actress or tries to make a go of it as a writer, I have to believe she will continue to astound with her creativity and authentic humanity.

The Island brought her back. She thought her mission concerned only Claire, finding her, getting her off the Island, and reuniting her with her toddler son. But this was an almost incidental, secondary mission. If the Smoke Monster had decided to do away with Claire, Kate's *raison d'être sur l'isle* would still stand. Her reason for being: a bullet, administered with sudden and destructive force, into the chest from the dorsal side. Hers was the highest calling: to destroy the Smoke Monster. Claire and Aaron, Claire's insanity and forced alliance with the Smoke Monster, Claire's suffering, Kate's many brushes with death, Christian's risking of Aaron's life—all of it was the dangerous, risky, inhumane but entirely necessary preamble to Kate's role as slayer of the world's most fearful nemesis.

On the black volcanic cliffs Kate did not run. She did not run from the Island. She did not run from the man she loved, did not run from her responsibilities. She stood firm, aimed the rifle, and delivered the final bullet.

Kate was Jack's salvation, the Island's salvation. She was the salvation of the world, though she must not have known that. It was just another day in the jungle for Kate Austen, for she still had work to do. She did find Claire, brought her home, and must have spent the next fifteen or twenty years ensuring Aaron's future.

I have heard nothing of the epilogue, save that it concerns Hurley as "Number One" and Ben as "Number Two". But we know already that Hurley was hesitant to take on the role. We also know that Walt was gifted in many of the same ways Locke was. Add to this the fact that Aaron's birth was pre-destined, known to the ancients, and a most inevitable evolution presents itself. Seems to me most likely that the eleven-minute epilogue we've been promised on the Season Six DVD will involve one simple storyline: Hurley will gladly relinquish his role as "Number One" to the young man surely destined to care for the Island: Walter Lloyd. And his "Number Two"? Someday, it will be Aaron. And if the kid has any brains, he'll invite Kate to the Island from time to time. She could arrive by plane on the Hydra runway. Plenty of Douglas

DC-3s are still in service; Kate would make a most appropriate passenger, visiting in style and comfort the Island whose future she assured.

The Chameleon

CHAPTER 4: THE CHAMELEON

I enjoy the fact that Juliet has become who she was because of the island.
—Elizabeth Mitchell, Interview with The TV Chick, May 11, 2010

She was every woman except herself.

Benjamin Linus idolised her because she was the very image of his dead mother. Jack found her attractive because she reminded him of his former wife. To Edmund Burke she was a means of making a name for himself. She found value in herself only to the extent that she served others: her sister, pregnant women, Mittelos Bioscience, the Others, young Benjamin Linus.

Her sole objective was to leave the Island. But to what end? On the Island or off, she could claim for herself only those identities that others had chosen for her. She was never herself because she had never claimed anything for herself, never given herself completely to anything.

In the end, she found herself only because a man needed her to be the woman she truly was. James Ford didn't need every woman. He needed the woman who believed in herself so that she could believe in him.

LOST is the story of the human need to discover identity in connection to a single, unchanging, enduring value. Juliet Burke found something enduring, claimed him, gave herself to him, and in this perfect connection, found herself.

The Coat of Many Colours

I find Juliet one of the easiest characters to like, but the most difficult character I have ever attempted to reduce to a single chapter. Whereas chapters on Jack, Locke, and Kate virtually wrote themselves, I have worried over Juliet Carlson Burke for several weeks, spending long hours pouring over her biographies, rewatching critical scenes, and never reaching the core theme of her character.

Over time I finally came to realise she was a chameleon. She wore a coat of many colours, and not only in the sense that everyone within her closest sphere saw her not as Juliet Burke, but as the person they wished her to be. Every one of these people saw her as something other than the woman she was precisely because she wore the coat—because she had been vested with abilities that others envied, exactly as in the Biblical story of Joseph and the coat of many colours.

Benjamin and Jacob were not the only names lifted whole from the Hebrew Bible, then. Juliet's true name, surely, was Joseph—the favoured son of Jacob who wore the coat of many colours. Both Benjamin and Joseph, sons of Jacob, were all things to all people. Benjamin was all things to all people because he manipulated and fabricated. Joseph (our Juliet) was all things to all people because of what they wished to see in her, and especially, the things they envied in her.

But assigning her a name brings us no closer to understanding her identity. We cannot know the Biblical Joseph in a single dimension as the son of Jacob who wore the coat of many colours. In order to understand him, we must be able to discern multiple attributes that form a unique person. In the same way, we cannot know Juliet through the single dimension of a name.

Envying the Coat

Edmund Burke wore very nice suits and worked in one of the richest offices we saw in the six years of LOST. He was a man who asserted and enjoyed power, and he attained that power through the determined effort of those in his employ. Why work hard—or work at all—when you can coerce underlings into working for you?

When Juliet made a groundbreaking discovery in fertility, Edmund pulled out all the stops in an effort to steal her glory for himself.

EDMUND: I want in.
JULIET: In on what?
EDMUND: I know what you're doing, Juliet.
JULIET: I'm not really sure what...
EDMUND: I read your notes. I know what you took from the lab...
JULIET: Ed, I've been doing my research in my own lab, on my own time...
EDMUND: It's your sister, isn't it? Look, Jules, there's two ways this plays out. One is your research is potentially genius. And the other — it raises some very serious ethical questions. Maybe even criminal concerns. But if you collaborate with me, based on my reputation, all this is viewed as cutting edge science. And we will win prizes and drink champagne. And do a lot of good for people.

In Juliet, Edmund must have thought he had the perfect lab rat. She was excited by research and she was very good at it. He didn't marry a lover. There was nothing in his bearing or very clear purpose that said anything about amorous concerns or even the most rudimentary empathies of romantic love. Edmund Burke didn't marry a lover. He married a publication mill. He married a productive researcher who could keep him in the limelight at technical conferences. He married a resource who would ensure his promotion into increasingly higher echelons of power and influence. When Juliet tired of his single-minded glorification of self and his inability to lift his narcissistic eyes away from untiring self-admiration, he nevertheless continued to exercise control over her. She was far too valuable a resource to allow any measure of independence.

At the beginning of her career, every scientist faces constraints imposed by society, the leaders in her field, the particular institution she works for, and so on. Juliet Burke, M.D., faced constraints much deeper and invasive than any experienced by her colleagues. The constraints on her were not professional, but personal. They were violations of her person, and they were imposed by a man so gripped by envy and desire to control that the only way Juliet finally achieved freedom from him was through his sudden death.

Oedipus

Envy was not limited to sentiments regarding Juliet's prowess in the laboratory. There are many kinds of envy, and probably all of them were present at one time or another on the Island. Benjamin Linus envied Juliet not for technical ability or beauty, but for nurturing skills. Ben never had a mother. In Juliet, he believed he had found the most adorable and sexually attractive correction of that deficiency. In fact, during their only dinner date alone together, they spoke of only one issue besides Juliet's relationship with Goodwin: Children.

BEN: I want to thank you for how wonderful you've been with Zack and Emma.
JULIET: They're really sweet kids. Ben, they've been asking me about their mother in Los Angeles. I'm not really sure what to say.
BEN: They'll stop asking in time.
JULIET: They're children. Do they really belong here?
BEN: They're on the list, Juliet.

Ben assigned Juliet to act as mother to the now-orphaned children from Flight 815. Since he sought no private time with Juliet before the arrival of the children, it seems quite likely he was using the kids to evaluate Juliet's mothering skills before seeking a closer relationship with her.

Ben had a special affinity for children, but he also had a special place in his heart for the mother he never knew. With Juliet, he would be able to pursue both of these personal interests. He wouldn't have to raise children alone, as he had had to do with Alex, and he could enjoy the company of one who looked and acted like his dead mother. She presented the additional attraction of being amenable to his control. Children were a natural focus for Ben because they could be manipulated. If he could find one such as Juliet, who had already proven herself malleable, life would be that much richer for Ben. "You're mine," he told Juliet. He would be able to control children and mother, bringing meaning to his life. Juliet was the perfect object of Ben's envy and control.

Surrogacy

Sarah was no longer a part of his life. Kate seemed to have fallen for one as much on the run from life as she was. Lacking steady feminine companionship, and finding on the Island a woman who bore striking resemblance to his gorgeous former wife, should we be surprised that Jack found himself attracted to Juliet?

Jack shared many of Juliet's interests. He was also a physician, also a surgeon, most assuredly also one who cared deeply about the welfare of his patients. Both he and Juliet established strong love relationships with at least one patient in their care: Juliet with her sister and Jack with his future wife, Sarah.

But similar interests do not a strong relationship make. Jack lacked female companionship not because of any accident of history or nature, but because he was in a state of mind entirely unsuited to the cultivation of long-term relationship. With the crash of Flight 815, Jack was beginning a three-year period of soul searching that would lead to his installation as the Island's greatest but shortest-lived Protector. His destiny was to become the hero of the series and the saviour of humankind. But because his task was so enormous, he had to dig deeper and come closer to failure than any other character. He was changing to such an extent he could never act as anyone's Constant—with one exception, of course. But this is neither Kate's nor Jack's story.

Jack could not accept Sarah for the woman she was. "I'm going to fix you," he told his wife-to-be. And true to his word, he did fix her. This should have been sufficient, and might have been the end of the story. But Jack could not stop there. He had to prove his worth every day. He had to fix people. When he finished with the grand project of fixing Sarah, he moved onto the next great project. She was not his wife, but a trophy, a proof of his valour as surgeon and doctor.

In his condition during the first hundred days after the crash, he could never have served as Constant to Julia. He, like everyone else in Juliet's life, would need her to be someone else—in Jack's case, he would have needed Juliet to be Sarah. But since being Sarah was not good enough even for the woman who was Sarah, the relationship between Jack and Juliet would never have worked. Juliet could never be surrogate for Sarah. Jack's brand of envy would not make Juliet into the person she needed to be.

Climb Every Mountain

This chapter was originally titled 'Climb Every Mountain'. Juliet had to find her destiny, discover her worth as a person. In the words of the wise Mother Abbess from the Sound of Music, Juliet had to "find the life you were born to live." As with Maria, Juliet's destiny was not to be found in humble service, but in the arms of a man.

Mother Abbess' song is the highlight of The Sound of Music and one of the most stirring bits of cinema ever put on film. You can watch—and listen—here:

http://www.youtube.com/watch?v=qxsCBIxr71M

The imagery does not fit perfectly. The major problem is that Juliet never indicated she understood that she was on a quest to discover herself. Events always seemed to overtake her. She did exercise judgment, she finally chose her identity and her destiny, but other than the clear desire to leave the Island, there was no quest, as far as I can tell. In the end, her desire to leave the Island was enough, for reasons I will make clear before the end of this chapter.

But Climb Every Mountain fits Juliet Burke in important ways. Juliet overcame obstacles as no one else could. She did not seek solution to fertility problems for her own glory or benefit. She sought them because they were good in themselves. She treated twelve-year-old Ben to the best of her ability, and when his injuries were beyond her abilities, she sought any other means of saving the boy's life. We can easily imagine in such a situation that Jack of the first one hundred days would have pounded away on the boy until he died, intent on proving his valour, not on saving the boy's life. Juliet had no pride to damage or protect. She showed time and again her selflessness and her drive to overcome every obstacle, to climb every mountain, to ford every stream.

Admiring the Coat

We do not have to envy Juliet her coat of many colours. We ought to take some time to admire it, though. Juliet was a talented, dedicated, intense young woman. Expert in fertility, fertility research, and pregnancy, her work helped women deliver healthy babies in the most difficult of circumstances. She became fluent in Latin at an age when most of us have difficulty absorbing simple elements of our own language. When she wasn't pulling a gun on adversaries or fabricating deceptions to support Ben's nefarious plans, she was able to get along with just about anyone. She became so adept at automotive repair that no one suspected the Dharma car pool was run by a physician.

Special attention must be given to her achievements in saving newborn lives. Treatments she developed allowed two unique births. First, of course, was her sister's conception and bringing to full term and safe birth a healthy child, even after she had gone through rounds of chemotherapy.

By far the achievement bearing most profound significance to the greater story was her development of medications and successful treatment of Claire. Thanks to her intervention, Claire gave birth to a very healthy baby boy, Aaron, who became critical to Kate's story and therefore to the endgame of the series. She overcame the pregnancy problems imposed by The Incident, thus tying up in a pretty bow one of the major sub-plots of LOST.

Finally, Juliet was midwife to the final successful birth on the Island before Aaron: Ethan Rom.

Her coat imbued her with a strength of character unlike any other. Would anyone else on the Island, battered, beaten, and broken by a fall of several dozen metres, have had the depth of character to perform the pure act of will she consummated in the detonation of the nuclear bomb? She was the right person at the right place at the right time because her coat of many colours was the best and brightest to be found anywhere.

Challenge and Destiny

No one questioned Juliet's desire to leave the Island. Her wish must have made sense to everyone, and so no one thought to question the logic behind her desire—until Sawyer, that is.

JULIET: I'm going to leave.
SAWYER: You do realize it's 1974, that whatever... you're going back to... it don't exist yet.
JULIET: It's not a reason not to go.
SAWYER: Well, what about me? ...
JULIET: You'll be fine.
SAWYER: Maybe... but who's gonna get my back?

Juliet had no valid reason to leave the Island, and especially not in 1974. Sawyer pointed it out to her, and at the same time demonstrated that she would have important work to do on the Island. At the very least, he could protect her and she could protect him—"get my back", as he was wont to express the idea.

Juliet obsessed on something that might have been attainable at certain times during her Island journey, but it never made sense. Her destiny was not about escaping anything, but finding something.

It must be considered a strange curiosity that no one had ever questioned Juliet's motives or objectives—until Sawyer. He stood out in this respect, but there was an even more important way in which he constituted a breath of fresh air to Juliet: Sawyer never told Juliet who she had to be. In fact, he insisted that she be the person she was. She did not have to perform grunt work to make

Sawyer look good in the eyes of others. She did not need to become Sawyer's mother or Sawyer's former wife. She needed to be herself, and she needed to be Sawyer's equal.

The end result of this necessary union was an unforeseen development. Sawyer became James. James Ford was no longer the vengeance-seeking scoundrel who had made the first months on the Island miserable for everyone. He was James LaFleur, literary scholar, leader of women and men, protector of Jack and Kate and all the others who could not protect themselves. Juliet turned James into a responsible, loving, caring human being. It was certainly one of the most remarkable transformations we were privileged to observe during the series.

Identity

SAWYER: [Gives Juliet a sunflower]
JULIET: Is that for me?
SAWYER: You were amazing today.
JULIET: Thank you for believing in me.
SAWYER: Ah.

James believed in Juliet and allowed her to become the woman she wished to become. By seeing the wisdom in Sawyer's ability to question her motivations and desires, she chose a life of freedom, she found an identity grounded in her own innate worth and James' uncompromising belief in her.

It worked.

It worked very well, indeed. It worked well enough, in fact, that there was not a dry eye anywhere in the world when the two of them found each other again at the vending machines at St. Sebastian Hospital. It was a marriage made in heaven, or the closest thing to heaven—an Island where a scoundrel and a woman without a purpose could become the best example of life, love, responsibility, and humanity the world has ever seen.

The Consigliere

CHAPTER 5: THE CONSIGLIERE

I don't want to die. I want to live forever.
—Richard Alpert, "Ab Aeterno"

"Ab Aeterno" is the most unsettling episode in the six seasons of LOST. But it is also the richest of all episodes, forcing us to confront ideas examined nowhere else in the series.

It is possible to watch Richard Alpert's story in the ninth episode of the sixth season of LOST and see nothing more than a simple, bittersweet love story. The love of Richard's life, Isabella, is dying. He rushes off to purchase the medicine that will save her life, and the cruelty of everyone around him not only brings about her death, but conspires to force him into slavery and a life bereft of hope.

Such a detached interpretation is possible. But for those in whom the greater story struck a chord, there is much more to this episode. Richard's meeting with two deceitful men in black is no coincidence. Father Suarez's denial of absolution—and denial of even the possibility of repentance—was not merely the sure evidence of the priest's utter lack of humanity, but it pointed to the core themes of LOST, and most emphatically to the central aspect of Richard's struggle—and every character's struggle—on the Island.

What is the centre of our concern as human beings? LOST posed this question 121 times, but never more forcefully and with as much unrelenting passion as during "Ab Aeterno." In the course of this episode, LOST rejected almost every conventional way of approaching the question of our humanity, insisting instead on our acceptance of a demanding, radical approach to understanding ourselves.

Even thirteen full months after this episode first aired, I find myself unsettled by the intensity of Richard's story, and the powerful emotions and ideas it elicits. LOST insisted that the path to finding ourselves is marked by truths antithetical to anything we've ever believed. Essentially, LOST said if we wish to find ourselves, we must disorient ourselves from the conventional partial-truths that blind us to the full reality of our complete selves. We are, as human beings, more than the sum of any possible set of superficialities. If we are to find ourselves, we will do so only by ensuring our authenticity at the deepest level of who we are.

Spiritual Connection

Doctors and priests exist to serve. Doctors take the Hippocratic Oath, pledging to treat all who come to them, even without payment. Priests take a vow of obedience to the Gospel, which calls on these doctors of the soul to have greatest concern for the needs of the poor. In the space of only a few hours, Richard experienced the violent upset of both of these truths, in a way that affected his life to its core. The doctor would not give Richard the medicine to treat his wife's affliction, even when Richard offered all the money he had. But this unconscionable affront to the sanctity of the Hippocratic Oath was not the worst of the doctor's sins.

DOCTOR: ¿Esto es todo lo que tienes? [English: Is this all you have?]
[Richard hands over his wife's cross necklace.]
RICHARD: Ahora lo tiene todo. [English: Now you have everything.]
[The doctor examines the cross and tosses it across the room.]
DOCTOR: Esto no vale nada. [English: This isn't worth anything.]

The doctor did not throw the coins across the room. In fact, the coins bore so little consequence to the outcome of this scene that their eventual disposition has no importance at all. However, we saw the little gold necklace several times throughout the remainder of the episode; it had a value far greater than its equivalent weight in any precious metal. The necklace was precious in itself.

We do not require advanced degrees in cinematographic analysis to know the necklace was symbolic of the spiritual connection between Richard and Isabella. From the greater context of LOST we know that Isabella was more than Richard's wife and lover. She was his Constant—the anchor in time and place that gave Richard's life meaning and value, the person without whom life would lack substantive connection to the passage of days and the significance of physical bearing. Richard's need for Isabella never wavered, even over a course of years and decades exceeding two or three lifetimes. LOST teaches that we need strong, deep, one-on-one, personal connections to significant others. A singular life divorced from these kinds of connections is simply not possible; it is in precisely this lonely kind of condition that we find ourselves most Lost. In trampling on Richard's deepest connection with another human being, the doctor was demonstrating his disdain for the healthy relationships that define our truest humanity, and doing more to spread discomfort and disease than he could have achieved by allowing illnesses to go untreated. He was attempting to destroy not only a physical human life, but the spiritual connections that make us who we are.

The creators of LOST were emphatic about the deeper meaning of the series. LOST is a character-driven show about the value of human relationships. Everything, including the dense, inter-woven mythology, the many-layered themes, and the thesis itself, are all oriented toward human personalities and the connections between one character and another. Many fans who disliked the series finale found themselves believing that LOST had not addressed the many mythological details and open questions they considered unresolved. In my first book, "LOST Humanity," I considered LOST from a strictly mythological and thematic point of view, demonstrating that the major questions were indeed fully addressed over the course of the series. The deepest themes of LOST, I showed, were those involving character relationships. I pointed out three distinct types of relationship, two of which—the Constant Pair and the Strange Attractor Pair—were unique to LOST.

In this second volume, we are going to consider the progression of LOST from the point of view of the characters. Each character's story is different, though the themes are often similar from one character to another. LOST believes that we learn most when we learn from the lessons of our lives, and from the lives of those with whom we share intimate connection. One of the most intimate connections we were offered over the course of six years was with Richard Alpert, husband to Isabella, advisor to Jacob, and beloved immortal of the Island.

Disorientation

LOST assaulted our senses with the insensible and the nonsensical. Polar bears roamed a tropical island. The Island itself, rooted to the ocean floor, nevertheless moved about freely. Though the Island had a history, it was unbounded by the normal constraints of time and place and cause/effect. Jack applied to the problems of 1977 the hard lessons he had learned three years before, in 2004. Richard remained untouched by time from the summer of 1867 to the winter of 2007.

The disorientation was intentional, and necessary to the greater objective of LOST, which was a restructuring of our understanding, a reordering of our priorities as they applied to the Island. In "LOST Humanity" I showed how this disorientation was the first pre-requisite on a path toward understanding each of the major mythological aspects of LOST and all of the questions outstanding. Although mythology and themes are not within the province of this book, the need for disorientation was just as important to our understanding of characters and their relationships with each other. In fact, in the case of Richard Alpert, disorientation had such deep importance that the writers went far beyond the storytelling constraints that had marked earlier episodes. Richard Alpert's story had to begin not with ordinary disorientation, but with a direct attack on our conventional understanding of the world. "Ab Aeterno" forced us to confront a world literally turned upside down.

Inversion of Humanity

In his prison cell, condemned to die, Richard knelt before the man he thought could bring him divine absolution. How could he have known that he was surrendering his soul to an incarnation of evil more despicable than even the Smoke Monster? The Island's Man in Black, at least, was motivated to save himself from what he saw as an island prison. The man in black who visited Richard in his prison cell betrayed the penitent kneeling before him, desecrated the holy vestments he wore, and blasphemed his Maker in denying absolution. It wasn't until the next morning that we understood the motivation for his cruelty. For a few silver coins from a slave trader he was willing to consign Richard to eternal spiritual torment. If there is a hell, men such as this priest must not even have to show an entry visa; they're granted immediate and eternal citizenship.

What the priest did in that prison cell was the worst and possibly unforgivable perversion of the Catholic faith. These men in black are supposed to be all about redemption and the undeserved grace of a beneficent Creator. The Roman Catholic faith does not allow a priest to withhold absolution from a truly penitent man only hours from death. If this man was truly a priest, he would have known that his unlawful, cruel, and unthinkably evil act would have placed his own soul in immediate peril.

The black vestments and black stole seemed to me an invitation to contemplate the meaning of Black and White on the Island. Are we to believe that the grand backgammon match going on these past millennia is a duel between Good and Evil? Are we to understand "Ab Aeterno" to refer to the ages-old, relentless struggle between heaven and hell? If a priest, who is supposed to be good, is instead the most visible representative of Satan on the Canary Islands, is it possible that the Man in Black, who is supposed to be "evil incarnate," may instead contain in him some measure of good?

We were witness to several important inversions during Richard's story. Almost all of them were theological in nature. I am convinced that they were intentional, and I trust that Melinda Hsu Taylor and Gregg Nations (the writers of "Ab Aeterno") were more reliable in their theological interpretations than the writers of "Deus Ex Machina" (Episode 1:19; the episode in which Emily Locke told her son "You have no father. You were immaculately conceived.").

I noted already the doctor's violation of the Hippocratic Oath. He perverted the Oath for his own gain, violating his sacred responsibility to heal the sick. This perverse attack on humanity was the first of dozens of inversions to follow.

The second important inversion occurred during Richard's confession to Father Suarez. Richard gave an emotional, heartfelt confession, begged for absolution. "Le ruego, le ruego, padre, por el perdón de Dios." Padre Suarez's response was shocking: "No. No puedo otorgar la absolución por un asesinato." The priest's words were false and self-damning. Not only could he give absolution, even for the crime of murder, but in the context of the situation, the priest was virtually obliged to offer immediate pardon. That he refused to do so was a severe perversion of the office of Holy Orders and the sacrament of reconciliation.

Inversion of Expectation

Richard's Bible was open to the Gospel of Luke, Chapter Four. The camera focussed on Verse 24: "Amen, I say to you, no prophet is accepted in his own native land." But the full context is crucial. I reproduce below Luke 4:18-30, from the six verses before Verse 24 to the six verses after:

> He [Jesus] came to Nazareth, where he had grown up, and went according to his custom into the synagogue on the sabbath day. He stood up to read and was handed a scroll of the prophet Isaiah. He unrolled the scroll and found the passage where it was written:

> "The Spirit of the Lord is upon me, because he has anointed me to bring glad tidings to the poor. He has sent me to proclaim liberty to captives and recovery of sight to the blind, to let the oppressed go free, and to proclaim a year acceptable to the Lord."

> Rolling up the scroll, he handed it back to the attendant and sat down, and the eyes of all in the synagogue looked intently at him. He said to them, "Today this scripture passage is fulfilled in your hearing."

> And all spoke highly of him and were amazed at the gracious words that came from his mouth. They also asked, "Isn't this the son of Joseph?"....

> And he said, "Amen, I say to you, no prophet is accepted in his own native place. Indeed, I tell you, there were many widows in Israel in the days of Elijah when the sky was closed for three and a half years and a severe famine spread over the entire land. It was to none of these that Elijah was sent, but only to a widow in Zarephath in the land of Sidon. Again, there were many lepers in Israel during the time of Elisha the prophet; yet not one of them was cleansed, but only Naaman the Syrian."

> When the people in the synagogue heard this, they were all filled with fury. They rose up, drove him out of the town, and led him to the brow of the hill on which their town had been built, to hurl him down headlong. But he passed through the midst of them and went away.

In this passage, Jesus is depicted as creating another disturbing inversion. The people in the congregation would have believed themselves "righteous before the Creator" but Jesus chose to hold up for them the example of Naaman the Syrian—a gentile who was cleansed (made righteous). The story—even though it was drawn from Hebrew Scripture—was an intentional affront to Jesus' listeners. In the context of the earlier claim that "this scripture passage is fulfilled in your hearing," Jesus' words could have been interpreted as being not only in bad taste, but possibly even blasphemous. He was subtly claiming divinity, and those listening would have none of it.

Luke 4:21 ("Today this scripture passage is fulfilled in your hearing") is nothing less than the thesis of the Gospel of Luke. The entire Gospel message is framed in an endless cascade of inversions, with frequent demonstrations of gentiles' fidelity to the Deity, long diatribes against those normally believed to have great piety (the Pharisees), and the centrepiece, the Sermon on the Plain, in which Jesus says the most blessed among us are the poor. Not the "poor in spirit" as in the Gospel of Matthew, but the literally poor, the destitute of the world.

The message I took from this lingering focus on the fourth chapter of Luke was simple: I should be looking for aspects of Richard's Island journey to convey the sense of a world turned upside down. I should accept nothing I see on the Island as having true value concordant with first appearances. I must question everything, because much of what I see will be an inversion not only of expectation, but of truth.

Inversion of Seafaring Culture

Only on a slaver could an Englishman named Jonas rise to become First Officer. The nineteenth century British Navy would never have promoted a man so named; he could never have earned the crew's respect. A Jonah (or Jonas) was one who brought bad luck or downright evil on board a ship. But Jonas Whitfield was Captain Magnus Hanso's right hand man, finding the slaves the nineteenth century entrepreneur would sell in the New World. Great Britain had abolished slavery over forty years before, but slaves remained abundant in the Americas. Even the "Land of the Free," the former British Colonies in North America, had tolerated and encouraged the practice of shackling fellow human beings up until short months before the Black Rock set sail from the Canary Islands.

Jonas Whitfield showed his true colours on the Island. He proved himself willing to flout British law on slavery, customs of the sea, conventions of social propriety. How many other laws did he bend or break to serve his master and his own enormous caprices?

He earned his keep at Hanso's side. It was hard work, but he was up to the challenge, whether hunting down slaves or seeing the Black Rock safely through any storm—except those great gales brought about by the clash of Island titans.

Inversion of Reality

Richard's first contact with the reality of the Island was obtained through the Man in Black. They were in hell, he told Richard. I don't believe the Man in Black was lying about this. He firmly believed he resided in the darkest, most tortured pits of the underworld, held prisoner by the devil who had been tormenting him for nearly 1900 years: Jacob. He required assistance, not only in killing Jacob, but in escaping the Island.

But he did lie about Isabella. He was not above posing as the dearest beloved of those he wished to bring over to his warped vision of the world. He proved this by coming to Mr. Eko as his brother, Yemi, by appearing to Ben as his daughter, Alex. So to Richard he became Isabella, and in her likeness, told Richard in all sincerity that they were in hell.

He sized up the prisoner, examined his thoughts, stole the images of the man's beloved Isabella, allowed him to hunger and thirst, and then came to him as the vision of his wife. It must have seemed entirely logical, even if he had not been in a deranged, thirst-induced hallucinogenic state. Where else could he be besides hell? Why would his dearest wife not come to attempt his rescue?

Even if we do not adopt the Smoke Monster's view of things, we could say Richard was in hell. He was in the part of the Island Rousseau dubbed "le Territoire Foncé" [sic; in French, the correct phrase is "le Territoire Sombre"—the Dark Territory"]. It was dark territory not for the presence of the Black Rock, but because of the many "Cerberus Vents" and the palpable sense of the Monster's awful presence.

Inversion of Baptism

There was to be no escape from this world turned upside down. Not for Richard. When he found Jacob, the Man in White kicked the knife out of his hand and threw him into the waves. Jacob dunked Richard four times. I counted. Why would I do such a thing? Why would the number of dunkings have any significance?

In the Christian tradition we are baptised "In the name of the Father, and of the Son, and of the Holy Spirit." Most of us are baptised with the gentle passing of a few drops of water over our foreheads. Some of us, like my son, are fully immersed in water. In a few Christian denominations there is a single dunking. But in most traditions, including the one I try to follow, the candidate is immersed three times, once for each Person of the Trinity. Jacob's four-fold baptism was intentionally devised so as to prevent any religious interpretation.

At this point we could move on and admit that Jacob's baptism was not intended to have Christian or generally religious undertones of any kind. However, I think it may be important to consider the wider context of Jacob's action.

Baptism, in Christian theology, is a sharing in Jesus' passion and death. We are forced under water—into death. It is only after the third time under water (mirroring the third day in the tomb) that we finally rise to new life. Baptism is not a denial of death, but an embracing of death. It is not a continuation of life, but the beginning of an entirely new life. It marks a turning point.

Richard's baptism was no turning point. The only goal of Jacob's violent exercise was to point out that Richard was not physically dead. "Still think you're dead?" Jacob kept dunking Richard until he admitted, shouted, that he was not dead, that he lived, that he wished to live. It was Jacob's way of telling Richard that he was not in hell, that the Man in Black was not reliable. I found the entire scene fascinating. Far from a baptism, this was an anti-baptism. Jacob forced Richard to say he was not dead. The "baptism" was not an acceptance of death—literal or figurative, physical or spiritual. It was, rather, a violent continuation of life as it had been. Richard remained among the damned of the earth—or at least he continued among those who considered themselves beyond redemption. The only change in Richard was the psychological awareness that he was not physically dead. Nothing truly important changed.

This "baptism" became a means of gaining control of Richard's soul. Richard would forever look to Jacob as the man who made him aware of being alive, but he enjoyed no more spiritual or physical freedom after the dunking than he had known before. The change in Richard was not for his benefit, but for Jacob's.

Jacob's Progress

In Richard's prison cell, the evil priest uttered words that were false for Richard, but true for everyone on the Island. "La única manera de regresar a su gracia es a traver de la penitencia." Penance may not have been necessary for Richard, but it seems to have been necessary for everyone on the Island. Even Richard ended up spending 140 years in indentured service to Jacob. Ben served without so much as having seen the man from whom he took orders. The few survivors of Flight 815 spent most of the three years of their journey in unending penitence for their sins on and off the Island.

The imposition of required penance was not justified in the case of Richard's jail cell confession, as was obvious from context. The natural extrapolation from this truth relates to conditions for Candidacy and service to Jacob. Why were the survivors, the Others, the Candidates required to submit to life-threatening rigours in order to prove their valour? Why, if grace is freely given, was Richard forced into eternal service of Jacob's desires? Why, if true love is unconditional, did Jacob impose lifelong service as a condition of healing Dogen's son? Why, if Jacob is the embodiment of perfect goodness, did he allow so many of his Candidates to die gruesome and unnecessary deaths?

Does a parent, claiming an interest only in her child's unencumbered freedom of choice, allow the child to run off a cliff? Does she, seeing a child drowning in a pool three metres in front of her, observe dispassionately as the child takes her last breath, or does she risk her own life by jumping into the pool to drag the child to safety? In what way can anyone claim or believe that Jacob's actions constitute some advanced awareness of and preference for "progress"?

Jacob's Sin

These were the most revealing twenty words of the episode:

"You aren't the only one who's lost something, my friend. The Devil betrayed me. He took my body. My humanity."

During his talks with Richard, the Smoke Monster spoke of Jacob, referring to him as the "Devil." Over a meal of roast boar, the MIB confided to Richard the nature of his feud with Jacob. Their disagreement was not philosophical, even if Jacob tried to paint it in that manner. Their hostility toward each other had its origin in a very personal set of events.

It was because of Jacob that the Smoke Monster had no tangible human form. It is because of Jacob that Cerberus had to fabricate a human image from whatever dead bodies he found on the Island. And it must have been at least in part due to Jacob that the MIB was left with a sour disposition and dark outlook on humanity.

"He took my body. My humanity."

Both the Man in Black and Jacob seemed to be missing important elements of humanity. The Smoke Monster said, "They come, they fight, they destroy, they corrupt. It always ends the same." He saw only darkness. Jacob said, "That man who sent you to kill me believes that everyone is corruptible because it's in their very nature to sin. I bring people here to prove him wrong." But if Jacob had not given his brother over to a condition worse than death, the Man in Black would never have become his supreme nemesis. Without Jacob's intervention, the Island would never have become the dark and foreboding place of hopeless terror that so many thousands over the centuries were obliged to endure.

Reversion of Perspective

Carmel Vaisman, in her analysis of Lost 6.07, "Dr. Linus" ("Find Lost With Carmel", http://www.youtube.com/user/FindLostWithCarmel#p/a/u/1/moKy-FPWr-A), said something important to Richard's journey. I transcribe a portion of the narrative here with her permission:

"I think that the episode sheds light on what are light and dark on LOST. We keep trying to figure out who's good and who's bad while both sides do questionable things. So here's the deal: Being in the light requires courage and truth. Your deeds can still be wrong, but as long as you regret it and truly share, you're in the light. Darkness is when you think you're beyond redemption, when you stop sharing and disconnect from the community. Maybe you haven't done a single thing wrong, but you are dark inside, dark from the pain eating you up. It's not about doing the right thing. It's about perspective."

Richard was in the light—he had proper perspective—as long as he followed the path carved out by his relationship with Isabella. Richard found his Constant in Isabella. Even when the Man in Black spewed lies, even when Jacob coerced him into eternal servitude, Richard knew a truth that could never be corrupted. No one could tell Richard he did not love Isabella. Even trying to convince him of this would be foolishness and a waste of time. Everything in his life has told him of the truth of her, of her love, of their need to be together regardless of cost. When the doctor threw the gold cross across the floor ("Esto no vale nada"), he was discarding Richard's great truth, that Isabella was worth everything. It was an act equal in rank with murder, for it took no account of the infinite value of human life. It was the act of a heartless and truly evil man.

Richard, in orienting all thought and action around the infinite worth and goodness of his beloved, established an incontrovertible truth. Truth is something Richard needed, if he was ever to make sense of events on the Island. He could rely on Isabella, the Angel in White. And he could rely on at least one other person.

Saint Hugo

Saint Hugo of Grenoble had a single-minded devotion to honesty and truth. These virtues have usually been in short supply among the world's leaders, and this was true in the Middle Ages no less than today. Saint Hugo was uncompromising in his forthright and sincere approach to even the intractable dishonesty of the church leaders of the time. His moral leadership led to important reforms that made the church truly responsive to the needs of the poor.

His namesake on the Island was likewise a man of unimpeachable integrity. Hurley's discomfort with lies was no mere matter of morality. It was the feature of his character that allowed his friends, and especially Richard, to discover truths that would otherwise remain obscured under the lies and deceptions of men like the Man in Black and Jacob.

Hurley was there to allow Isabella to reaffirm the truth Ricardo had always known.

RICHARD: I—I don't see her.
ISABELLA: Dile que su inglés es magnifico.
HURLEY: She's right there. She says your English is awesome.
RICHARD: ¿Estas tú realmente aquí?
ISABELLA: Cierra tus ojos.
HURLEY: She wants you to close your eyes. It's okay, I'll tell you what she says.

They were the same words she used 140 years before, the last words that passed her lips before she died. Thanks to Hurley, Isabella was able to do something Jacob, or anyone who truly cared, should have done long ago. She told Ricardo he had suffered enough.

ISABELLA: Ya has sufrido suficiente, Ricardo.
RICHARD: Te extraño, yo... Yo haría cualquier cosa para estar juntos de nuevo.

He didn't yet realise the full force of her words, the full reality of her presence with him, because he told her he'd do anything to be with her again. She reminded him of the fact he had kept in his heart since leaving El Socorro.

ISABELLA: Mi amor, ya estamos juntos.
"My love," she said, "We're already together."

Thanks to Hurley, Richard learned of the truth he really knew already: He and Isabella were together, they had always been together, and always would be together.

Direct Link to the Island

Richard's immortality and his eternal connection to his Constant were not his greatest legacies. Richard was granted something only Protectors had ever gained: communication with the Island.
Hurley carried an important message from Isabella. It was directed at Richard, but it had implications for everyone on the Island.

HURLEY: She kinda said one more thing. Something you have to do.
RICHARD: What?
HURLEY: She said you have to stop the Man in Black. You have to stop him from leaving the island. 'Cause if you don't... todos nos vamos al infierno. [English subtitles] We all go to hell[sic].

This was not Isabella's message. She was acting as the agent of another entity. Clearly she was not the Man in Black's agent. He had already impersonated Isabella, and he did so in order to make Richard believe that he and his beloved were in hell already. Her warning that they would end up going "al infierno" meant they were not in hell, but would end up in the place of torments if they allowed the Man in Black to pursue his agenda.

The most important truth to take from this brief sequence is that Isabella was not acting on behalf of Jacob. Jacob did not have the ability to speak with the dead. This was made quite clear in "Across the Sea." Jacob did not share his twin's ability to see or talk with dead people. Jacob's inability to bond with his dead mother was the most important factor in his emotional reliance on the Guardian (the woman who killed Jacob's biological mother). Neither could Jacob take on the form of anyone other than himself. Even after his own death, he was able to appear only as his younger or older self and in no other form.

If Isabella was not speaking on her own behalf, and if she was sent neither by the Man in Black nor by Jacob, some other powerful party was responsible for her appearance. Miles knew nothing of Isabella's appearance. He is the only other character we know to have had the ability to speak with or sense dead people. However, he is not the only character known to have been able to influence the dead.

In my first book on LOST, "LOST Humanity," I make the case for the deep influence of the story's most important conscious entity. In Chapter 14, "Advanced Topic I: The Source," I present several pages of argument, drawing from dozens of scenes over six years to show that the Island had its own thoughts and exercised its own judgment. In fact, the Island was the most important character in the series.

Isabella's message about the Man in Black came neither from the Smoke Monster nor from Jacob. Isabella spoke as the messenger of the Island. It was the Island that wished to warn Richard of the menace posed by the Man in Black.

Richard became the recipient of the only communication we know to have originated with the Island. Others received instruction that may have been from the Island. For instance, Christian Shephard, claiming to speak on Jacob's behalf, instructed John Locke to move the Island. He was probably not speaking as Jacob's messenger; most analysts, in fact, believe Christian's apparition in the cabin was just one of the many forms of the Smoke Monster. Although Christian may have been acting in some sense as an agent of the Island, the associations are difficult to make. Causal connections are likewise tenuous at best for any of the other possible Island interventions through Locke, Jack, Michael, and Jacob. Isabella's message is proof of Richard's unique connection to the Island.

Siempre Juntos

Richard was our first and best example of a life lived with other human beings. If "live together, die alone" defines LOST, there could be no better definition than the one provided by Richard Alpert and his beloved Isabella. "Siempre estaremos juntos," she said. We will always be together. It is the truth and the promise most elusive in any life, and the bittersweet reality that earns LOST a cherished place in our hearts. Over the years we may begin to forget some of the details—how Jack learned to count to five, why Kate broke into a bank in New Mexico. But we will never forget Richard, his heartbreaking story, his dedication, and his hope. Most of all, we will never forget that he found himself, was no longer Lost, because of his Constant, his beloved—his Isabella.

The Flower (La Fleur)

CHAPTER 6: THE FLOWER

"Son of a bitch."
—James ("Sawyer") Ford
(said at least 38 times during the six years of LOST)

Without him there is no LOST.

If nothing dwelling within drives us to commit foul acts, there is no tragedy, no drama, and no story to tell. If we do not cultivate a noble heart, there are no accomplishments, no drama, and no story to tell. But humanity has ever been and always will be a chaotic mixture of good and evil, selfishness and nobility. LOST is the greatest of stories, for it explores every dark corner of the human heart, and brings out every one of the good and better angels of our nature. Two players, two sides, one light, one dark. In Sawyer we have both sides—every darkness, every angel, in a turbulent broth of pain, vengeance, and deceit. Sawyer is LOST, because Sawyer is tragedy, comedy, and complexity. We think him selfish, but without his selfless leadership, the time-travelling survivors would not have endured Dharma times. We think him narrow-sighted, the cause of the submarine explosion, but without his broader vision, no one would have survived the sinking.

Despised and rejected, adored and respected, Sawyer is the most interesting character in LOST, and a most difficult subject for a chapter. Here's a short take on the long con.

The Letter

What are the forces that drive the human heart? I suppose we do not have to become psychologists or priests to understand that the boy sitting outside the church after his parents' funeral service is suffering pain we cannot even imagine. Will the pain motivate him to excel? Will sadness overwhelm him in an adulthood of depression and drugs? Will he be driven to crime?

Or perhaps he will seek out that which gives his life greatest meaning. We accept this option as a good and perhaps even noble undertaking. We say she is driven to paint. It has been her passion—her obsession—since childhood. He was born to practice law. His mother was a court judge, his father was a lawyer, the law was all he ever knew growing up. In both cases these noble pursuits were not noble at all, but simply the most visible and accessible components of childhood. We are what we eat, and we become that which we are most aware of.

James Ford was most aware of Tom Sawyer, the man who talked his mother into adultery, who stole his father's life savings, who so enraged the man that he shot his wife and then himself. James was left without parents, without a home, and with a very large empty place in his heart. He had to fill that empty place, and it could only be filled by the most prominent thing in his boyhood awareness. He filled that empty place with Sawyer.

James Ford did not intend to obsess on vengeance. He did not intend to become that which he despised. His uncle must have done his best, but anyone's best could not have been enough to deter James from focussing on the single greatest presence in his childhood. Tom Sawyer was the boy's passion—his obsession—it was all he ever knew growing up. He had to find the man who killed his parents. What better way to locate a man skilled in the art of deception than to become an accomplished deceiver oneself? Birds of a feather flock together, and even if confidence men could not stand each other's presence, they surely hunted the same prey and frequented the same types of seedy establishments. James would find Sawyer, because James would become Sawyer.

Compassion

The Island dispatched its representative, Christian Shephard, to take Claire's baby from her. We don't know to what extent, if any, Christian had an independent awareness of what he was doing. If he did have any uncoerced means of seeking understanding, he may well have wondered at the Island's very specific instructions: Find some way to take the boy from Claire, get her away from the immediate vicinity, then leave the baby on the path to the survivors' camp.

Why would the Island ask anyone to leave a defenceless child in a place where predators might take him? Because the Island knew who next would walk down that path, and that man had already proven he would not allow children to be harmed by predators. The Island knew this because it knew Sawyer, and knew also that he had reneged on a deal to make hundreds of thousands of dollars. He refused to take the money from David and Jess only because of their eight-year-old son, and the realisation that in taking the money he would have caused the boy as much pain as he was still experiencing, twenty years after the same event occurred to his parents. The predator from whom he protected the boy was himself.

It is certainly not coincidental that the two individuals on the Island most devoted to the welfare of children were the Island's two greatest deception artists, Benjamin Linus and James Sawyer Ford. The lesson is worth absorbing:

Even the worst scum of humanity are likely to possess at least a few of the greatest virtues.

Let us not start bubbling over in our appreciation of the man. Sawyer was no hero at this point; he hadn't even the rudiments of the sacrificial temperament required to care for an infant. In the last twenty years a few high schools in the United States have begun to teach teens about parenting by giving them a five-kilo sack of flour for a week. Hold the sack wherever you go, or make sure it is safe; if you lose any flour, you've harmed the baby. Sawyer, surely, would have had flour all over the ground and an empty sack after a week's time. But Sawyer was not alone, and the Island did not intend for him to raise the infant, only to rescue it. He handed off the boy to his sweetheart, Kate—and the remainder of this chain is an entirely separate story (see the chapter on Kate, "The Candidate").

Winston Churchill

Winston Churchill is the most admired European leader of the twentieth century—on this side of the Atlantic, anyway. I have no feeling for his stature in his home country or on the continent. But over here in North America you'd better have an exceptional basis for comparing anyone to the man who stood up to Hitler and wouldn't give an inch, even when London was in flames. They don't make 'em like that anymore—never made 'em like that, actually. Winston Churchill was a breathtaking accident of history, and the primary reason little girls and boys in London schools are not reading and writing and singing in German and being taught about the superiority of Aryans and the inferiority of Englishmen and Scotsmen.

JACK: So where do we go from here?
SAWYER: I'm working on it.
JACK: Really? Because it looked to me like you were reading a book.
SAWYER: [Chuckles] I heard once Winston Churchill read a book every night, even during the Blitz. He said it made him think better. It's how I like to run things. I think. I'm sure that doesn't mean that much to you, 'cause back when you were calling the shots, you pretty much just reacted. See, you didn't think, Jack, and as I recall, a lot of people ended up dead.
JACK: I got us off the Island.
SAWYER: But here you are... [sighs] right back where you started. So I'm gonna go back to reading my book, and I'm gonna think, 'cause that's how I saved your ass today. And that's how I'm gonna save Sayid's tomorrow. All you gotta do is go home, get a good night's rest. Let me do what I do.

Saying what Sawyer did takes balls, as they say. But did he have a basis for comparing himself to the man who saved the Western world from the goose-stepping nonsense and sheer terror and inhumanity of Nazism?

Our first thought is, of course, no. Sawyer was known almost entirely for one quite unsavoury quality of character. If anyone was above reproach in this regard, surely it was Winston Churchill. Churchill would never have deceived to advance his own selfish projects, as Sawyer did.

But we need to look closer. Churchill did deceive, and he performed such deeds on a regular basis. He was a master manipulator. He routinely lied to his own people about their capabilities and the extent of damage inflicted by the enemy. One of the greatest lies, in which the Americans' own Franklin Roosevelt was an enthusiastic participant, was Lend-Lease. Roosevelt gave Churchill ships, jeeps, war matériel of almost every kind (though not airplanes as far as I can tell. Perhaps a student of WWII can correct me—I believe the only Lend-Lease airplanes were provided to Russia) with no expectation of full reimbursement. The matériel was not given gratis—Great Britain paid dearly for Lend-Lease, making the final payment just four years ago, in 2006. But payment was less than ten cents on the dollar. The deception was in presentation. Roosevelt compared the attack on Britain to a fire at a neighbour's house. If the neighbour needed my garden hose to put out the fire, I wouldn't charge her fifteen dollars for the hose, I'd just ask for the hose back when she was done. Britain kept the equipment, of course. But it was a marvelous and necessary deception.

All leaders in war need to deceive. Roosevelt deceived. Churchill deceived. In fact, these leaders fabricated more deceptions than Sawyer could ever have hoped to create in his three years on the Island. In retrospect, and from a strictly logical point of view, we understand a wartime leader's need to deceive. But we understand, also, that the leader is acting on behalf of an entire country, not on the basis of selfish whim.

When Sawyer—Jim LaFleur then—deceived during his time with the Dharma Initiative, he was not saving only his own skin. His deceptions saved everyone else with him, and that was Jim LaFleur's intent. Like a wartime leader, he was not motivated to save himself first, but to ensure the safety of everyone in his care.

The comparison with Churchill may be a bit lopsided, but we ought to take a fresh look at the way Jim LaFleur operated during those critical days in 1974. LaFleur created for Horace a magnificent deception, a grand lie, about having been shipwrecked on the Island. But the bit of oratorical artistry that truly saved him, Faraday, Juliet, and Miles involved only a white lie and a great deal of truth. The event occurred in the summer of 1974, on a park bench in the middle of the barracks commons area. Sawyer went to see the Leader of the Leader of the Others, the ageless one, Richard.

SAWYER: Hello, Richard.

RICHARD: I'm sorry. Do we know each other?

SAWYER: I'm the guy that killed your men. Heard some gunshots, saw two men throwing a bag over a woman's head. Gave 'em a chance to throw the weapons down and walk away, but one of them took a shot at me, and I defended myself.

RICHARD: Is that so?

SAWYER: That's so.

RICHARD: Your people know that you're telling me this?

SAWYER: They ain't my people, Hoss. So if you got some kind of a truce with them, it ain't been broken.

RICHARD: If you're not a member of the DHARMA Initiative, then what are you?

SAWYER: Did you bury the bomb?

RICHARD: Excuse me?

SAWYER: The hydrogen bomb with "Jughead" written on the side. Did you bury it?

RICHARD: How...

SAWYER: Yeah, I know about it. I also know that 20 years ago, some bald fella limped into your camp and fed you some mumbo jumbo about being your leader. And then poof... he went and disappeared right in front of ya. Any of this ringin' a bell? That man's name is John Locke, and I'm waitin' for him to come back. So... you still think I'm a member of the damn DHARMA Initiative?

Sawyer didn't have to take responsibility for killing Richard's men, but in doing so he deflected Richard's anger away from Dharma. Sawyer was not deceiving here, but he was manipulating. I think in these types of exchanges Sawyer was demonstrating a kind of kindred nature with Churchill. He was using language to effect change and influence people in much the way Churchill did during the war.

LaFleur et la fleur

Sawyer proved his mettle by building a life—"and a damn good one"—in Dharmaville, and in so doing, saving Juliet, Faraday, and Miles. He proved it again by saving Kate, Jack, Hurley, and Sayid. But more than anything, he showed us his true colours in his relationship with Juliet. Sawyer's colours, we learned, were yellow and green. He was LaFleur—the flower—at heart, and it took Juliet to make him and everyone around Jim LaFleur realise the kind of man he was.

Jim LaFleur didn't have to try to save Sayid, but he did. He didn't have to risk his life and Juliet's life, but he did. Juliet joined the martyrs—Charlie and

Locke—and the future martyrs—Sayid and Jack—who gave their lives for the Island. Jim LaFleur paid an even steeper price than Juliet. But because of his selflessness, Sayid lived through the Dharma days to be on the submarine. Because Sayid was there to give up his life, Jack and Kate lived to kill the Smoke Monster.

It worked. The candy bar fell, and Jim LaFleur recognised the woman he loved, the woman he was destined always to love, the one who pulled him away from morbid intent on vengeance and into liberating appreciation of amorous fidelity.

Without him, there could have been no LOST.

Rogue, villain, leader, scoundrel, and hero. He is the worst and the best, selfish and selfless, a brute, but at heart a flower, waiting to be appreciated for his true worth. Juliet found this rare flower, and when she did, neither she nor the flower was Lost anymore. His story was tragedy, comedy, and complexity, and the most interesting and compelling story of LOST.

.

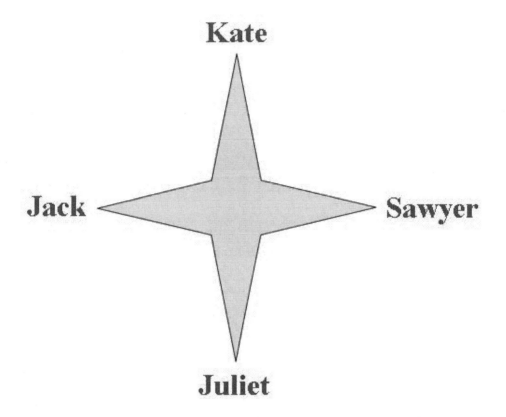

The Four-Pointed Star

CHAPTER 7: THE FOUR-POINTED STAR

"Have you ever sat next to someone at a bar and felt that your paths have crossed before? Has the thought ever crossed your mind that the stranger behind you at the store would become a significant part of your life?...seemingly random people. Do you know any of them? Do any of them know you? Do any of them know someone you know? Odds are that the answer to anyone of these questions is yes... Throughout the world, connections are constantly being made. Which begs the question; are chance encounters a matter of coincidence, or a matter of fate?"

—Damon Lindelof, "Lost Connections," 2007

I truly disliked only one part of the LOST storyline, a major sub-plot that captivated millions around the world. I must have been immune to its magic, because I never joined the ranks of Jaters, Skaters, or Suliets. Until the very end, I didn't see much point in the romantic entanglements of the lead characters. The great love quadrangle collapsed under its own weight, I thought. It was the weakest structure in the LOST universe, a shameful storytelling exercise that dragged a genre-bending television series into the realm of daytime soap operas. The Jack-Kate-Sawyer-Juliet love connection devalued LOST and wasted the prodigious talents of extraordinary actors on a six-year-long guessing game that served only to infuriate dedicated fans and serious devotees.

We can certainly look at the romance sub-plot in this way, but as with just about any other facet of this multi-dimensional series, alternative viewpoints are not only valid, but their plausibility is supported by well-engineered character depth and plotline substance. The build-up to Sawyer's embrace of Juliet followed by Kate and Jack's kiss on the cliffs did not end with the destruction of the quadrangle. We know this because we realise Sawyer did not leave the Island alone.

Most of you reading this are scratching your heads at this point, wondering what oddball idea Pearson has come up with this time. Sawyer, you're saying to yourselves, sat alone on that Ajira plane. Kate wasn't with him, she was two seats away, holding Claire's hand. Juliet wasn't with him, either; she was long dead and buried on the Island. So how can I say Sawyer was not alone? What strange scheme has Pearson devised?

It's not my scheme, though, it's Jacob's. It was Jacob, after all, who said it only ends once, and that all the fighting, destruction, and corruption before then is just progress. The quadrangle was indeed destructive, but it was also the best example of Jacob's Progress. I was the most vocal critic of the love quadrangle, even into Season Six when it was clear that Sawyer had cast his lot with Juliet. I didn't see the point of it then, blinded as I was by the brilliant mythology of the story. But LOST, in the end, is a story about people, and the great love quadrangle turned out not only to be a terrific sub-plot in itself, but it served to unite four character arcs with the grand mythology of the show. Every one of the characters, diverse as they were, ended the show by asserting the primacy of a single, overwhelming concern. This chapter is about that concern, the axis of symmetry in the Great Quadrangle that perfectly resolved the story of LOST.

Signs of Compatibility

Opposites attract, they say. Men are from Mars, women are from Venus. James Carville drives political campaigns for Democratic candidates, while his wife, Mary Matalin, works in high-profile capacities for his Republican opponents. Yet if ever there was an example of marital bliss, surely it is most fully exemplified by the dynamic duo from New Orleans. I stated in "LOST Humanity" that the Strange Attractor connection—the struggle relationship—is more important than even the Constant-type love relationship. In the common wisdom that "opposites attract," could it be that we somehow inherently recognise the value of strife in a relationship? Is it possible that the occasional or frequent argument between wife and husband is not only inevitable, but is actually the glue that holds a life-long relationship together?

Any of us who have survived a few decades of marital discord chafe at this notion. We have intimate and unpleasant knowledge of points of irreconcilable contention that at one point or another have threatened to render asunder that which was never threatened by any outside force. Adultery is not the leading cause of divorce. The leading causes are these far-flung, sometimes amorphous areas of contention that divorce briefs reference as "irreconcilable differences." People leave each other because they are too different from their mates and not because of any extra-marital temptations. Perhaps there is some attraction between those of opposing temperament, but hard-won experience tells those of us in enduring relationships that elements of belief and practice held in common and close to the heart are the most reliable anchors in any clash of will and desire.

The way we considered the first love triangle (Jack-Kate-Sawyer), as a legitimate competition between Jack and Sawyer for one woman's heart, makes a good deal of sense in light of the durable wisdom of those who have made relationships work. The Carville-Matalin marriage is the rare exception upholding the otherwise broadly applicable rule that couples who survive the slings and arrows are those who share common and deep concerns. Kate was attracted to Jack because he represented stability—the central feature of his personality that directly challenged Kate's need to be always on the run. But

Kate was more attracted, or so we believed, to Sawyer. Kate and Sawyer were both criminals, they had both murdered, and both of them had devised and executed elaborate cons. If the Island ever brought couples together, it must have seemed to many of us—perhaps most of us—and even the Jaters!—that Kate would eventually succumb to Sawyer's wit and charm. Jack, of course, would see in Juliet the perfect reflection of his life-long pursuit of medical expertise and his deep concern for patient well-being. Theirs was a perfect romance, born in a heavenly jungle. Juliet could no more fall in love with bad-ass Sawyer than she could abandon a patient.

Deep Fissures

Kate seemed to bounce back and forth between Jack and Sawyer. We were aware of the frequently-expressed rationale for Kate's eventual decision to choose Jack. Ben communicated nothing novel to Sawyer when he articulated the reason in Episode 4.02, "Confirmed Dead":

BEN: I know its not pleasant but, let's face it, you really don't stand a chance now...
SAWYER: Chance of what?
BEN: James. Look at yourself. Yes, on this Island you're brave, daring, handsome, you're someone, but if you left with them, back in the real-world a low-life scam artist like you could never compete with a first class surgeon. I think Kate was really upset when you made your choice to come with us. Thank god she has Jack there to comfort...

Sawyer's charm, so the thinking went, would never overcome Jack's ability to provide financially and in quality of life. Perhaps Jack wasn't as exciting in the emotional department—not as sexy, maybe—but he would more than make up for any deficits through his quality of character.

In a similar manner, we knew to expect fractures in any relationship between Juliet and Jack. Juliet knew his background, after all, down to the most minute detail of the divorce settlement between him and his wife, Sarah. By all accounts, Sarah was a good woman, and yet she found life with Jack, the man who fixed her, to be intolerable. As Juliet came to know Jack, and especially in experiencing his less-than-admirable response to difficult situations, she must have found herself feeling increasingly concerned about any romantic involvement with him.

But these fissures, deep as they were, and as convincing as they might be to an independent observer, did not constitute the origin of discord between Jack and Juliet or Sawyer and Kate. If we are to understand the way this four-pointed star collapsed, we need to dig deep into the characters.

The Constant

The Constant is not the deepest or strongest connection between characters. It is not even necessarily the most enduring. Romantic relationships can be resolved in almost any way in fiction, but LOST is not just any fictional work. There are rules in the LOST universe, and the establishment and unfolding of relationships adhered to patterns unique in fiction. This fidelity to process was demonstrated most convincingly in the orderly collapse of the romantic quadrangle. Before we can understand that process, we need to understand two important features of the Constant.

The Constant need not be a lover. Recall Faraday's explanation in Episode 4.05, "The Constant":

DANIEL: ... I think Eloise's brain short-circuited. The jumps between the present and the future ... she eventually, she couldn't tell which was which — she had no anchor.
DESMOND: Wh...what do you mean, anchor?
DANIEL: Something familiar in both times. All this, see this is all variables, it's random, it's chaotic. Every equation needs stability, something known. It's called a constant. Desmond, you have no constant. When you go to the future, nothing there is familiar. So if you want to stop this, then you need to find something there ... something that you really, really care about ... that also exists back here, in 1996.

The Constant is nothing more than an anchor in space and time. Faraday had no romantic attachment to Desmond, but he wrote in his notebook, "If anything goes wrong, Desmond Hume will be MY constant."

The important aspect of this advice from the master of time travel, at least for the purpose of our discussion, is not the fact that anything or anyone can serve as a Constant. The crucial property is choice. The Constant relationship is established through the free choice of the person or persons creating the connection. Desmond was free to choose Penny, but he had to know that she had also chosen to retain Desmond as her anchor. Penny could have refused. Desmond could have sought a spacetime anchor in someone or something else. But they both made a decision to maintain an intimate relationship despite all obstacles. The hallmark of the Constant relationship, then, is choice.

This fact is one of the reasons for my statement in "LOST Humanity" that the Constant anchor is not the primary human relationship, at least according to LOST.

Primary Concern

The fundamental concern of life does not come about as the result of caprice. One does not choose a primary concern. Rather, it is the centre of attention itself that takes root in the souls of those it calls and directs their journey. The innermost concern fuels our opinions, our resolve, our courage, and our will. But the deepest concern of our lives is not itself any of these things. Opinions change. People lose their determination. We believe our ability to shift focus, to make a conscious decision to shift our allegiance from one worthy cause to an entirely new locus of commitment indicates our complete freedom of thought and action. But at our core we are never in flux. The deepest concern never wavers. Its manifestations, in the form of the opinions and decisions informed by temperament and history, are constantly in motion. The fundamental concern, however, the force of nature guiding our will, is unmoved.

Are human beings ruled by destiny or free will? Do we have a purpose or are we subject only to the whim of the moment? This was the question posed by the adoptive mother (the Guardian) of Jacob and the Man in Black. She appears to have considered the question one of good versus evil. But this is not the form of the question that became Jacob and the Man in Black's primary concern over the next two thousand years. Their mutual concern, the object of their contemplation that captured them in an eternal struggle, was the idea of fate. "They come, they fight, they destroy, they corrupt, and it always ends the same," the Guardian said. The Man in Black in subsequent years reiterated her position without deviation. His captive partner in this lifelong struggle, Jacob, provided the essential nuance that allowed us to understand the focal point of their strange attraction. "It only ends once," he said. "Anything that happens before that is just progress."

According to Jacob there is an endpoint. That is, we have a destiny toward which we orient our lives. We have purpose, our lives have meaning, because our life journeys have a final destination not determined by the vagaries of choice, but by the sure and steady fundamental orientation of our lives. Struggle —whether with oneself or with others—is inevitable, because the human soul is on a trajectory toward fulfillment of its goal. Not only that, but as a society, as a civilisation—indeed, even as a species—all of us collectively participate in a grand trajectory that aligns with progress toward the attainment of the common elements of our humanity. All the fighting and destruction and corruption that occurs in the meantime is just progress toward that final and shared goal.

We need not believe Jacob. We may find ourselves in agreement with the Man in Black. Our decisions affect us more than any imposition of concern. There is no destiny as such, only human choices given in response to the ever-changing world. Choice, being subject to no unifying force, becomes entirely capricious, and leads to the endless suffering and death and corruption that are the true hallmarks of our humanity. There can be no hope of rising above. We are caught in endless conceptual, spatial, and temporal loops of repeating clash, discord, and violence. It always ends the same.

The Necessity of Struggle

LOST sides with Jacob on the question of destiny, at least to the extent of proclaiming that human life has purpose. "All of this matters," Jack told Desmond. There was a place in the pews for Desmond and Penny, but only because of the struggle that preceded the trip to Nirvana. Every instant of Jack's suffering and struggle to overcome his misplaced emphasis on the wonders of science and logic had meaning and value because it was in conflict that Jack attained new understanding. It was only through the testing of convictions in the crucible of battle that he came to have a more profound awareness of the true meaning of Mittelos.

Struggle is necessary, according to LOST, because it is in struggle that we gain intimate understanding of the topography of our deepest concern. What is science, if not the desire to understand and accept the structure of the universe around us? What is faith, if not the desire to understand and submit ourselves to the universe around us? Understanding is nothing more than another way of saying acceptance. "I understand that life evolves through natural selection of genetic mutation," is a statement of acceptance of the theory of evolution. I understand it. I accept it. From a spiritual point of view, I understand there is a Creator. I accept this, I submit myself to this truth. Science and faith may believe different things, but they both believe. They both consider exploration of the universe to be the primary focus of human life. Whether we call this understanding or acceptance or submission is a bit of semantics upon which the struggle gains its meaning.

Jack's struggle focussed on science. He became the primary advocate of faith not because his fundamental concern had changed, but because he finally understood the true nature of his concern. In the light of the laboratory and the operating room Jack understood that concern to be labeled "science." But in the much more penetrating Light of the Island, Jack finally discerned the truth that logic comprised only a small, almost insignificant subset of all ways of discovering knowledge, and that faith was a more appropriate term to describe the reality of his concern.

The Personalisation of Struggle

Jack did not come to this awareness by himself. Neither did he find a comfortable place on the sand near the ocean and contemplate his navel or the meaning of life or the significance of science to his existence. His understanding of science and faith were born of struggle. It was not just any type of conflict, though. He certainly faced an opposition of values within himself that nearly resolved as suicide over the side of a bridge. But the proddings that pushed him onto the bridge were not questions or doubts or battles of his own making. The tumult in his soul was not the result of a detached contemplation of objective truths known to all. He arrived at his understanding of science and faith through intimate struggle with a single individual: John Locke. Without John Locke, Jack Shephard could never have become the saviour of the Island.

The primary struggle of our lives, according to LOST, is the principal driver of our emotions, beliefs, thoughts, and actions. It is not something we decide, and not anything we discover on our own or through disinterested consideration of abstract ideas. The struggle affects the character to the core, because the very concrete aspects of that struggle are uniquely manifested in the single person the character engages in battle. Struggle, in LOST, is always a one-on-one conflict between two advocates for diametrically opposed understandings of the same fundamental concept. For Jack and Locke, the concept was Faith/Science. For the Man in Black and Jacob, the concept was Destiny/Free Will. For Hurley and Ben, the concept was Honesty/Deception.

The concepts were driven by the peculiarities of both members of the odd-couple (or "strange attractor") pair. Thus, Jack struggled with the effects of science and faith on the Island, because his strange attractor twin, John Locke, brought precisely these concerns to their heated discussions. The argument regarding destiny and free will centred on human beings in general, and was not limited to any effects on the Island, because this was the nature of the conflict that Jacob and the Man in Black engaged. The struggles were personal, but they had far-reaching implications.

Incompatibilities

Kate and Sawyer could never have attained compatibility as a Constant couple. In fact, Kate was drawn to him not because he nurtured her, but because he stood in the way of achieving her goal of detached freedom. Kate's deepest struggle was toward instability. She ran. It was the single most defining feature of her character. She ran from everything, from everyone. She liked Sawyer because he was closest in bearing and temperament to the one person she most despised: Her biological father, Wayne Janssen. She struggled with Wayne, and then she struggled with Sawyer. But at some point she must have realised the struggle had neither meaning nor value. Whether she understood it or not, she had been seeking to emulate Wayne—in her thoughts, in her words, in what she did, in what she failed to do. In fact, she was in temperament and behaviour so similar to Wayne that she could have adopted his name.

We know of strong precedent for this close emulation of vile personality. James Ford might have retained some of the innocence of youth if he had taken to heart his uncle's words. "Listen to me, Jimmy. I know you're angry at the man that did this to your momma and daddy. And hell, you got every right to be. But you gotta move on, boy. They're gone, and there ain't nothing you can do to change that. [pauses] What's done is done. Now promise me you're not going to finish that letter." He promised, but he went ahead and wrote it anyway, made firm in his resolve for retribution thanks to the pen that Jacob had given him. He became Sawyer, as Kate became Wayne.

Their romance had no future, because it had no present, it had no value to either of them. Their attraction was not to each other, but to the idea of stability, and in LOST there are no abstractions, no ideas over which one can fight or take a stand. There are only individuals who articulate a truth diametrically opposed to our own. Each character had to seek out the other character whose view of life was most contrary to her own. Kate had to seek out the character who valued stability above all things.

Kate understood stability in familial terms. Both of her fathers were unstable. Wayne was a carousing drunkard. Sam Austen was an absentee soldier-dad. Diane was working all the time, when she wasn't off carousing with Wayne. When Kate settled down for a plain, stable life of taco night and domestic bliss in suburban Miami, she tolerated the strange state of personal security until she missed her menstrual cycle. Missing a cycle could mean pregnancy, and pregnancy would bring a fast end to life on the run. Parenthood, for Kate, was the very definition of stability, for she could not imagine imposing on any child the awful, fragmented life she had known in her youth.

So it was that nothing scared her more than the stability, responsibility, and domesticity that she saw in Claire. Wayne and Sawyer and Ed Mars worked the same side of the Instability = Stability equation that Kate believed she was pursuing. They could not serve as strange-attractor agents of her personal growth because they were on the same side of the conceptual divide. Claire, on the other hand, was the perfect twin for Kate's odd-couple dance toward personal enlightenment.

Jacob's Progress

Kate found emotional strength in Jack because his attractor was entirely different from hers. Jack's obsession was Science/Faith, not Stability/Instability. They found comfort in each other's arms because they neither competed for nor complemented the other's primary concern. Sawyer never could have provided this emotional strength for Kate, because his primary concern was too much like hers.

When the players in this strange quadrangle reached emotional and spiritual maturity, they came to see the truth. Only Juliet, in her unyielding commitment to others, could provide the foundation for James Ford's growth into a true leader. Only Kate Austen could keep up with Jack on his lonely journey.

The final state of maturity assures the eternal bond promised by the Constant. This is not something achieved by choice, and neither is it achieved through strange-attractor struggle alone. All facets of character must be developed to their fullest potential, and this includes that part of human character that seeks reconciliation. Kate's mother wronged her, and Kate wronged her mother. Jack's father hurt him, and Jack hurt his father. The back-and-forth retribution across the generations had to be addressed, and this was most fully achieved in the sideways world. Kate delivered Claire's baby—again—and remembered. But she was not just remembering. In bringing Claire's baby into the world she was accepting Aaron's role in bringing an end to the legacy of emotional pain in the Janssen household. Kate was able to finally embrace Jack without inhibitions only after Aaron freed her to be the mature Kate Austen.

Jack was not free to move on into eternity until he had addressed his family's wounds. He accomplished this in the sideways reality by raising a fine son, and by not bringing pain into David's life. It was only after this work was complete that Locke told him the truth that set Jack on the path toward full maturity: "You don't have a son, Jack." Just as Kate needed Aaron to become fully Jack's Constant, Jack needed David to become the one man who could stand at Kate's side for their trip to Shambala.

Sawyer's union with Juliet was assured not by killing Anthony Cooper, but by providing for Clementine's future. And Juliet, whose childhood in its own way had been no less tortured than Sawyer's, became the only woman who could stand at his side when she dedicated her life to bringing new life into the world.

In the end, romantic ties were made neither through struggle nor through choice, but through children. The cheery disposition of everyone in the pews just before they were engulfed by the Light was the result of the purity and goodness of Aaron, David, Clementine, and young Ben Linus. The children shall lead us, because the children are our future and our legacy. They are the flesh-and-blood manifestations of the truth that it only ends once. They are Jacob's Progress.

I rewatch the old episodes now. I see Kate bouncing back and forth between Sawyer and Jack, and this time, I'm enjoying it. I like this strange little love quadrangle, and I'm glad it's part of my favourite television series. The four-pointed star collapsed, but it collapsed into something beautiful. I'm not immune to the magic anymore.

The Leader

CHAPTER 8: THE LEADER

You'll understand soon enough that there are consequences to being chosen. Because destiny, John, is a fickle bitch.

> —Benjamin Linus, "Cabin Fever

He lied.

The topic before him had no bearing on his words: he deceived in matters large, in details small. The consequences of dishonesty figured into his thoughts only to the extent of laying the groundwork for the next deception, which in turn would provide the foundation for subsequent misdirection. He manipulated facts and fabricated stories to suit his purpose, to frame conditions to his liking, to cause those he controlled to believe he was advancing their agenda so that he could nefariously implement his own well-engineered plans.

He manipulated, coerced, forced those under him to commit the worst offences. When lying was insufficient to his ends, he murdered. He killed with his bare hands or with weapons, with guns, gas, or rope. He actively participated in mass murder. A reasonable jury of his peers would be obliged to find him guilty on all charges and pass down the severest of sentences.

Benjamin Linus was arguably the most villainous, hateful character on the Island. But we found ourselves liking him. Ilana, who knew his crimes, was never taken in my his tricks, pardoned him. The man who was his opposite, who endeavoured never to fabricate an untruth, took him on as advisor. At Ben's own death he was found worthy to make the voyage to the Church of the Holy Lamp Post, having served well as Hurley's faithful consigliere.

It is appropriate to ask what might reasonably be considered the greatest unanswered question in the six years of LOST: Who was Benjamin Linus?

Original Innocence

The circumstances of his youth were most similar to those of his future nemesis, John Locke. Both men were born several months premature to a woman named Emily. Both endured a tortured childhood of neglect and abuse without the care of a mother. Each of them later in life would methodically engineer his own father's death.

At some point their paths diverged. Locke never seemed to grow up. He insisted that the world around him conform to his understanding, that those in charge allow him to be the person he believed himself to be. Locke's innocence was so integral to his being that he could not conceive of the notion of deception. Even after fifty years of navigating the real world, he never figured out that at every turn people had been taking advantage of his trust in them. His gullibility would be his undoing. He lost his money, lost a kidney, lost the use of his legs, and finally lost his life. Every bit of suffering in his sad life was the bitter outcome of his own innocent trust in the good will of others.

We don't know which events in Ben's early years led to his adoption of deceit and manipulation as a default *modus operandi*. The example of John Locke indicates we cannot blame a motherless childhood or the capricious vagaries of life that placed more than a boy's fair share of suffering in their paths. Apparently neither of these conditions was sufficient to induce either life-long innocence or habitual deceit. Every generation provides examples of children neglected and abused who become sterling examples of trustworthy industry and responsibility in their adult years. We must look to some other cause of Ben's manipulative lifestyle.

Both men came to hate their fathers, but at different times, and for different reasons. It is in the Darltonian expression of malignant fatherhood that we see the most vivid contrast between Ben and Locke.

Anthony Cooper, like Ben and James Ford after him, earned his livelihood from a keen facility with manipulation. But a lifetime of seducing women and conniving to take their husbands' savings made him too busy to check in on young John Locke, even once.

Sins of the Fathers

Roger Linus was a very different kind of father.

Roger might have left his son, if he'd had the opportunity to do so. But on a janitor's wages, and with most of his meagre income dedicated to nightly rounds of liquid amnesia, he would never get off the Island. So he took the time-honoured path of many men in the same situation: he ignored his son. Child neglect was not a punishable offence in the Dharma Initiative, and besides, these were the disco-drenched 70s; no one was sober enough to figure out what anyone else was doing.

The situation was sad for young Ben, but many boys have grown up under similar situations without becoming psychopathic liars. But few boys under such conditions were exposed to the species of psychological abuse that Ben suffered on a nightly basis. Roger planted in his son's heart an idea of the kind that should never be expressed to a child, even in a fit of anger. Especially not in a fit of anger. Roger told his son that he, Ben, was responsible for his own mother's death.

Perhaps this was the unbearable burden of undeserved guilt that caused Ben's visions of his dead mother. He didn't question her apparition, but others did. When he entered the deactivation code for the sonic fence and slipped into the Hostiles' territory, he came upon Richard Alpert. When Ben explained he was looking for his dead mother, Richard's interest in the boy increased immediately.

RICHARD: Did she die here, on the Island?
BEN: No. When I was a baby.
RICHARD: Did you see her, out here, Ben, in the jungle?
BEN: She talked to me.
RICHARD: What did she say?
BEN: That I couldn't come with her. She said it wasn't time yet.

In hindsight we know that the apparition of someone who had not died on the Island would be taken as unusual by any of the Others, and especially by the one member of the League of Jacob who lived through the ages. What did the apparition of Emily Linus mean to Ben? To the Others? Was Ben possibly among those being groomed by Jacob for Island leadership? Did Ben's visions point to some other "special" aspect of his character that would have significance for Jacob's band?

Roger's frequent refrain that Ben had caused his own mother's death was the inexcusable ranting of a man entirely unfit for the care of a child. I don't imagine there is any way to accurately calculate the deep psychological damage that must have been inflicted by Roger's deplorable contempt for his own son's mental health. The wounds to Ben's soul must have been painful beyond anything a human being should have to endure.

I don't believe, though, that Roger's thoughtlessness and his unsuitability for parenting were sufficient to have caused Ben's manipulative temperament and his comfort in deception. I believe going to the root of Ben's character requires that we spend time contemplating a concrete object in Richard's possession at the time of his meeting with Ben. If we understand this object, we will understand Ben.

The Compass

We saw this compass for the first time in Lost 4.11 ("Cabin Fever"). It was one of the six items Richard showed to young John Locke in 1961, asking the boy, "Which of these things belong to you already?" The compass was one of the items Locke identified as belonging to him.

The boy was correct. The adult John Locke gave the compass to Richard in 1954 during the period of erratic time travels as a proof that he was from the future. Richard kept the compass for the next 53 years. He surrendered the compass to the wounded, time-traveling John Locke in 2007, instructing Locke to give the compass back to him the next time Locke saw him. That next meeting turned out to be their short conversation in 1954, since that was Locke's next stop on his time-travel tour. Richard accepted the compass, showed it to young Locke in 1961, and returned it to Locke in 2007, who transported it back to 1954, gave it to Richard, who...

With most of the human players in Jacob's two-thousand-year-old game of backgammon, the compass was caught in an endless time loop. The compass existed in concrete form, but it was never created. The compass had no possible entry point into the loop. It had no beginning, it would never have an end. It just *was.*

The Man in Black, posing as John Locke just before the real Locke's time-travel appearance in 2007, asked Richard about the compass Locke had given him in 1956. "A little rusty," Richard said, "but she can still find north." Perhaps it was a manifestation of the MIB's sense of humour, perhaps it was a deeper intention to control people, events, and time itself, but it was the Smoke Monster who told Richard to give the compass back to Locke during that critical rendez-vous in 2007. By instructing Richard to return the compass to Locke, Smokey was ensuring the perpetuation of an endless time loop. If nothing else, the endless circularity through time of people, events, and objects supported the MIB's understanding of human behaviour. " They come. They fight. They destroy. They corrupt. It always ends the same."

If all the important events on the Island were captured in endless loops, the Smoke Monster would always turn out to be correct. If every occurrence of any importance was relegated to a time loop, Jacob's vision of human progress finally ending the loops would never come to pass. Perhaps by controlling all the defining events in this manner he could gain the upper hand over Jacob and make the final move that would end their perpetual game of senet to his advantage.

Destroying the Loop

We were witness to the end of all time loops. The selfless heroism of Boone, Charlie, Locke, Sayid, Kate, and the greatest hero, Jack Shephard, ended for all time the eternal, circular game of senet. The destruction of time loops was the final grand objective of Lost. By accepting Jacob's gauntlet, these men and women not only showed their mettle and proved their valour, but demonstrated for all the stuff of which humans are truly made.

Those who were "special" were the immortal heroes, the women and men who did not shirk the call of destiny, even when the Island called them to self-sacrifice. "You were special, John," Ben told Locke outside the Church of the Holy Lamp Post. Indeed. Locke's heroism was the most magnificent demonstration of the divinity of his soul, for he knew his mission had to end in his own death.

Jack's mission was the single most important calling anyone had received since Biblical times. Everything else had to be put on hold, even the reconciliation of Jack with his own father. How fitting it was, then, that the Island summoned not Kate, not Sarah, not his sister, Claire, but Christian Shephard, to bring his son back to consciousness after the crash. "I need you to go find my son," Christian told the yellow Labrador Retriever, Vincent. "He's over there in that bamboo forest, unconscious. I need you to go wake him up.... He has work to do."

Ray Shephard never had faith in his son, Christian. Christian never had faith in his son, Jack. Jack ended the cruel, circular Shephard heritage of father-son enmity by raising a fine son, David, and connecting with him. Jack was allowed this final resolution not in his life on earth, but in the life after his heroic act.

Ben's Loop

Ben was a tragic figure. For many years he thought himself "special". Perhaps Richard, knowing of Ben's visions of his mother, considered him "special", too. Perhaps most or all of the Others considered their leader somehow different from themselves. He had inherited the Island from Charles Widmore, after all. But Jacob didn't grant him even a perfunctory audience, not a word of gratitude for his long service. Ben never was special. Finally grasping the truth of that fact must have hurt Ben to the very depths of his being.

I believe the tragedy of Ben, the endless, almost unbearably monotonous quality of his grand deceptions and fabrications, and the genesis of his flawed character were all wrapped into a single momentous event in 1977 that captured him forever into a great time loop.

In Season Five, Sayid gave us his understanding of Benjamin Linus:

"He's a liar, a manipulator...a man who allowed his own daughter to be murdered to save himself...A monster responsible for nothing short of genocide."

In Sayid Jarrah's mind, Ben Linus was of the same ilk as Adolf Hitler. Sayid brought young Ben into his confidence, allowing Ben to believe he was one of the hallowed "Hostiles". The adolescent Ben trusted Sayid so much he engineered an elaborate jail break for the man. Alone with Ben far away from the Dharma barracks, Sayid saw the chance he had been waiting for. He aimed the gun directly at the boy's heart and fired. Ben fell to the ground, apparently dead.

The waters of the Temple eventually saved Ben. Richard claimed Ben would not remember anything that happened before the immersion in the waters, but he would be changed forever. He would no longer have the innocence of youth.

I believe it was not Jacob's healing waters that robbed young Ben of his innocence. I believe it was Sayid's betrayal of Ben's trust that forever removed any possibility of trust from the boy's range of conceivable dispositions. After he had placed complete faith in a man he believed a "Hostile", one of the "good guys" in the boy's mind, only to become the object of the man's unjustified but complete hatred, how could he ever again trust anyone? How could he tell anyone the truth ever again? If the only person he ever found worthy of his trust could shoot him in the chest, fully intending to murder him with a single shot, how could he ever place even a modicum of faith in anyone's professed intentions?

In spite of what Richard claimed, I believe Ben could never have forgotten this event. Perhaps he didn't remember Sayid, but how could he have forgotten a bullet to the chest? A wound that very nearly killed him? No amnesia-inducing waters would carry a force sufficient to overcome a reality that strong and dark and full of corruption. Ben remembered. Those memories made him into the man he became. And what he became was another tragic loop, just another example the Smoke Monster could point out as proof of his thesis regarding the most enduring and contemptible qualities of the corrupt and rotten human soul.

Redemption of a Soul Lost

Charles Widmore's instructions to Ben in 1988 could not have been any clearer: Ben was to find Danielle Rousseau's camp, murder the woman, and kill her child. The young man had wanted to join the Others since his arrival on the Island fifteen years before. He must have been a constant pain in Widmore's side, this young man who thought himself "special". A young man who even then must have been using every waking moment of his life trying to discover the means by which he might wrest control of the group from Widmore's hands. Did Widmore send young Ethan Rom on the mission to ensure Ben's faithful execution of the gruesome task?

I don't believe Ben refused Widmore's orders in an attempt to amass political power. I don't think he saved Danielle and baby Alex to spite Widmore or usurp his authority. I think his decision to spare baby Alex's life was the only response Ben could have made in the situation. Just as life experience had turned him into a psychopathic liar, I believe the earlier and even more painful events of life—beginning with separation from his own mother—instilled in Ben Linus a natural affinity for children and an unquenchable desire to ensure the fulfillment of their needs. Roger Linus was the worst father one could imagine. Ben must have had such a deep desire to correct the evils his father had wrought that the prospect of raising a girl with the full intensity of a father's love must have driven him more than any consequences Widmore might have chosen to mete out for Ben's insubordination. Baby Alex's life must have meant as much to him as his own life. When he looked into the little baby's eyes, he must have seen only one possible outcome.

The Final Blow

Perhaps raising a child to adulthood could have made up for Ben's earlier genocide. In the Richard Attenborough film, "Gandhi", one of the most moving scenes occurs near the end of the movie. A Hindu man, Nahari, rushes up to the Great Mahatma, who is weak from the nearly month-long food fast he began in response to Muslim/Hindu bloodshed. The man's eyes are wide in sheer terror.

Nahari: I'm going to Hell! I killed a child! I smashed his head against a wall.
Gandhi: Why?
Nahari: Because they killed my son! The Muslims killed my son!
Gandhi: I know a way out of Hell. Find a child, a child whose mother and father have been killed and raise him as your own. Only be sure that he is a Muslim and that you raise him as one.

Ben almost fulfilled the self-imposed assignment. Sixteen-year-old Alex had grown into a beautiful young woman, capable in many ways, but still a child, still in need of a father's care. Ben took a gamble when Widmore's thug, Keamy, held a gun to Alex's head. The gamble was almost sure to succeed. Ben and Widmore both knew the rules, and those rules prevented either of them from assassinating family members.

"I stole her as a baby from an insane woman," Ben said. "She's a pawn, nothing more. She means nothing to me. I'm not coming out of this house. So if you want to kill her, go ahead and—"

Ben didn't get to finish his statement. Keamy put a bullet in the girl's brain and her lifeless body dropped to the ground.

Final Reckoning

He was a sad and lonely figure seated on the marble bench outside Our Lady of the Foucault Pendulum.

Perhaps he could have entered the church, Alex or Danielle accompanying him as his Constant. He had served admirably as Number Two to the Protector of the Island, Hurley. He was a sad man because he realised the enormity of his crimes. But more than anything, he continued to suffer the devastation of Alex's death. Sadness and devastation kept him outside, alone, spiritually unable to cross the threshold to the final antechamber before... moving on.

But he was there. Charles never made it anywhere near the church. Keamy died in a place where everyone was already dead—his soul forever expunged from the rolls of those who could call themselves human beings.

Ben was there.

Ben, despite a life of lies, tortures, and murders, mass murder, the cold-blooded execution of his own father—in spite of everything, Ben sat outside the church.

We might think it an instance of undeserved grace. I find myself believing something else entirely. Possibly none of us, other than the great heroes—the Jack Shephards and Kate Austens and John Lockes—could be said to deserve the grace that allows us admittance to the final antechamber. Perhaps that grace is extended even to those among us, undeserving as we are, who nevertheless think ourselves somehow a cut above, that in spite of our foibles we somehow are granted redemption. Perhaps even arrogant fools such as these are extended an undeserved and unappreciated grace.

Ben is not among these delusional fools. The pain in his soul is real. He is lonely, devastated, aching in the deepest recesses of his spirit. He stays on in his purgatory because to do otherwise would be to deprive himself of the single honest objective of his life: Raising a helpless girl he was supposed to have murdered, teaching her everything that is good and noble and true in the hearts of women and men, and seeing his helpless baby turn into a capable and beautiful and *trusting* young woman.

Benjamin Linus was allowed this grace, not because he begged for it or deserved it or thought himself worthy. He was allowed this final grace precisely because he knew himself unworthy, and because the death of Alex forever marked him a sad and lonely and pained man.

In Ben's pain and humility he found pardon and redemption. And someday, someday soon, taking Alex's hand or Danielle's hand in his own, he will cross the threshold, sit with his beloved Constant in a pew, surrounded by the Rousseau family friends and relatives and those cherished and adored, those Ben trusted, and experience the bright light that will carry them to a happier and eternal destiny.

The Man in Black

CHAPTER 9: THE MAN IN BLACK

The Devil betrayed me. He took my body. My humanity.
—The Man in Black, "Ab Aeterno"

His is a hardened heart of pure darkness.

So evil is he that no name attaches to his character. Even the most forgiving among us felt relief when Jack pushed him over the cliff to his death. How to feel compassion after two millennia of vile deeds? How to feel empathy, when he was so completely unlike any of us?

Many who have spent a few years thinking about the Man in Black are disquieted by our mixed emotions. The Island is at peace now that he is gone, but our thoughts about this character remain conflicted. This should not be the case. The story is over, and the Man in Black is most definitely dead. Why, then, our inability to drive this most evil of all characters from our thoughts?

He was dissatisfied, always on the move, wishing above all else to leave his island abode—he wanted to run. In this regard, was he any different from Kate? He was the original Man of Science, spending decades studying the Light and water he believed capable of releasing him from his island prison. In this regard, was he any different than the later Man of Science, Jack? Who among us would find fulfillment in meek submission to an eternity in shackles, never permitted to rejoin his own people? Can any one of us claim the Man in Black's goal of freedom was any different than ours would have been? In fact, in what way are we any different from the Man in Black?

We were told the Man in Black had no name. But we know his name. He bears seven billion names. We know him well, for this Man in Black, this most evil of all human beings, is no stranger to us. We know this most evil of all beings, for the Man in Black is us.

Guardian of Contempt and Lies

We create excuses for him—for ourselves. His own mother didn't even think to give him a name. The woman who became his Guardian murdered his mother and never showed him even a modicum of love. His brother hated him, and took every opportunity to beat him bloody. The Guardian lied to him about anything that mattered: his origins across the sea, his mother, his identity as a human being. As soon as the boy was old enough to reason, the Guardian taught him not human virtues, but contempt for anything related to humanity.

"All men [are] dangerous," she said. "They come, they fight, they destroy, they corrupt... and it always ends the same." She repeated this teaching at every turn, relentlessly transforming her perception of the world into the boys' complete understanding of existence. "You're special," she told the Man in Black, as if to say he was unlike men, unlike even his own brother. Can we blame him for believing his desires outweighed the needs of others? Of what value were the needs of men, when their very nature was base, when men were "greedy, manipulative, untrustworthy, and selfish"?

The woman the boys addressed as "mother" not only taught them contempt for humanity, she valued deceit above honesty, control above personal autonomy. She lied about every aspect of life the boys would ever become familiar with. The Island was the only refuge of life in an ocean world. There was nothing "beyond the sea," and certainly no human beings. She was their mother, and the boys came from her.

The Boy in Black was "special," though, and the Guardian should have known he would discover the truth on his own. But even after her favoured one learned the truth—from his dead mother's own lips—she attempted to control him, to mold him to her will, to prepare him for duty as the Protector.

None of this was the Boy in Black's fault. He had not asked for a psychopathic guardian, for a mama's–boy brother who hated him, for a sterile and hostile environment that was conducive only to the most warped understanding of life. If the Boy in Black was never shown love, if the only person who ever loved him was violently removed from his life, if he was taught to hold humans in contempt, if his only example of humanity lied to him about everything, can we blame him for demonstrating that contempt in his adult life?

Reality and Childhood

As dark as the Guardian's assessment of humanity was, we know her words to be true. Not a woman or man who has ever walked the earth has had a heart devoid of greed and selfishness. No one who has ever drawn breath has shown herself trustworthy in all matters. If a man proclaims that human beings are good, that we are motivated only by pure intentions, we say the man is delusional. On the other hand, if a woman declares that human beings are foul, that our deeds are rooted in selfish desires, we know we ought to defend her stance as realistic and almost always correct.

If, then, the Guardian raised the Man in Black to recognise truth, how can we fault his childhood, or believe her teachings to have planted in him any motivations antithetical to a life well lived? Can it be anyone's fault other than his own that he became the most dreaded being ever known, and that he turned an island paradise into hell on earth?

But this argument is a paper tiger. That an aspect of human existence adheres to reality is no justification for its inclusion in the teaching of our children. War, for example, has always been a part of the reality of human existence, but we do not include in our bedtime stories the grisly accounts of men losing life or limb because other men are shooting at them, or throwing bombs and missiles in hopes of inflicting harm. Childhood is a time for the inculcation of good habits and ideals of behaviour and ambition.

Even the darkest stories of the Brothers Grimm began from the instinctively-recognised premise that human life is good, that parents are good, that children are good. Even if a story ended badly, the child could distill from it the lesson that she and her parents were immune to the ills suffered by the story's less than perfect characters. The child and her parents, after all, were virtuous, while the characters had well-noted faults.

Any parent with the least awareness of the needs of children knows to protect her own flesh and blood from the less savoury realities of life and to instead emphasise the virtuous possibilities of human existence. That the Guardian did not follow this tack is again her fault, not the fault of those who suffered under her misguided and hurtful tutelage.

Absolution or Accountability

I suppose a fair number of those reading this chapter—perhaps a strong majority—favour the position that we cannot absolve the Man in Black his sins against Island visitors and residents. Adulthood is nothing if not rooted in the notion of accountability. From a legal point of view, ignorance of the law is not a positive defence. So too, from a moral point of view, ignorance of the elementary values of humanity provides no ethical basis for life as a human being.

We are all subject to legal, social, and moral laws. As adults, we are expected to face the consequences of our actions, whether or not we enjoyed *a priori* understanding of those consequences. If the Ministry of Natural Resources officer finds bass in my cooler when I was allowed to catch only trout, I may argue as much as I like that bass season has not ended, and how was I supposed to know that bass fishing has always been prohibited at Minnow Lake? But I am equally at fault whether I knew of the restriction or decided to flout it. It was my responsibility to look into any special restrictions at the lake; it was not the responsibility of the MNR or anyone else to inform me beforehand.

The case of Socrates is illuminating in this regard. Socrates was charged with the corruption of the young people of Athens, specifically for teaching about "things in the heavens and below the earth." He was the most visible of the itinerant teachers known as Sophists, and he was certainly aware of the growing social hostility toward those who taught eristic—winning a debate by any means possible, even through deceit or obfuscation—and that as the premier instructor in the sophistic arts he would be held accountable to Athenian law. It seems unlikely that he was the innocent teacher of pure dialectic ("the Socratic Method") that his most famous pupil, Plato, asserted in his later dialogues. In fact, he owned up to his guilt, at least to the point of agreeing to accept the penalty for his illegal activities, which in 5th century BCE Athens was death by ingestion of hemlock.

The most fascinating aspect of Socrates' short post-trial life is that he could have chosen a long and happy life. I do not embellish when I say he *chose* to accept the penalty. Socrates had so many friends in high places that his detention was an unnecessary formality. His friends had bribed the guards, and he would have been allowed virtually free passage out of the city. He could have escaped to Naxos or Thyra or any other Greek-speaking enclave beyond the long arm of Athenian law. That he could have escaped, but chose not to do so, is important to the argument I wish to make on behalf of the Man in Black.

Exile From Athens

Socrates had several solid reasons for his decision to face punishment. But the causal relation of greatest interest to this chapter was his recognition of social contract. The less thoughtful of his many followers considered only Socrates' potential future life. They didn't see his life as a whole, as a teacher who had benefitted from the philosophical diversity and free inquiry that had been essential to Athenian culture for decades. Socrates saw himself as integral to Athens. If he were to flee to some far abode outside Athens' laws, it would mean surrendering an essential part of his identity.

Socrates was a teacher, but also a man consumed with the desire to learn. He practiced and taught that the ideal life should concentrate on the acquisition of knowledge and wisdom, not wealth or comfort. Since he sought knowledge above all else, he tended to seek the company of those considered to be the wisest of Athens.

Without a doubt, his relentless questioning of learned citizens and accomplished soldiers and politicians proved embarrassing, since his questions would inevitably reveal the wisdom of even the most experienced leaders was founded on superstition or incorrect understanding or irrational belief. But embarrassment or not, the conversations with the most intelligent leaders in the most intellectually-driven centre of learning in the Mediterranean constituted the aspect of Socrates' life that excited him more than anything else in his experience. If he fled Athens, he would be giving up forever these conversations with the most experienced and fascinating individuals in the world. Facing a choice between death and a life devoid of the only joy that life can bring—the acquisition of new knowledge—Socrates chose death.

Some may think his choice too severe. If you are among those who believe he could have extracted some happiness from a life in exile, consider the other preoccupation that gave him pleasure: teaching. Athens provided the most attentive students of any city in the world. Since no other location could afford him students as committed to the pursuit of knowledge as he required, death again was the better choice.

I do not wish to argue that we should be like Socrates. My argument is simpler: We *are* like Socrates. More than anything else, we seek meaningful learning and teaching, give and take—sharing—with other human beings. In this respect, no one who has ever lived is different from Socrates or from you and me. If the Man in Black was to exercise his humanity, he had to be able to engage in the give and take that is essential to our identity as human beings.

But note what the Guardian taught him about his identity, and about his relationship with other human beings:

BOY IN BLACK: We saw people! Men!
...
JACOB: ...They looked like us!
GUARDIAN: They're not like us. They don't belong here. We are here for a reason.

...
BOY IN BLACK: Why didn't you tell us about them?
GUARDIAN: Because they're dangerous and I didn't want to frighten you.
JACOB: What makes them dangerous?
GUARDIAN: The same thing that makes all men dangerous. They come, they fight, they destroy, they corrupt...
JACOB: Why would they hurt us?
GUARDIAN: Because they're people, Jacob, and that's what people do.
BOY IN BLACK: But we're people. Does that mean that we can hurt each other?

These words from the Guardian were the worst imaginable instruction to young children. Her words meant that she considered the two boys to be above human beings [we have a reason for existence, men (humans) do not], and in fact they were not human beings at all. Humans—these beings who were different from the Guardian and the two boys—were to be feared and distrusted, because they were dangerous, they would hurt the boys ("that's what they do"), and everything they did resulted in destruction and corruption.

Since they were not human, nothing the boys said, did, or believed could be considered to share in any way with humanity.

The Boy in Black was aware of his identity as a human being, but the Guardian sought to deny him any attachment—physical, psychological, or otherwise—to humans. By the time he reached his early forties, after a lifetime of being told that he was not a human being, that he was special and unlike anyone else in the world, he was used to considering himself to be set apart, higher than humanity:

JACOB: ...I wanna know if Mother's right.
MAN IN BLACK: Right about what?
JACOB: About them.
MAN IN BLACK: Oh, you mean my people. You wanna know if they're bad. That woman may be insane, but she's most definitely right about that.
JACOB: I don't know. They don't seem so bad to me.
MAN IN BLACK: ... Trust me, I've lived among them for 30 years. They're greedy, manipulative, untrustworthy, and selfish.
JACOB: Then why are you with them?
MAN IN BLACK: They're a means to an end.

People have no intrinsic value, and they have nothing of value in and of themselves (as objectives in themselves) to offer the Man in Black. They're merely objects—tools—to be exploited toward the attainment of an objective of intrinsic value.

In this sense, the Man in Black became much like Archibald Beechcroft (http://en.wikipedia.org/wiki/The_Mind_and_the_Matter)in his outlook. A more widely-known analogy with the Twilight Zone is Henry Bemis (http://en.wikipedia.org/wiki/Henry_Bemis) , from TZ 1.08, "Time Enough At Last," but the themes in this benchmark episode were so densely layered and interconnected, the extraction of a clear, single theme is quite difficult. Even though Henry Bemis sought books more than other human beings, he suffered the same loneliness that afflicted Archibald Beechcroft. Neither man, in the end, could endure the psychological torments of a world without people or their ideas.

Despite the best efforts of the Guardian, and despite the natural tendencies of the Man in Black to segregate himself from other human beings, the Man in Black recognised that he was a human being. Saying that he was not human was a lie, and he recognised the Guardian's words as a lie. Even though he never would have spoken the words himself, somewhere deep inside he knew that he needed other people. With Archibald Beechcroft and Henry Bemis, he knew he could not live alone.

Time Enough At Last

The Man in Black ordered his life according to the philosophical underpinnings provided by the Guardian. But in spite of all her efforts to segregate him in every way from human beings, he maintained connections.

Intellectually he may have understood himself to be something greater than and different from a human being, but emotionally he was as connected as any human could be to another.

The Guardian must have recognised that she had raised the Man in Black with such an exclusive orientation toward his own desires and urges that he had no concept of the Island's needs. He was experimenting with the Light and the water. The mindset that could even envision such activity was foreign to the Guardian. The Light was not something to be controlled. It was something beyond human control. Even if, as independent observers, we saw nothing inherently evil in his experimentation, to the Guardian his desire to control the Light was the worst imaginable evil. She knew she had to move quickly to end the experimentation. She knocked out the Man in Black, destroyed the village, and killed every one of its inhabitants to prevent any future collaborations with her wayward dark-haired charge.

When the Guardian killed all of the Man in Black's friends, she immediately deprived him of the human support that had sustained him for all the years he had been away from her. We know that the Man in Black had more than a detached interest in the people. He had strong emotional connections to them. The Guardian's deliberate, hurtful action left the Man in Black only one possible course of action.

By murdering the Guardian, the Man in Black was extracting an eye for an eye, but he was also destroying the source of everything that had brought order to his life. Intellectually, emotionally, psychologically, and spiritually, he was completely alone. He was left in such a deep morass of rudderless confusion and spiritual pain that he had no strength to battle anyone, least of all his own brother.

Everything in the Man in Black's environment conspired to rob him of his humanity. Although he felt a connection with his birth mother, we have no evidence that he established with her a true emotional bond. It seems more likely that the truths he learned from her served only to further alienate him from the Guardian and from his own brother. We might see in his choice to pursue scientific studies with the other survivors of the shipwreck an attachment of sorts, but again, the value of his interaction was substantially degraded due to his pre-existing attitude that "my people" were beneath him and could be counted on only to act in a "greedy, manipulative, untrustworthy, and selfish" manner.

By the time he killed the Guardian, he was not much more than the shell of a real person. Thanks to the Guardian's misguidance, he was entirely oriented toward selfish pursuits. I don't think we could say he evinced any sign of evil tendencies until the afternoon the Guardian killed all his friends. It is tempting to think that he should have understood that tampering with the Light was not a permissible activity, but we have no evidence that the Guardian had ever told the boys any such thing. He had natural curiosity, and the Light promised a means of leaving the Island, which was his final goal.

It seems to me likely that the Man in Black could have returned to his scientific studies, even after he murdered the Guardian. He might have been able to enjoy "time enough at last" to pursue his dream of leaving the Island. He could have had an unhappy but otherwise uneventful existence if not for the final blow to his humanity.

Exile From Humanity

Jacob took away the last remaining vestiges of his brother's humanity when he threw him into the Source. The Man in Black was no longer entirely human; he was exiled, as it were, to an existence that was truly inhuman. In his exile he achieved something denied to Socrates. He could go into this Smoke-Monster exile only because he was no longer a human being. But his roots were in humanity. Everything he had been, and everything he ever wished to be had its origin and its completion in being human.

Even if his exile from the human race was physically possible, it was emotionally and psychologically impossible. All of us have to identify with something. We are not sufficient unto ourselves. At the very least, we identify with the truth that we are human beings. Exile from our own humanity is not tenable, because exile destroys everything with which we can identify ourselves. It falls apart under itself—physically, morally, philosophically. The Man in Black could not exile himself from the human race, because he could not exist without identity.

The Man in Black existed as the Smoke Monster—as a human/island hybrid who was neither human nor Island. He judged not as a human, not as a non-human, but as dictated by the strictures of the Source, as executed by the Island itself. He desired in the same way he always had, but now he had absolute power to pursue his desires.

The Man in Black became evil, not of his own desire, but because he was no longer entirely human. He could only desire as a beast and judge as an Island. But men are not beasts, and no man is an island; neither of these things offered him what he truly needed, which was human identity.

The Man in Black was an impossible lie. He could never have achieved happiness, even if he left the Island. Even if he somehow managed to identify the specific Roman province or city that had long ago been his birth mother's home, the people there would have felt no kinship with him. No one on earth, in fact, would have felt anything in common with him.

I believe the emotion I feel most when I think of the Man in Black is pity. I am sad for him. Jacob and the Guardian robbed him of everything that makes us human. Even though he sought to be reunited with his people across the sea, what he most lacked was something he would never be able to obtain, regardless of the degree of effort he put into its attainment: ordinary human life.

I feel relief and satisfaction, though, too. In the end, I believe we are correct in expecting—demanding—that intelligent entities demonstrate at least the rudiments of respect and an understanding that selfish pursuits cannot be put ahead of the basic needs of other sentient beings. The Smoke Monster was willing to kill, even to exterminate, to achieve its ends. It had to be destroyed, even if he was a pitiable being.

I feel another emotion, too, that probably will not seem to have any place in sentiments weighing toward pity. Nevertheless, it is there. Just as Christians during the Easter Vigil can express their delight in the "happy fault...[the] necessary sin of Adam" (hear the full chanted version here: http://www.youtube.com/watch?v=JGI6-9wQidg) that resulted in human redemption, I too take delight in the necessary fault that led to the Smoke Monster, for it was the precursor to the Island's redemption. Explaining that one will take a bit of doing. In fact, it will be the last thing explained in this book, in the final chapter, "The White Rabbit." You see, it was because of the Smoke Monster that Jack Shephard first saw his "white rabbit," and it was because of that white rabbit that Jack came to understand his true calling as Protector and saviour of the Island.

Add to the emotional mix, then, a feeling of deep gratitude to the being who gained for the Island so great a Protector.

The Man in White

CHAPTER 10: THE MAN IN WHITE

It only ends once. Anything that happens before that is just progress.
—Jacob, "The Incident"

The only person he ever loved killed his birth mother.

She did not return his love. The centre of her world, the focal point of all her attention and affection, was his brother. She demanded goodness, honesty, and devotion, but relegated him to the recesses of her heart. She awarded him second place in a game that could have only one winner. He was not good enough. He was the loser.

He should have grown up bitter, angry, eager for vengeance. People are "greedy, manipulative, untrustworthy, and selfish." It was what his brother believed. It was what the woman taught both of them. Instead, he became the world's most determined optimist. Emperors came and went, power shifted from Rome to Mecca to Madrid to London, but this one man, protecting the Light of the world, never gave in to pessimism. "People are good," he preached. Human beings made mistakes, but these were not the signs of a weak and sinful species, but rather the proof that humankind reached for something better. Humans sinned only because they were endowed with the free will to make progress on their own terms.

He represented the best of the human tradition. He grew up in adversity, faced a world always on the brink, but rather than becoming defeated and cruel, he chose to see in others the Light he was sworn to protect. Such was the quiet greatness of the world's most devoted leader, Jacob, Protector of the Island.

The Guardian

She was not their mother. She was a murderer.

Jacob referred to her as "Mother", and this is the appellation preferred by Lostpedia and most Lost analysts. I favour the title of "Guardian", or "adoptive mother", at least because this was her true role, but more importantly because the boys never belonged to her. The idea of belonging is crucial to LOST, as I detailed in the chapter on the Man in Black (Chapter 9).

The Guardian murdered the boys' mother, Claudia. She had been Protector of the Island perhaps since the days of Tunis, when Egypt was a hope centuries in the future and the Phoenicians who would found Carthage had not yet even set sail. We will never know the length of her reign as Protector. Moments before her death, Claudia posed the question, but the Guardian cut her off. "Every question I answer will simply lead to another question," she said. Perhaps she had arrived only years before. Possibly she was the historical Queen Elissa of Carthage, who became enamoured of the hero of Troy, Aeneas. When Aeneas left her bed to found Rome, the great Roman poet, Virgil, would have us believe she fell on Aeneas' sword. Perhaps instead she became so disenchanted with the ways of humankind that she exiled herself on the island near Carthage, where she found new purpose in the shadow of the statue.

The Guardian murdered Claudia. She felt she had to commit the deed. Her logic was unassailable. After all, the Island needed a Protector. She had grown tired of the responsibility, but she could not simply walk away. Therefore, she needed a reliable replacement. Humans were untrustworthy, so she would have to raise the replacement herself, from infancy. Claudia's womb would provide the replacement the Guardian required.

The Guardian made sure pregnant Claudia was on the Roman ship she had chosen, and gave the master of the vessel a map to his final destination, putting him on a course to intercept the Island. We know this because we know the story behind every shipwreck and plane crash on the Island. The crash of Oceanic Flight 815 was not an accident. The Elizabeth did not happen upon the Island by chance. Magnus Hanso steered the Black Rock according to an itinerary devised by Jacob. Crashes were not accident, but destiny—a fate dictated by the Island itself. Every Protector honoured the custom of seeking replacement Candidates; the task was implicit in the job description. The Island demanded no less.

She raised the boys to feel contempt for humanity. Humans, she told them, were greedy, manipulative, untrustworthy, and selfish. "They come, they fight, they destroy, they corrupt... and it always ends the same." Since human beings were base, predictable, and dangerous, nothing good could result from any interaction with them.

The Game

It's the oldest game in the world. "Archeologists found sets when they excavated the ruins of ancient Mesopotamia. Five thousand years old."

The game always has two players. "Two players. Two sides. One is light... one is dark." The game had much greater significance than an afternoon diversion at the shore of the sea. Although senet apparently involved chance—in the throwing of painted bones—the game's designers did not believe in luck. Every event in life and death was determined by fate. The game revealed one's connection to the gods.

The Boy in Black (BIB) was the Guardian's choice to become Protector. We know this from the context of Jacob's conversation with her many years later at the Source.

GUARDIAN: It has to be you, Jacob.
JACOB: No, it doesn't. You wanted it to be him. But now I'm all you have.
GUARDIAN: It was always supposed to be you, Jacob. I see that now. And one day, you'll see it, too...

The Guardian's response reveals her deception. Her first statement is a lie. The second statement is key: "I see that *now*." That is to say, until *now* she didn't see the truth of Jacob's destiny as Protector. She saw some other truth prior to this moment. That truth, of course, was that the BIB was destined to replace her as Protector. This had been her plan all along.

The BIB was resourceful, inquisitive, creative. He had the ability to understand the full truth as revealed in fragmented observation and incomplete information. He was crafty, cunning, and yet dependable. Such were the requisite qualities of the one who would guard the most important treasure on earth. These were not characteristics inherent to the position, but they were the ones recognised by the Guardian as effective. They were the qualities she believed herself to possess; that the Boy in Black evinced them could only mean he was destined to the leadership function.

The BIB would require an opposing force. Human beings were untrustworthy, and as much as the Guardian placed her hope in the boy, he was as human as anyone else. He possessed the guile for leadership, but he would need a companion very different in outlook and character. The companion would provide unvarnished truth to balance the BIB's dreams and schemes. Eventually this companion would prevent the BIB from rendering decisions based entirely in selfish desire. Protecting the Light required unselfish devotion, and no single human being could be trusted to act without self-interest.

The Guardian devised a game. She would be the boys' sole source of affection and affirmation. She would make Jacob completely dependent on her.

GUARDIAN: Do you love me, Jacob?
JACOB: Yes.
GUARDIAN: Then tell me what happened.

In this conversation she was seizing an opportunity. She had no interest in what had occurred on the beach between the two boys. She did have enormous interest in ensuring Jacob's psychological attachment to honesty. So she made honesty a condition of Jacob's love of her.

Being Mama's boy, Jacob would fight tooth-and-nail to explain to the BIB the course he felt the Guardian would have advocated. Since the BIB was attached to the Guardian in his own way, Jacob's arguments would make their mark, and the BIB would be shamed into a more appropriate course of action.

Such was the game the Guardian placed in motion from the earliest days of the boys' youth.

The Rules Change

Boys will be boys, and these two boys were no different from any other in that respect. Every teenager discovers truths that indicate a priority different from those a parent tries to establish. The BIB discovered the truth that "Mother" was not their mother at all, and he pleaded with his brother to leave the vile woman.

The BIB's discovery didn't affect Jacob to the core, as it had affected his brother. But Jacob's confrontation with the Guardian over the BIB's discovery revealed two beliefs that would eventually separate him from her.

JACOB: He said you killed our mother... Is that true?
GUARDIAN: Yes... If I had let her live, she would have taken you back to her people; and those people are bad, Jacob—very bad. I-I couldn't let you become one of them. I needed you to stay good.
JACOB: Am I good, Mother?
GUARDIAN: Yes, of course you are.
JACOB: Then, why do you love him more than me?
GUARDIAN: I love you in—in different ways.

Jacob believed himself to be good because this was the truth the Guardian had expressed again and again. But she had an odd way of phrasing the truth. Here, trying to keep Jacob in her good graces, she said, "I needed you to stay good." Was "being good" a temporary state? Why did the Guardian favour the BIB? Was he "better" than Jacob in some way? If the BIB was "better", was Jacob good at all, or was the Guardian only telling him what he wished to believe? She lied about being their mother; couldn't she be lying about other important matters?

The second matter causing his consternation was the nature of humankind itself. The Guardian said people were "bad... very bad". If Jacob wished to believe he was good, he was basing his belief entirely on the authenticity of the Guardian's word. In the "Mother" deception she had already proven herself untrustworthy. Jacob needed a second validation of his innate goodness. He did not achieve that validation through the Guardian or by making wonderful tapestries for her. He found validation of his worth in others.

MAN IN BLACK: Why do you watch us, Jacob?
JACOB: ... because I wanna know if Mother's right.
....
MAN IN BLACK: Oh, you mean my people. You wanna know if they're bad. That woman may be insane, but she's most definitely right about that.
JACOB: I don't know. They don't seem so bad to me.

110

MAN IN BLACK: ...Trust me, I've lived among them for 30 years. They're greedy, manipulative, untrustworthy, and selfish.

Jacob and the MIB had very different agendas. The MIB wanted to get off the Island, and used the Romans as "a means to an end". Jacob sought validation of his goodness. He ignored selfish deeds and evil words, choosing instead to see in the Romans only good and noble acts and intentions. Believing in the goodness of humanity, Jacob was able to validate his own goodness. In doing so he found spiritual reconciliation with the only person he had ever loved. Paradoxically it was that reconciliation that caused him to all the more vigorously oppose the Guardian's ideology.

Hundreds of years later, Jacob and the MIB were opposed at the spiritual core of their persons. To the MIB's constant refrain of the long litany of human failings, Jacob would reply that human beings were on a trajectory aimed at perfection. "It only ends once," Jacob said. "Anything that happens before that is just progress."

The Torch is Passed

The Guardian realised almost too late that she had made a grave miscalculation. The MIB would eventually murder her, she knew. That was not the grave error; she would even thank the MIB for killing her. The mistake she made was in placing her hope in the MIB and not in Jacob. Jacob would have to become Protector, even though he had spent a lifetime living in the MIB's shadow. Jacob had been loyal, submissive, and honest. The MIB was focussed on the impossible objective of leaving the Island. He would be unable to leave until she made him Protector, but she knew, from thirty years of hearing the pronouncement from the MIB's own lips, that he would use the power of his office to leave the Island forever. He would become the worst among the people she despised. She couldn't allow that; her power had to devolve to Jacob.

"Nam non accipimus hoc quasi vulgarem potionem, sed ut ille sit quasi unus mecum," she said. "Because we don't accept this as a simple potion, but so that he shall be as one with me." Jacob chanted the same invocation when he passed the torch to Jack. As educated as Jack was, Latin was not a part of any curriculum he had followed. When the time came for Hurley to become Protector, Jack simplified the ritual to two words: "Drink this." It lacked European charm, but the command remained effective.

Jacob approached the responsibility of protectorship with sober appreciation and indefatigable effort. He sought the perfect Candidate, and to find her, he would have to coerce people in her vicinity to help him achieve the goal of bringing her to the Island. He would have to speak languages. Many languages. He brought people to the Island and learned their native tongues.

Perhaps he lived off the Island for months or years at a time, possibly putting Candidates in charge of protecting the Source in his absence. He became fluent in modern Russian, English, and Korean. Since he sought out the largest populations from which to draw Candidates, he almost certainly became proficient in French, Spanish, Mandarin, Hindi, Swahili, and a dozen other languages.

The early attempts must have sought a Robert Conway. But Mittelos was significantly more complicated than the James Hilton vision of Shangri-La in Lost Horizon. Jacob could bring accomplished statesmen, business people, and philosophers to the Island, but they must have shown no sign of being adaptable to the requirements of Island life, to say nothing of the absolute requirement of unswerving allegiance to the final objective. Who in the civilised world would choose to spend her days on an Island threatened at all times by a ruthless, destructive, deceptive, unopposable man bent on leaving the Island at any cost?

The Black Rock

Jacob initiated a new strategy at some point in the late nineteenth century. He revealed the strategy to the Final Four (Hurley, Kate, Jack, and Sawyer). "I didn't pluck any of you out of a happy existence. You were all flawed. I chose you because you were like me. You were all alone. You were all looking for something that you couldn't find out there. I chose you because you needed this place as much as it needed you." Those who lacked something important, who needed a purpose beyond the ones life had presented, were the people most likely to accept a centuries-long challenge.

Jacob must have thought long and hard. I don't mean over a period of days or weeks. I mean over periods of time that would consume the longest of lives. He needed Candidates ready to leave the world and commit themselves to a task greater than any person.

The answer must have become clear only in the years of the American Civil War. Slavery was disappearing around the world. The last major hold-out was the United States, with over six million slaves treated worse than animals. Here were six million possibilities, six million souls who would do anything to find a place in paradise. Jacob must have been crushed to learn of the Emancipation Proclamation, followed by the Union victory. Humanity had been served, yes, but the largest remaining pool of potential Candidates had just been taken away from him.

But the world was full of individuals willing to skirt international law for personal gain. One such selfish thug was Alvar Hanso's great-grandfather, Magnus Hanso. Young Alvar would learn from his father the craft of selling arms at hugely inflated prices to combatants in time of war. They were the Krupps of the twentieth century. He and his father came from a long line of Hansos happy in their ability to extract personal fortunes from the human need to inflict suffering on other human beings. Magnus had no difficulty at all in the enlightened nineteenth century finding powerful men who thought nothing of enslaving other men. The Royal Navy reject was the eager supplier of their criminal lusts.

Jacob did not think out the problem, perhaps because he knew he was running out of time. Eventually dark souls of Hanso's ilk would be imprisoned or would move on to other means of illicit profit. Getting Hanso to sail along a route taking his ship to the Island was not difficult. But Jacob showed no forethought regarding the disposition of crew and slaves after their shipwreck. The Smoke Monster killed all of them, with the exception of the one man he thought he might be able to persuade to carry out his bidding. But Richard was too weak for candidacy. If he could not execute a plan engineered by the Smoke Monster, he would not be able to outwit the man, either.

Jacobian Philosophy

Richard was not the first person Jacob brought to the Island.

RICHARD: Before you brought my ship, there were others?
JACOB: Yes, many.
RICHARD: What happened to them?
JACOB: They're all dead.

We don't know the mechanism of death, but it seems certain that many—perhaps hundreds over the millennia—suffered the same fate as Richard's peers on the Black Rock. Richard witnessed many gruesome murders. Jacob's rationale for allowing this bloodshed seemed to be the first thought in Richard's mind.

RICHARD: But if you brought them here, why didn't you help them?
JACOB: Because I wanted them to help themselves. To know the difference between right and wrong without me having to tell them. It's all meaningless if I have to force them to do anything. Why should I have to step in?

I wonder if Richard accepted this explanation. Perhaps in his confused, dehydrated state he was not yet able to process thoughts clearly. I want to believe he would have followed up with questions aimed at a more enlightening response. If he had been a bit more clear-headed, perhaps he would have thought to ask, "How could they have proven their knowledge of right and wrong when the Monster killed them before they even had a chance to speak?"

The paramount objective, at least in Jacob's mind, was to prevent the Smoke Monster's escape. Temple Master Dogen had it right: The Man in Black "is evil incarnate." In fact, the entire Island could be thought of as a prison cell, holding the most violent, destructive person in the world. Jacob lifted a bottle of wine. "Think of this wine as what you keep calling hell," he told Richard. "There's many other names for it too: malevolence, evil, darkness. And here it is, swirling around in the bottle, unable to get out because if it did, it would spread. The cork," he said, holding the device in his hand, "is this island and it's the only thing keeping the darkness where it belongs."

Consequences

This is as good a place as any to stop for a few moments to consider Jacob's callous behaviour. He sought flawed people, but he wanted them to know the difference between right and wrong. He wanted people who could stand up to the Smoke Monster, but the only way they would be able to do so was through Jacob's protective touch. He touched no one on the Black Rock; consequently every man and woman on board was immediately killed. Richard survived only because he was in a state amenable to the MIB's coercion, exacerbated by three days in jungle heat without water. In the centuries before the Black Rock surely hundreds more had died due to Jacob's lack of foresight. More important to the story of LOST, they died because of Jacob's lack of compassion.

He could not bring people back from the dead, even if his brother apparently enjoyed this privilege, though probably in only the most limiting of circumstances. He could not absolve sins, confer grace, or perform any other function we might associate with divine prerogative. He could touch people, elevating them to Candidate status, in this way calling upon them the Island's full protection. Suicide and death from the elements (even an unrestrained fall from twelve thousand metres) could not touch the Candidates. The greatest benefit of candidacy had more meaning than the prevention of accidental death: The Smoke Monster could not touch them, either.

Few enjoyed the Jacobian privilege of candidacy. The Others had to labour on their own. Even their penultimate leader, Benjamin Linus, had never been touched by Jacob. Perhaps they lived only due to Jacob's neglect and the opportunity his high-minded philosophy provided to the MIB. By leaving the Others to find their own way to survive, he neglected to realise that his brother was manipulating Ben and probably many of the Others.

Possibly the consequence of greatest moment deriving of Jacob's peculiar way of looking at the world was the efficacy of Candidates over the centuries. A lesser man than Jack Shephard would have taken Jacob at his word: The Island is a prison cell, nothing more. It is just a cork. Having figured out how to kill the Smoke Monster, such a Protector would have made a mistake of Biblical dimension.

KATE: You killed the Smoke Monster, now let's go home.
JACK: Yeah [Grinning]. You're right.

SAWYER: It's Miller Time! There's beer on the boat. C'mon!

Serving as prison to the MIB was nothing more than an accident of history. The true purpose of the Island was much greater than anything Jacob understood, even after two thousand years of walking sandy shore and jungle path. His lack of understanding must have misled dozens or even hundreds over the centuries. There must have been instances in which people went to heroic lengths, thinking they were fulfilling divine mandate, but instead were pursuing entirely the wrong goal, or making the Island situation worse than it had to be.

Ille Qui Nos Omnes Servabit

Second-guessing Jacob is easy. In the end, though, his plan succeeded, and in positive ways he could not have foreseen. With meticulous planning over several decades he brought wounded, sometimes deceitful, selfish people to the Island. They overcame their tendencies toward self-fulfillment and became the best leaders Jacob had ever seen. Many of them, like Charlie, Sayid, and Locke, sacrificed their own lives for the good of the Island.

Jacob's survival over such a span of centuries was testament to his courage, resolve, and humanity. The guardian he loved as mother killed the woman who gave birth to him. His brother hated him, and plotted unceasingly to kill him. No one understood him, cared about his problems, or even wanted to be around him. Other than Richard, he had no friends, and even Richard doubted him. Everyone, with the exception of the Man in Black, feared him. He lived in that reality without complaint for two thousand years. But he was not content with mere survival. He enjoyed life, found the silver lining in every dark cloud, and saw goodness in every person he met. Jacob was the model of a purpose-driven, optimistic, happy life.

We point to his failings, but would that everyone had his failings, and his greatness. He made a place in his heart, even for murderers like Kate Austen and James Ford. Even for a murderer like the Guardian, the one he loved as mother. He carried all of us in his wounded heart. Ille qui nos omnes servabit. Indeed. For two thousand years he did just that. With Charlie, Sayid, Locke, and his brother, Jack Shephard, he did not fear the final sacrifice. Requiescat in pacem, frater noster.

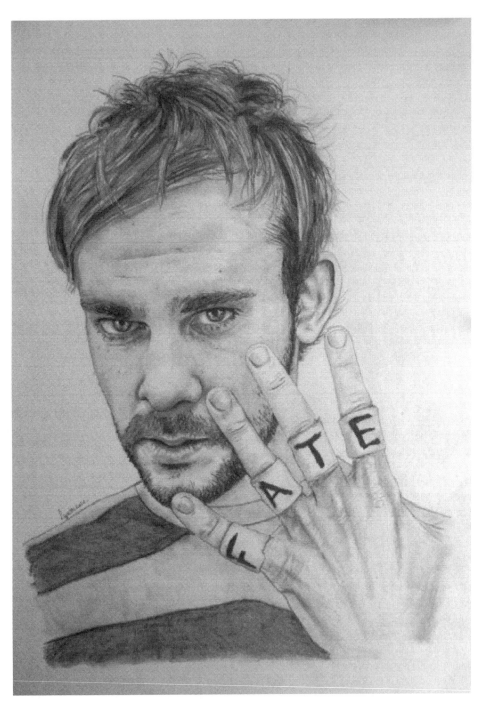

The Martyr

CHAPTER 11: THE MARTYR

"Guys, where are we?"
—Charlie Pace, "Pilot"

"Not Penny's Boat".

We know him by these three words. Words of warning. Words of caring. Words of sacrifice. He is the heroin addict who mustered the courage to defy his body's demand for the drug. He conquered fear of death to swim thirty metres below the waves, to his destiny, to his greatest and final accomplishment.

Tragic life meets tragic end. He gave warning, but no one listened, and the mercenaries came. Greater love hath no man than this—but what do we make of a heroic death whose final plea goes unheeded? Claire would never again take her soul mate's hand. Liam would never reconcile with his younger brother.

Perhaps we believe Charlie's heroism wasted in alarms disregarded, but if so we have missed the point of his life and death. His greatest accomplishment was not the final notice of a three-word warning, but the final entry on a five-sentence list. But neither Greatest Hit nor greatest sacrifice went unheeded. We know this because Liam was not Charlie's brother. Sayid was Charlie's brother. "Think not of him as slain; nay, he lives," the Quran tells us of Sayid. "He who believes in me will live, even though he dies," the Gospel of John tells us of Charlie. He lives, not only in memory, but on the Island, in eternity. He is not tragic death, but heroic life. Charlie is the soul of the Island.

Music Is A Gift

#5: The First Time I Heard Myself on the Radio.

Charlie Pace was a musician, and for a brief period in time, Manchester's most famous bass player and vocalist. But to record his vocation in this manner tells us little about his true impact on society, or indeed what his true function was. I might as well have said Charlie picked locks for a living. Our estimation of Charlie would depend on his true function. If his business card said "locksmith", we would not hesitate to invite him to join the neighbourhood association. But if his vocation were Mafia safe cracker we would have quite a different reaction. And if he picked locks for MI-6 or Mossad we would probably feel more uneasy about his presence in our neighbourhood than if we learned he was a criminal.

To say that Charlie was a musician is not sufficient. For the last sixty years those who produce popular music have been at the cutting edge of culture. Charlie was a "rock god", as Liam said, because our society holds no one in greater esteem than a rock-and-roll musician.

Music has always enjoyed cultural importance. Vocal and instrumental creations provide common cultural ground, enrich our days, and fill us with optimism and good cheer. LOST would be a weaker and less compelling drama without Michael Giacchino's grand score. In fact, I imagine most would find themselves in agreement with the statement that life without music would be very dull, indeed.

"Music hath charms to sooth the savage breast", as William Congreve wrote in the late seventeenth century. Note well that Congreve stated that music is not inherently but only potentially a civilising force. "Music hath charms"—has the ability—to civilise, but does not necessarily always do so. We do not need to turn to misogynistic rap lyrics or racist country-western songs to understand the potential of music to reduce civility and decorum. Back in the early seventeenth century, William Shakespeare provided poetic notice of this potential in his play, Twelfth Night. "If music be the food of love," Duke Orsino said, "play on." Orsino's true feelings are revealed only upon recitation of the full quote, however. "Give me excess of it; that surfeiting, the appetite may sicken, and so die." That is to say, Shakespeare's Orsino did not wish to be entertained with good music, he wished to be overwhelmed and finally sickened by it so that he would no longer have an excuse to love.

Even if You All Everybody expressed an egalitarian philosophy of human worth and social cohesion, the song did not prevent its creators from pursuing personal choices that led to the band's disintegration. Charlie and Liam could choose to sink or swim in the cultural environment they created for themselves.

Learning to Swim

#4: Dad Teaching Me to Swim at Butlins.

We all have legs to swim, but we have no idea how to use them. Without a teacher, we would flail about and drown. Charlie was fortunate in having a father who sacrificed time to teach his son an important skill. He would need every bit of that ability on the Island, on the day of his final challenge.

I remember well the frustration and embarrassment of not being able to dance, unable to coordinate the movement of feet to the music. When the night of the waltz drew near I had a date but not even the most rudimentary ability. A friend came to my rescue the day before. I must have been the worst pupil she had ever attempted to teach. I like to believe it was the challenge of teaching me that gave her the patience to spend so many hours demonstrating the same steps over and over again. But she accomplished her task, I thanked her, and the next evening took another woman to the dance. My friend longed for more than an appointment as dance instructor, I know. I had spent weekends at her parents' home, sleeping in her absent brother's bed, one thin wall separating us. Her sacrifice meant something in the end. The woman I danced with that night became my wife eleven years later.

Charlie needed teachers throughout his life. Every one of us needs teachers in just about any endeavour we might attempt. When Charlie became a "rock god" he had only one teacher, and that teacher led him astray.

CHARLIE: [in a confessional with priest] Bless me Father, for I have sinned. It's been a week since my last confession.
PRIEST: Go ahead, my son.
CHARLIE: Last night I had physical relations with a girl I didn't even know.
PRIEST: I see. Anything else?
CHARLIE: Yeah. Uh, right after that I had relations with another girl. Then... straight after that I watched while they had relations with each other. You see, it's, it's my band, Father, Drive Shaft. We've been playing the clubs in Manchester. And, uh, we've been getting some heat, a following, you know, and, uh, the girls. There's some real temptations that come with the territory, if you know what I mean.
PRIEST: Well, we all have our temptations, but giving in to them, that's your choice. As we live our lives it's really nothing but a series of choices, isn't it?

Charlie seemed content to accept whatever came along, largely unburdened by the knowledge that the choice was always his. The closest teacher would do, and during the Drive Shaft days the closest teacher was his older brother, Liam. Liam surrounded himself with admiring women and little bags of semi-refined heroin. Sex, drugs, and rock and roll. It was by then a well-accepted course of study, with entire drug trafficking routes and eager instructors in place to welcome new students. And the most honoured students, by far, were the famous musicians themselves, purveyors of the culture that earned traffickers wealth, respect, and legitimacy.

By the time he reached the Island, Charlie's drug habit had destroyed Drive Shaft, driven a wedge between him and Liam, and turned Charlie into a sweating, trembling junkie, living from one fix to the next.

Our Father, Who Art On the Island

Liam didn't board Flight 815 for Charlie's gig in Los Angeles. But plenty of other teachers did make it onto the plane and survived the crash on the Island. Charlie's drug addiction made him a loner, but withdrawal brought symptoms to the fore and made his condition obvious to those with any familiarity with drug culture.

Jack Shephard had treated drug addicts, and John Locke spent several weeks helping to grow marijuana. Both men understood Charlie's addiction and became his friends. Locke became Charlie's mentor.

CHARLIE: I want my stash, Locke. I can't stand feeling like this.

LOCKE: Come here. Let me show you something. [They walk to a plant with a cocoon on it]. What do you suppose is in that cocoon, Charlie?

CHARLIE: I don't know, a butterfly, I guess?

LOCKE: No, it's much more beautiful than that. That's a moth cocoon. It's ironic, butterflies get all the attention; but moths — they spin silk, they're stronger, they're faster.

CHARLIE: That's wonderful, but...

LOCKE: You see this little hole? This moth's just about to emerge. It's in there right now, struggling. It's digging its way through the thick hide of the cocoon. Now, I could help it, take my knife, gently widen the opening, and the moth would be free. But it would be too weak to survive. The struggle is nature's way of strengthening it. Now this is the second time you've asked me for your drugs back [he raises the bag of heroin]. Ask me again and it's yours.

Locke clarified the issue for Charlie and became a sure teacher in time of dire need. But the hard work of digging through the cocoon was left entirely to Charlie.

When Jack became trapped after a cave collapse, Charlie volunteered to crawl through the narrow tunnel Michael had dug to rescue Jack. He was smaller than anyone else, and this is the rationale he might have invoked, but he did not. Jin had a wife, Michael had a son, but Charlie had no one. He was alone on the Island. His rationale was simple: No one depended on him, and if he died in his attempt, no one would miss him. He was wrong about that, of course.

Having the right knowledge allows informed choices. Anyone could begin digging to rescue Jack, but the digging would have been in vain if the tunnel collapsed around the diggers. Michael was uniquely qualified to lead the recovery effort because he understood load distribution and support. The digging itself was just physical labour and could be performed in shifts to reduce hardship for all.

Digging their way out of the collapsed cave was not the difficult part of rescuing Jack. The challenge again revolved around knowledge. Jack and Charlie could have surrendered themselves to death in a dark cave, but Charlie was alert to possibilities. When he saw a moth fly up to the ceiling and disappear, he knew there was a way out of the cave.

Locke gave Charlie the knowledge of possibilities in his battle to free himself from drugs. But he alone would have to choose to apply that knowledge, as he had chosen to dig his way to freedom out of the cave.

When Charlie requested his bag of heroin a third time, Locke was disappointed. Locke gave the young man three chances to succeed and he failed every opportunity. Locke was not just sad when he handed over the bag, he was in anguish, and the pain was evident in the deep creases of his brow. But when Charlie threw the bag into the camp fire, without so much as a moment of hesitation, Locke's expression changed immediately. He didn't have to say the words, but he did anyway. "I'm proud of you, Charlie."

Lord of the Rings

#3: The Christmas Liam Gave Me the Ring

Rings have power because they bind us to one another. I wear a ring signifying that I belong to my wife. Liam wore a ring to indicate he belonged to a rock band, and also as a bond to his maternal grandfather, Dexter Stratton, from whom Drive Shaft acquired its name.

A ring is not only a symbol of responsibility. A ring is a symbol of identity. We are who we are because of responsibilities. I am my wife's husband. I am my daughter's father. I am my father's son. These are expressions of familial bond, bonds of commitment and responsibility, but more than anything these bonds and commitments—these rings—define who we are.

Centuries ago life was recognised as gaining individuality from its origins. When John's wife gave birth to a son she named Henry, the boy was known to everyone in town as Henry, John's son. Over time the name of a boy like Henry would be simplified: Henry John's son became Henry Johnson. The townsfolk would expect certain behaviours. When Henry spoke as his father had, or began courting a woman from his mother's village, neighbours would nod and say with grin and a wink, "He is his father's son" or "The apple doesn't fall far from the tree."

Charlie inherited the "DS" ring because he demonstrated responsibility.

[Liam pulls off his "DS" ring]
CHARLIE: Liam, no. Mum gave you that. You're the first born. It was her father's and his father before that...
LIAM: And it's a family heirloom, and that's why we named the band after Dexter bloody Stratton. I know. But Charlie—let's be honest—we both know I'm a sodding mess. But you, you're different. You're gonna get married, have a family, a baby. I'll be lucky if I hit thirty.
CHARLIE: Don't say that, Li.
LIAM: The ring has to stay in the family, Charlie. So please, take it. Mum would have wanted it this way. Pass it on to your little one someday. I need to know it's safe.

Liam recognised the responsibility of the ring bearer. A ring is a beautiful but also frightening and sobering thing. There is no Lord of the Rings. Freedom and individuality can be acquired only through commitment and adherence to tradition. One cannot become Lord of the Rings because no single person has power over commitments that bind one to another. To say I am committed is to say that I surrender power to that which owns my fealty. For good or for bad, the ring is lord over me. Responsibility is the only possible source of human freedom. We recognise maturity as the sober and deep joy that comes of accepting and zestfully applying this paradoxical truth in our lives.

Could Charlie wear the ring?

Life and Death Decision

I don't often think on things as they might have been, but I did wonder, when I saw Sayid break open the ceramic statue before Charlie's eyes, what might have happened had Locke been the one to discover the heroin. Sayid knew nothing of Charlie's heroin addiction, but Locke had helped Charlie through withdrawal, had given him powerful choices to work himself free of the shackles of drug-dependent slavery. Would Locke have quietly burned the statues' contents? Perhaps Charlie's mentor could have prevented the pain of a long relapse into addiction.

If Charlie had been spared this pain I am not sure of every particular, but I believe one critical element of Charlie's future would have changed dramatically: Charlie would not have accepted death under thirty metres of water. He would not have given his life for his friends. He couldn't. Until he faced real temptation—a free, lifetime supply of blissful oblivion—he could never know who he truly was.

This time around Charlie forced a response. When he set a fire and abducted Aaron he endangered the entire group of survivors and threatened a baby's life. His friends were no longer free to nurture him to chemical freedom. With the lives of so many in jeopardy because of Charlie's behaviour, only a few actions were possible. His friends chose the gentlest course, showing restraint out of love for the young man. A very stern John Locke carefully took the baby from Charlie's arms, gave the infant back to his mother, swivelled on his foot and thrust his hard fist into Charlie's face. He hit Charlie hard, slugged him once, then again, and again, knocking him down into the cold ocean water. The group that had gathered left him there.

Charlie was *persona non grata,* banished from the group. His only contact was the single person less despicable than himself, Sawyer. Charlie threw a bag over Sun's head, dragged her into the jungle, and there knocked her unconscious and tied her to a tree, leading the survivors to believe she had been attacked by the Others. This incited almost everyone in camp to demand an armed response, and Sawyer entered the Swan to warn Locke of the approaching mob. When Locke left to prepare a hiding place for the guns, Sawyer took the guns himself. Working together, Charlie and Sawyer executed one of the most elaborate con games ever perpetrated on the Island.

Redemption was not an easy process. Sayid was the most approachable of the group, probably because he knew of his own capacities to inflict pain. Charlie had caused physical harm to only one person; Sayid had tortured and killed. Eko, seeing that Charlie had become useful again, recruited him to assist in building his church.

As Charlie worked on the church, Vincent approached, a Virgin Mary statue in his mouth. It was the third and final temptation. Hours later, having gathered all the remaining statues, Charlie stood at the shore and pitched them as far as his arm could throw into the deep water. Unbeknownst to him, Locke stood behind him, looking on with approval as Charlie destroyed the last of the Nigerian plane's cache of the deadly drug. Near the end of Season Two, at Libby's funeral, Charlie stood next to Claire and she took his hand.

Charlie wore the DS ring and accepted responsibility toward Claire and Aaron. No longer Lord of the rings, instead he submitted himself to the commitments they represented, and in so doing, discovered the highest freedom available to any human being. Charlie, at last, was free.

Hero and Holy Martyr

#2: Woman Outside Covent Garden Calls Me a Hero

In truth, Charlie had never been abandoned, even in his darkest hour. His father not only taught him to swim, but instilled in him a respect for himself and for others. Weekly confession was not an action Charlie took out of desperation in Drive Shaft days, it was a habit, long engrained as the result of a traditional childhood in very traditional Manchester.

In the course of 121 episodes of LOST we saw only two men rescue a woman from unsavoury villains in a dark alley. In Episode 6.18, Sayid was a beaten and dejected man who thought himself untrustworthy. But as soon as he saw a man slug a woman he rose from his seat in the Hummer and ran to her rescue. In Episode 3.21, Charlie was a washed up musician and a useless drug addict. But when he saw a man mugging a defenceless woman, he ran to her protection.

Of all the characters we met over six years, Charlie and Sayid were the only two who consciously attempted to adhere to their faith traditions. The accidentals of their faiths were devotional books and the particular words they used in prayer. But the true meaning of their selfless witness to the Creator's love and justice played out in dark alleys. In both cases, their faith was rendered whole and their lives made holy and joyous and perfect in a single heroic act performed deep under water.

How like Charlie, to rescue a woman he didn't even know from lawless thugs. He did know her, though, even if he didn't recognise her. The woman, Noor Abed Jazeem, was the most important person in the world to the one who called her Nadia. In this light we know the truth. Charlie could not but help Nadia, for Nadia was beloved of Sayid, and Sayid was, in all ways that have enduring significance, Charlie's closest and dearest brother.

It Is Finished.

After the close-up shot of a suddenly opening eye, the image of a three-word warning scrawled on a musician's left hand may be the most iconic image of LOST, and not without reason: The words on Charlie's hand determined the course of the next three years, rippling outward from this single moment to become the initiator of the final cascade of events leading to Hurley's installation as Protector.

Literally with his last breath, Charlie warned Desmond that the people on the freighter were not the rescuers they claimed to be. Desmond reported Charlie's death, and his warning. Charlie's best friend, Hurley, knew Charlie's last words had validity. His decision to remain on the Island with Locke was informed not only by his close friendship with the musician, but by the truth of Charlie's warning.

Claire was devastated. More vulnerable than ever, she became susceptible to her dead father's pleadings, and surrendered her son to his care. This led to Kate's adoption of Aaron and her growing realisation that she had to return to the Island to find Claire and reunite mother and son. Charlie's death, unexpected by both Jacob and the Smoke Monster, was exploited by the Island to force Kate's return for a single, critical action: firing the rifle shot that would cripple the Man in Black (see my essays on Christian Shephard, and also the chapter on Kate Austen, "The Candidate").

Safe and sound in the "civilised" world, Jack had time to reflect on his Island experience. Locke's defence of the Island at first seemed insane. Locke's devotion alone may never have been enough to cause Jack's enlightenment. But as Jack continued to work out the significance of the Island, he did not have to rely exclusively on Locke's feelings and faith. He could recall also Charlie's warning about the freighter, and Hurley's absolute trust in Charlie's words. As Jack slipped deeper into his own drug-induced insanity and hell, he came to realise Hurley had a stronger grip on reality than anyone he knew. Hurley was sane and trustworthy, ergo Charlie was likewise trustworthy. With two men of integrity supporting Locke, with every event on the Island supporting Locke, Jack was faced with a stark choice. He could continue in his denials and endure a life of pain and insanity, or he could embrace the faith his closest friends knew to be true. Charlie's heroism was almost certainly the final straw that forced Jack back to the Island.

Maiorem caritatem nemo habet. No greater love has any man than this. And no death had greater meaning than this. Charlie's death was the central defining act of LOST.

Eternal Friendship

#1: The Night I Met You

We think of Charlie's final act as his greatest. But he himself counted one event far greater than any other. We witnessed this Greatest Hit in the opening minutes of our six-year adventure.

It was not an act he could achieve on his own. One may love another silently, secretly, in perfect charity. But this is not the love that LOST holds in highest regard. Love, in LOST, is something shared, something built by those weak and flawed into something strong and perfect. We are Lost until we find each other, until we find that single, flawed person willing to build with us something perfect, beautiful, an edifice enduring all ages, testament to infinite capacities to give, to help, to sacrifice, to love.

CLAIRE: You didn't? Peanut butter? No way.
CHARLIE: Just like you ordered. Oh, there is one thing. It's extra smooth.
CLAIRE: That's okay.
[Charlie opens an empty jar.]
CLAIRE: It's empty.
CHARLIE: What? No, no it's not. It's full, full to the brim, with stick-to-the-roof-of-your-mouth, oh, god, makes-you-want-a-glass-of-milk extra smooth. It's the best bloody peanut butter I've ever tasted. You want some?
[Claire, smiling and laughing, dips her finger into the jar.]

Few of us have ever tasted peanut butter so rich. Charlie didn't find it, or make it. Charlie and Claire made it together. To anyone else, an empty jar. To Charlie and Claire, their final and perfect destiny.

Years before Jack, Charlie discovered the Light. He is not tragedy and death, but heroism and life. He opened a jar, tasted life's richest fare, and shared it with another. Charlie is the soul of the Island.

The Mother

CHAPTER 12: THE MOTHER

Imagine 16 years from now. You thought he was still alive. But in your heart you know that he wouldn't remember you. He wouldn't know you. He wouldn't even know that you ever cared about him. I haven't asked you questions about my daughter, because I do not want to know the answers.
   —Danielle Rousseau, "Par Avion"

[The following is a loose English translation of the original essay, which I rendered in French. The original essay follows immediately after the translation. I believe the French version better conveys the idea I sought to express.]

She was completely crazy.

She set traps, not for animals, but for people. She kidnapped Aaron, tortured Sayid and who knows how many other men during her sixteen years on the Island. She dressed like a monkey, smelled like a goat, looked like a demon. It was the Island sickness, the infection caused by the column of black smoke, the malady from which no one recovered. The blackness inside her made her kill the members of her scientific team. Those who survived the Monster were felled by her rifle. Danielle was in the service of the Island's unholy spirit, as was Claire after her.

This idea, though consonant with common wisdom, was nevertheless false. If we consider closely the reality of the situation, Rousseau never even touched the Monster. Far to the contrary, she fought against him. If so, what was the force that held her in its grip? A tropical fever? The disorientations of time travel? Malaria? Amoebic dysentery? Intestinal worms? Maybe she got up on the wrong side of bed a few too many times?

None of these reasons explains her behaviour. The most difficult fact about Rousseau is this:

Danielle Rousseau was never crazy.

She exhibited the same emotions as you and I, and her actions contributed to the human voyage that constitutes the grand narrative arc of LOST.

The Evidence is Clear as Claire

The rifle was different, but the hair and the facial expression remained the same. The traps did not change. She, too, was dressed like a monkey, smelled like a goat, and looked like a demon. Claire tortured, hunted, and killed because the same thing happened to her that had happened to Rousseau: her baby was stolen from her. The motivations were exactly the same for both women. Alex and Aaron were both babies at the time of their abduction.

I often go camping with my family in the Rocky Mountains. The only thing that I hope never to see on one of these trips is a baby bear. If I see such an adorable little ball of black fur, there's a very good chance that a ferocious and none-too-adorable mother bear is close behind. Anything I do, even if I merely feed the baby bear, the mother bear will consider an act of aggression against her children. The bear would track down and kill the offender. A mother remains a mother, whether she be a bear or a human being.

In the normal course of events, we would accept Claire's behaviour as simply the action of a mother to protect her offspring from danger. In this way, we can likewise consider in similar fashion the actions of Rousseau, given the abduction of her child. We have already seen that the acts of these two women were at times harsh and cruel, and sometimes far beyond the constraints of normal justice.

Again, law, reason, and a realistic evaluation of human nature come to our assistance. In the old common law of France, England, and the United States, there were situations in which homicide was not considered a criminal act, and the perpetrator was not penalised. If a spouse (usually referred to as "husband" in the law—women, considered "chattel," had no rights) found his wife in bed with another man, in flagrante delicto, he could kill the other man without significant consequence. This was the law of the State of Texas until 1974, for example. As a result, we can see that the law recognises that situations exist in which an extreme response is acceptable.

What is the value of a child? What are the legal rights of a tiny human being who can neither defend herself nor even walk? We recognise intuitively that the mother of kidnapped children constitutes an extreme case, calling for broader tolerance and understanding of her behaviour and actions. A mother from whom a child is kidnapped is naturally insensitive to the needs of others, even to her own needs. Because of this, she is capable of sacrificing for her children. She is "programmed" by nature to be particularly sensitive to the needs of her children, and insensitive to the needs of others. This is no infection, but rather the normal consequence of motherhood—it is the insensitivity of motherhood.

But in the end, there was much more than a mother's nature.

CLAIRE: Tell me where my son is.
JUSTIN: I don't know where your son is.
CLAIRE: Stop covering for them. They're not going to help you anymore. All you gotta do is just tell me the truth.
JUSTIN: I am telling you the truth. We don't have your kid. We never had your

kid.

CLAIRE: Stop lying to me! Your people took me to the temple and tortured me.

JUSTIN: No, we captured you because you were out here in the jungle picking our people off.

[Claire swings axe to strike him, pausing when Jin interrupts.]

JIN: Claire wait! Hold on.

CLAIRE: Hold on? Jin, they stuck me with needles. They branded me. [she shows scar on her shoulder] And if I hadn't been able to escape from the temple, they would have killed me.

For a mother, the response to the kidnapping of her child is never limited by law. But Claire Littleton and Danielle Rousseau were not offered a simple kidnapping. They were confronted with a war. An unending battle to survive on the Island. In this context, Claire's action of putting Justin to death was not a homicide. The act must be considered a just act in time of war. Claire proved her sanity in the assassination of Justin. "Look, if I hadn't killed him, he would have killed me." The first time we saw Rousseau in the jungle, we were not thinking "crazy." We were thinking *soldier*. I think this first impression is correct. Rousseau and Claire were at war with the Others.

Here we discover an important difference between the two women. While Rousseau battled against the Smoke Monster, Claire worked *for* the Monster. Evidently, then, Claire was infected by the black smoke. But we need to consider that the comparison between the two women may not be correct. We need to take a close look at the relationship between Claire and the Monster.

Claire and Her "Friend"

We know well that Montand, Robert, and the other members of Rousseau's team were taken and then infected by the Smoke Monster. If they were infected after such a brief contact, Claire's infection must have been much deeper, having had three years of intimate contact with the source.

We don't know with any certainty the nature of Claire's relationship with the Man in Black. But we have enough information to offer a strong theory. In Episode 6.10, the Man in Black told Claire she could not kill Kate, because he needed her to convince the Candidates to leave with him in the Ajira airplane. Once his plan was in place, he would no longer have need of Kate, and "... then whatever happens, happens." That is, the Man in Black told Claire she could kill Kate once Locke had collected all the Candidates onto the plane.

Congreve, in "The Mourning Bride," said "Hell hath no fury, like a woman scorned." There is no question of illness. There was neither hypnotism, nor trickery, nor even magic on the part of the Monster. Claire's state was such that it was possible for him to conform her to his will. Anger, fueled by the emptiness inside her mother's heart, consumed the young woman. This open wound in her soul could never be closed. Her condition could not improve, but only change and develop. With careful little suggestions, the Monster arranged the choices before Claire's eyes. His explanations were strong and direct, and appealed to her wounded heart.

Such is the strength of a mother's anger. It is a force stronger than any incantation or malevolent spell. Claire did work for the Smoke Monster, but she aligned herself with him only in hopes of finding her baby.

In the end, there was no difference between Claire and Rousseau. They acted in the same way, independent of any interaction with the Smoke Monster.

The Quest of Motherhood

During the third season, the reunion of Rousseau with her daughter was a revelation. But the meeting did not go smoothly.

KATE: Can I ask you something? I told you that your daughter was living with them, and you haven't asked me a single question about her, you haven't—
ROUSSEAU: Your friend, Jack. Do you care about him?
KATE: Yes.
ROUSSEAU: Imagine 16 years from now, you're told he's still alive, but in your heart, you know that he wouldn't remember you. He wouldn't know you. He wouldn't even know that you ever cared about him. I haven't asked you questions about my daughter because I do not want to know the answers.

Kate knew Claire would have the same problems after her reunion with Aaron. There could be only one solution: Kate would have to make Aaron and Claire her highest concern. Her quest was two-fold. Kate would have to help Claire find Aaron and also restore her sense as a mother. The relationship between a mother and her child is a concern for all of society. The evolution of collective social consciousness did not originate with Kate, but rather with Hillary Clinton.

It Takes a Village to Raise a Child

Hillary Clinton said "It Takes a Village to Raise a Child" is an African proverb. But the idea is European, and specifically French.

If we share the responsibility for motherhood—as Kate did in committing herself to serving both Claire and Aaron, and as Hillary Clinton believes we all must do as members of the village—we are equally obliged to share fatherhood and brotherhood. The Rights of Man and the Citizen are contravened if the responsibility of one person toward another is not shared equally across society.

This idea, celebrated every year on Bastille Day, is revolutionary. On the Island, three terms come to mind: Liberty, Equality, Maternity.

The balance pans of justice took on their complete meaning when Jack reilluminated the light in the cave. The balance of justice became reality when Rousseau and Alex (or Claire and Aaron) realised their full potential, and none of this was possible except through the assistance of Kate and the other protagonists.

Danielle Rousseau was never crazy.

Her quest was the quest of LOST: The search for trust of one person toward another, working together in the construction of a common edifice. For sixteen years, the Island was in disequilibrium. But with the reunification of Rousseau with her daughter, the Island was just a bit closer to paradise, with results on a par with those obtaining after the destruction of the Smoke Monster. Everything was in balance again. Rousseau had fought for this day with her weapons, her traps, her tortures. Thus was born the insensitivity of the strongest possible relationship, shared between mother and child. In the end, this bond came to represent a kind of Constant, a necessary corollary to the spirit of LOST.

L'insensibilité maternelle :
La quête culturelle de Danielle Rousseau dans « Lost »

Elle était folle.

Elle dressait des pièges, non pas pour les animaux, mais plutôt pour les hommes. Elle a kidnappé Aaron. Elle a torturé Sayid et qui sait combien d'autres hommes pendant les seize années passées sur l'île. Elle s'est habillée comme singe, sentait la chèvre, ressemblait à un démon. C'était le mal de la fumée noire qui la rongeait. Cette maladie dont on ne peut jamais guérir, l'avait gagné. Cette femme a tué les membres de son expédition scientifique. Ceux qui avaient survécus au monstre, ont péri par ses armes. Danille était au service de l'esprit de l'île, comme l'est aujourd'hui Claire.

Cette idée reçue n'est pourtant pas vraie. En effet, Rousseau n'a jamais touché le monstre. Bien au contraire, elle luttait contre lui… Quel mal la rongeait ? Une fièvre tropicale ? La désorientation des voyages spatio-temporels ? Le paludisme ? Une dysenterie amibienne ? Des vers intestinaux? Peut être s'est-elle levée du pied gauche trop de fois?

Aucune de ces raisons ne justifie son comportement. Le fait le plus difficile à croire est ceci :

Danielle Rousseau n'a jamais été folle.

Elle a vécu les mêmes émotions que vous et moi, et ses actions ont contribué au voyage humain qui constitue l'arc narratif de « Lost »

L'évidence est... Claire

Le fusil était différent, mais les cheveux et l'expression faciale étaient identiques. Les pièges n'ont pas changé. Elle aussi s'est habillée comme singe, sentait la chèvre, ressemblait à un démon. Claire a torturé, chassé et tué parce qu'on lui a retiré la même chose que Ben a prise à Rousseau : son enfant. Les motivations sont exactement les mêmes pour ces deux femmes. Alex et Aaron étaient encore des bébés lors de leur enlèvement.

Avec ma famille, je me rends souvent en camping dans les Rocheuses. La seule chose qu'on ne veut pas approcher, ce sont les petits oursons. Si l'on voit cette adorable boule de poil, il y a de grandes chances qu'une mère féroce ne soit pas loin derrière. Toute action, même l'alimentation du petit ours, sera admise comme un acte d'agression. La mère traquera et tuera l'offenseur. Une mère reste une mère, qu'il s'agisse d'un ours ou d'un homme.

En temps normal, nous pourrions accepter le comportement de Claire comme une simple défense pour protéger son enfant de la menace. A cet effet, nous pourrions également considérer de façon semblable l'acte de Rousseau, face à l'enlèvement de son enfant. Nous avons constaté que les actes des deux femmes étaient dans ce sens durs et cruels, et parfois démesurés.

Une fois encore, la loi, la raison et une compréhension réaliste de la nature humaine volent à notre secours. Dans l'ancien droit coutumier de France, d'Angleterre, et des États Unis, il y avait des situations où l'homicide n'était pas considéré comme un acte criminel, et où l'auteur n'était pas pénalisé. Si un conjoint (habituellement appelé «mari» dans la loi - les femmes, considéré comme biens personnels, ne disposaient pas de droits) a trouvé sa femme au lit avec un autre homme, in flagrante delicto, il pourrait tuer l'homme sans conséquences notoires. C'était la loi de l'État de Texas aux USA jusqu'à 1974, par exemple. Par conséquent, la loi reconnaît qu'il existe des situations dans lesquelles une réponse démesurée est acceptable.

Quelle est la valeur d'un enfant? Quels sont les droits d'un petit être humain qui ne peut ni se défendre ni même marcher? On reconnaît intuitivement que la mère dont les enfants ont été enlevés constitue un cas particulier, méritant une plus large considération dans son comportement et ses actions. La mère dont les enfants ont été kidnappés est naturellement insensible aux besoins des autres, même à ses propres besoins. De ce fait, elle est capable de se sacrifier pour ses enfants. Elle est «programmée» par la nature pour être particulièrement sensible aux besoins de ses enfants, et insensible aux besoins des autres. Il ne s'agit pas là d'une maladie mais plutôt de la conséquence normale de la maternité—c'est l'insensibilité maternelle.

Mais au fond, il y avait beaucoup plus que ça.

CLAIRE: Dites-moi où est mon fils !
JUSTIN: Je ne sais pas où est votre fils.
CLAIRE: .... Dites-moi la vérité !
JUSTIN: Je vous dis la vérité. Nous n'avons pas votre enfant. Nous n'avons jamais eu votre enfant.
CLAIRE: Arrêtez de mentir! Votre peuple ... m'a torturé.
JUSTIN: Non, nous vous avons capturé car vous chassiez ... notre clan !
[Claire brandit la hache pour frapper sa victime mais s'arrête à l'appel de Jin]
JIN: Attends!
CLAIRE: Attendre? Jin, ils m'ont torturé avec des aiguilles. Ils m'ont marquée .... ils m'auraient tuée s'ils avaient pu.

Pour une mère, la réponse à l'enlèvement de son enfant n'est jamais proscrite par la loi. Mais Claire Littleton et Danielle Rousseau n'ont pas eu à faire à un simple enlèvement. Elles étaient confrontées à une bataille. Une bataille incessante pour survivre sur l'île. Dans ce contexte, la mise à mort de Justin n'aurait pas été un homicide, elle aurait été considérée comme un acte juridique, en temps de guerre. Claire fit preuve de lucidité à propos de l'assassinat de Justin : «Tiens, si je ne l'avais pas tué, il m'aurait tué». La première fois que l'on aperçoit Rousseau dans la jungle, on ne pense pas «folle».

On songé à soldat. Je crois que l'impression est juste. Rousseau et Claire étaient en guerre contre les Autres.

Ici nous découvrons une différence importante entre les deux femmes. Alors que Rousseau s'est battue contre le monstre, Claire a travaillé pour le monstre. Évidement, Claire a été infectée par la fumée noire. La comparaison entre les deux mères est peut- être fausse. On doit examiner soigneusement la relation entre Claire et le monstre.

Claire et Son «Ami»

On sait bien que Montand, Robert, et les autres membres de l'équipe de Rousseau ont été happés, puis infectés par le monstre. S'ils ont été infectés suite à un bref contact, l'infection de Claire est beaucoup plus grande avec trois ans de contact avec le mal...

Nous ne connaissons pas avec certitude la nature de leur relation. Mais il existe des preuves suffisantes pour appuyer une théorie forte. Dans l'épisode 6,10, l'Homme en Noire (le Monstre) a dit que Claire ne pouvait pas tuer Kate, parce qu'il avait besoin d'elle pour convaincre les candidats de partir avec lui dans l'avion. Ses plans menés à bien, il n'aurait plus eu besoin de Kate, et cela «quoi qu'il arrive». Selon le Monstre, Claire aurait eu l'occasion de tuer Kate après l'embarquement de tous les candidats.

Congreve, dans The Mourning Bride, a dit, «L'enfer n'a pas de furie, comme une femme dédaignée». Il n'était pas question de maladie. Il n'y avait ni hypnotisme, ni tricherie, ni même de magie. L'état de Claire était tel qu'il était aisé pour le Monstre de la faire plier à sa volonté. La colère, celle d'un manque, a écorché vif la jeune femme. Cette blessure liée à la maternité ne pourra jamais se cicatriser. Son état ne pouvait pas s'améliorer, mais plutôt s'orienter. Avec de petites suggestions, le Monstre a su orienter les choix de Claire. Ses arguments étaient fermes et directifs.

Telle est la puissance de la colère d'une mère. Il s'agit d'une force plus puissante que celle d'un maléfice. Oui, Claire a travaillé pour le monstre, mais elle a fait son appel uniquement dans l'espoir de trouver son bébé.

En fin, il n'y avait pas de différence entre Claire et Rousseau. Elles ont agi de la même manière, indépendamment de toute interaction avec le monstre.

La Quête de Maternité

Dans la troisième saison, les retrouvailles entre Rousseau et sa fille étaient une évidence. Mais la réunion ne se fit pas sans embûches.

KATE: Puis-je vous demander quelque chose? Je vous ai dit que votre fille vivait avec eux, et vous n'avez pas m'a posé une seule question à son sujet ?

ROUSSEAU: Votre ami, Jack. Vous vous souciez de lui?

KATE: Oui.

ROUSSEAU: Imaginez-vous dans seize années à partir de maintenant… On vous apprend qu'il est toujours en vie. Mais dans votre esprit, vous savez qu'il ne se souvient pas de vous. Il ne vous connait pas. Il ne sait même pas que vous vous êtes toujours soucié de lui. C'est pour cette raison que je ne vous ai pas posé de questions sur ma fille : je ne veux pas connaître les réponses…

Kate savait que Claire aurait les mêmes problèmes lors de ses retrouvailles avec Aaron. Il n'y avait qu'une seule solution: Kate devait attacher de l'importance à Aaron et Claire. Sa quête était double. Kate devait aider Claire à retrouver Aaron et son état de mère. La relation de la mère et de son enfant est une préoccupation sociétale. Cette prise de conscience collective ne vient pas de Kate Austen mais plutôt d'Hillary Clinton.

Il Faut Tout Un Village Pour Élever Un Enfant

Hillary Clinton a dit que «Il Faut Tout Un Village Pour Élever Un Enfant» est un proverbe africain. Mais l'idée est européenne, et spécifiquement française.

Si nous partageons la responsabilité de la maternité, nous sommes également obligés de partager la paternité, la fraternité. Les droits de l'homme et du citoyen sont contrariés, si les responsabilités d'une personne à une autre ne sont pas partagées à parts égales. Cette idée que l'on célèbre chaque 14 juillet est révolutionnaire. Sur l'île, on évoquerait les termes suivants : «Liberté, Egalité, Maternité».

L'équilibre de la justice a pris tout son sens lorsque Jack a rallumé la lumière de la grotte. Elle est devenue réalité lorsque Rousseau et Alex (ou Claire et Aaron) réalisent leur plein potentiel, et tout cela ne fut possible que par l'assistance de Kate et de autres protagonistes.

Danielle Rousseau n'a jamais été folle.

Sa quête était la quête de « Lost : Les Disparus » : la quête de la confiance d'un homme envers un autre, de travailler ensemble pour la construction d'un édifice commun. Pendant seize ans, l'île était déséquilibrée. Mais avec la réunification de Rousseau et de sa fille, l'île était au plus près du paradis, au même titre que la destruction du monstre. Tout était à nouveau en équilibre. Rousseau luttait pour ce jour-là avec ses armes, ses pièges, ses tortures. Ainsi l'insensibilité nait d'une relation forte, partagée entre une mère et son enfant. Au final, il est question d'une sorte de constante, entrant en corolaire avec l'esprit même de « LOST ».

Pearson Moore

Grands remerciements à Vincent de lost-site.com pour son assistance. Il a transformé mon «français massacré» en prose claire et élégante; si vous avez apprécié cet article, votre plaisir est entièrement due à l'excellent travail de Vincent.

The Perfect Example

CHAPTER 13: THE PERFECT EXAMPLE

"I will never leave you again."
—Kwon Jin-Soo

"Let's elope."

"No. I'll get your father's blessing."

Sun all but rolled her eyes at Jin's quaint ideas. She must have wondered if he had spent his life in the nineteenth century. He would never obtain the great Woo-Jung Paik's permission. "You don't know my father." He didn't pause even for an instant. "I know me," he said, and gave her a beautiful white orchid, symbol of purity and eternity.

She was overwhelmed the day he brought the ring. "I have his blessing." But what she took for traditional charm turned into matrimonial slavery. "Clean the house. Wash yourself. Button your dress!" Mr. Nineteenth Century was not charming anymore. He was an overbearing, domineering chauvinist. She did what any modern woman would do: She plotted an escape, seduced a lover, learned English. Jin would never find her in America.

The day came at the Sydney airport. While he looked forward, she backed away. But then he did something not in her plans. He peered back at her with enchanting eyes, a beautiful white orchid in his hand. She cried, because she knew. She knew Jin.

In an epic tale replete with romance, theirs was the greatest love story of them all, but more than that: The story of Sun and Jin was the central lesson of LOST. We must come to know Jin and Sun, for it is through their story that we understand the Heart of the Island.

Reconciliation, Redemption, Rewatch

This was to have been a chapter about Jin-Soo Kwon alone. His story was distinct from Sun's, and they were separated for nearly two full seasons. More important to an essayist, their redemptive paths were different, virtually demanding separate essays. But then I rewatched House of the Rising Sun (1.06), and everything changed. By the end I was shedding tears over a story that meant so much more after the final submarine scenes of Season Six, but I also realised Jin's story did not stand alone. Writing about Jin without Sun would be as pointless as attempting a portrait of John Locke containing no reference to the Island, or a blizzard with no mention of snow. They are distinct persons, but theirs is a single epic, breathtaking story.

I argued in my early essays that LOST was not about free will or destiny, but rather it centred on personal identity. LOST required much of its main characters. They had to overcome personal histories and limitations, redeem themselves in thought and deed, in most cases they had to reconcile with someone, usually a father—and all of this in some way had to serve the interests of the Island. These objectives were achieved out of individual volition, and they represented the will of the Island (and thus they were *destiny*), but they were most of all the necessary steps toward realisation and assertion of identity.

Portraits of Jin and Sun could probably be relayed in separate essays, but this would not reflect well the intent of their character arcs and the much larger story, of which their sub-plot is a major strand. In fact, if we do not understand Sun-Hwa Paik and Jin-Soo Kwon, we don't understand the sideways world, and we don't understand LOST. Their story is the very thesis of LOST, relayed in the most compelling of human terms.

Juxtaposition

A poor fisherman from a small village. A millionaire industrialist from the largest city in the country. One would show kindness to a complete stranger, the other would kill his best friend to get ahead. They shared a common language, but the similarities ended there. They lived short kilometres away from each other, but they were so far apart culturally, in their priorities, in what they believed and stood for, they might as well have been from different planets. When Mr. Kwon dies no one will notice. When Mr. Paik dies the country will mourn. But the mourners would do well to forget Mr. Paik and lament instead the passing of a truly great man who taught tradition, confidence, and respect.

Mr. Kwon has one of the shortest entries at Lostpedia. He appeared in only two of the 121 episodes. We have been given only a single name: Mr. Kwon. What you are reading in these lines may constitute the longest continuous discussion of this man anywhere in the world. We can say only that we know practically nothing about him.

If we say this, though, we are wrong. We know much about Mr. Kwon. In fact, we know more about him than any of the other minor characters, and most of the supporting characters. Every time Jin did a good deed, we saw Mr. Kwon. Every time Jin used reason and good judgment and appealed to human dignity, we saw Mr. Kwon. Every time Jin respected his wife rather than claiming ownership over her, we saw Mr. Kwon.

Without a wife, without help mate of any kind, Mr. Kwon raised his son to honour and respect tradition, to cultivate a love of life and people, to fearlessly confront even the most difficult situation. Mr. Kwon was homemaker, janitor, housekeeper, school teacher, and money earner. He was anything and everything Jin needed. Above all else, Mr. Kwon was arguably the best father depicted in the six years of LOST. Jin-Soo Kwon has one of the longest entries at Lostpedia. I do not overstate at all when I tell you Jin's impressive résumé should be understood as a much abbreviated statement of his father's long list of accomplishments, most of which were never recorded on paper. You see, Mr. Kwon's accomplishments were all recorded in the good character of his adopted son.

We also know Mr. Paik. Cut from the same cloth as Charles Widmore, Martin Keamy, and Stuart Radzinsky, he was not all bad. In fact, he respected everyone—as long as a bribed official did exactly as Paik wished and did nothing to upset any of his plans, he wouldn't cut off his hands, or have one of his thugs beat his wife until her jaw cracked and she vomited, or shoot the family dog in front of the children. Al Capone is credited with the adage, "You can get much farther with a *KIND WORD* and a *GUN* than you can with a *KIND WORD* alone." To this Mr. Paik would add, "And brass knuckles will get you even farther."

Progeny Recapitulates Phylogeny

As she grew into adulthood, Sun came to be more and more like her mother and distanced herself from her authoritarian father. Then a man steeped in Korean tradition came into her life. A quiet, gentle, caring man. Jin was the very opposite of Paik Woo-Jung, the perfect man to give her a new life free from her father.

When Jin went to work for Mr. Paik, he destroyed Sun's dream of a happy future. Nothing good could come of this, she was sure. Probably even she never would have imagined that every characteristic she despised in her father would be magnified ten-fold in Jin. Sun was living a nightmare: her husband was becoming her father.

Jin had no history with Mr. Paik. He didn't enjoy being used as a thug and hitman, but there was a price to be paid for sleeping in Sun's bed, and her father enforced the highest possible toll.

SUN: [Subtitle: We can start a new life. We'll go away...]
JIN: [Subtitle: A new life? If we run away, your father would...]
SUN: [Subtitle: He won't know where we are. And you won't have to do this anymore—you won't have to...]
JIN: [Banging the table] [Subtitle: I do this for you, Sun! I do this because your father expects it. I do this because that's what it takes to be married to you.]

When his marriage was on the line, Jin learned quickly. He learned how to perform tasks he never would have chosen to do. He had to be good at what he did, because Paik Woo-Jung would demand nothing less than perfection.

Perhaps there are in this world criminals who lie, cheat, steal, and beat their enemies into a pulp but are otherwise exemplary members of society. Is Tony Soprano all that different from corporate wheelers and dealers who, if it were legal to do so, would bribe, steal, and murder? Doesn't Tony Soprano care for his family as much as those cut-throat corporate executives do?

The noble criminal, Tony Soprano. It's an interesting myth, but I see no connection to reality. Human beings just don't align their thoughts in one way during the business day and then arrange an entirely new set of priorities on the way home. A fundamental lifestyle option has repercussions through all facets of life. Jin began to exhibit every behaviour Sun hated because permeation of vile thought and action into every relationship was inevitable, and a much more realistic depiction of a man in his situation than anything written for the six years of The Sopranos. We are what we eat.

Jin consumed massive quantities of arrogance, absolute patriarchal control, and violent speech and action. He delivered all of these to the men Mr. Paik sought to discipline—and he delivered them to his wife, too.

The Bridges of Gyeonggi-do Province

Everything in Sun's demeanor and words brought absolute clarity to her feelings about her father. She wanted nothing to do with the man. She conveyed this fact repeatedly to Jin. Was he not listening? Did he not understand the most obvious and essential part of who Sun was? She was not a person to be held as chattel, not a woman to be treated as child, object, or beast of the field. She was her own person, equal in stature with Jin, equal to anyone in this world.

Jin did not act in any way to accommodate Sun's needs. He did not understand. He did not listen. He did not hear. Didn't he know the gifts were unnecessary? When he brought her an expensive purebred puppy, her response was, "Remember when all you had to give me was a flower?" The white orchid would have been enough. She could have sacrificed everything, lived in abject poverty, if only he gave her his heart. Everything else was unnecessary, superfluous, harmful to their marriage.

She had already endured a lifetime of her father's unbending will and the suffocating atmosphere of his toxic presence. Now she knew with certainty what her father was. She saw the truth of him in the blood on Jin's hands, in the gun he strapped to his side. Jin became her father, and worse. Everything she ever tried to escape now lived in her house, slept in her bed, ruled her, directed her, owned her.

She had to escape. Leaving Seoul would not suffice. Her father could track her anywhere in the country. But speaking only Korean, she was trapped in the Republic of Korea and its barely one hundred thousand square kilometres. She began studying English with a passion. Finding time was not difficult. Jin was away most of the day, enforcing her father's self-serving and evil will. She spent those long hours every day memorising words and meanings and pronunciations, absorbing rules of grammar, syntax, and intonation.

Her teacher was adorable. Jae was quiet, kind, gentle, sure of himself but not arrogant or proud. He was skilled and gentle in bed. His fluency in English was her ticket out of Korea; his generous heart was the guarantee of her freedom.

Did she wish her plan to fail? She could have been more discreet, but she almost flaunted her affair, meeting at her place or his, not even bothering to disguise herself or take circuitous routes to the sites of their trysts. She knew her father and his thugs watched her; he had been doing so all her life.

She should not have been surprised, then, when Paik Woo-Jung showed up at the door, catching them *in flagrante delicto*. She must have known the inevitable outcome, too. In those darkest days of her life, she must have reflected on the possibility—the likelihood—that Jae Lee would have lived if not for her own unyielding selfishness, her lack of concern for Jae's safety.

Jin arrived early one evening, for once not absorbed in his terrible duties. He must have felt her depression. "I have to deliver a gift for your father," he said, looking at her with compassionate eyes. He produced two Oceanic tickets. "Come with me."

The plan was so simple it could not possibly fail. She would lose Jin in the Sydney airport, stay a few days, and leave for the United States under an assumed name. She would finally be free of her father's tyranny.

They were in the Oceanic check-in line. Jin was absorbed, as usual, and Sun took slow steps, backing away from him. It was then that it happened. Her looked at her with those eyes again. No one had ever looked at her in that way—not since their courtship. Not since the day she knew in her heart that he loved her and only her. There he stood, looking back at her, loving her, raising a white orchid to his nose.

A Good World

Days before the flight, Jin was distraught. Paik was forcing him to commit increasingly violent acts. Sun was depressed and wouldn't tell Jin anything. He turned to the one person he trusted.

FATHER: Jin!
JIN: Father. Please forgive me. I was—ashamed of you.
FATHER: [giving him a hug]
[Shot of them with a trap, working on the boat.]
FATHER: What is she like?
JIN: Beautiful. Intelligent. Hardheaded. We don't talk anymore.
FATHER: Why not?

JIN: Because I can't tell her—about her father. In a good world—she would hate him, not me.
FATHER: It is a good world.
JIN: You don't know what I've done.
FATHER: You are my son. It does not matter what you've done.
JIN: I wish I could start over.
FATHER: Why can't you?
JIN: I have responsibilities.
FATHER: More important than your wife?
JIN: Her father wants me to deliver watches to his associates in Sydney and Los Angeles.
FATHER: Then let that be the last thing you do for him—then walk away. Don't come back. Go to America. Save your marriage.

Mr. Kwon understood perfectly the truth that had escaped Jin. Nothing was more important than his marriage to the "beautiful, intelligent" woman who would give up anything for him. Jin had been too long under Paik's dirty and bloody thumb. Sun and Jin belonged to each other, not to Paik Woo-Jung. In a conversation lasting not even five minutes, Mr. Kwon cleared away years of rotting filth from Jin's mind. "It is a good world." Everything Jin ever wanted was in the marriage he already had.

He knew what the white flower meant to Sun. It was the revelation of everything in his heart. "Go to America. Save your marriage." And there they were, in the check-in line at Oceanic Airlines, minutes away from a trip to Los Angeles and new freedom in the United States. When Jin drew the flower from his bag, brought it to his nose, and peered back at his lovely wife, she knew—he could feel it. Nothing would ever keep them apart.

Betrayal

Jin became the most physically abused survivor in Season One. He attacked Michael over Paik's watch and ended up in handcuffs, sweating and burning in the hot sun. When Walter burned the raft, Jin tried to put out the fire to save it. Later, seeing the burn marks on Jin's hands, Michael was sure he'd found the arsonist. If the man would beat him senseless over a watch, would he stop short of burning Michael's raft? Michael slugged him. And again. He pummeled Jin until his face was bloody.

Unable to take anymore, Sun shouted in English, "Stop it! Leave him alone!"

No one was more shocked than Jin.

How had she learned English? Thirty-two days on the Island could not possibly have been long enough to become fluent in such a difficult language.

She had been leading another life, not for weeks, but for years. Who was this woman he had been sleeping with?

Perhaps the world was still good, even if Sun was rotten. Jin went into the jungle and came back with a long bamboo pole on his shoulder and approached Michael. When Michael looked at Jin, a puzzled expression on his face, Jin said one word, in English: "Boat."

Redemption

Jin spent the next two months helping everyone. He helped Michael rebuild the raft, cutting construction time in half. Weeks later, he volunteered his sailing skills, piloting the Elizabeth to the other side of the Island to rescue Jack, Kate, Sawyer, and Hurley. After their rescue, when Hurley and Sawyer got into a fight, Jin broke them up. When Jack revealed the Others' plot to invade their camp and take the women, Jin was first to volunteer to stay behind and kill the invaders.

Over a period of two months Jin accomplished more good, helped more people, and felt better about himself than he had since he left the Southern village of Namhae for the big city in the north. He was a different man than he had been in Seoul. He was kind-hearted, as he had been in his youth. But now he brought wisdom and courage and balanced consideration to everything he did.

He and Sun began sleeping together again, and their happiness was evident to everyone. Hurley knew what was going on, and gave Jin a big "thumbs up" sign when he rose from their tent in the morning. Jin could only smile.

This was not the man Sun had married years before. He was more considerate, compassionate, and caring than he had ever been. He did not scold or reproach, even when she chose to wear a bikini. During the day, while he was away helping others, Sun thought of their nights together, full of more passion, romance, and happiness than they had ever known.

Pregnancy should have been their greatest joy, but Juliet knew it was a sentence of death. When Sun told Jin they would stay on the Island with Locke rather than leave with Jack, Jin confirmed her choice. "Wherever Sun go, I go." But Juliet knew Sun had only days to live if she made such a choice; she would die in the second trimester. Juliet decided to violate doctor-patient confidentiality. It was the only way to save Sun's life.

JULIET: Jin. Your wife had an affair.
[Sun turns around]
JIN: What?
JULIET: Sun was with another man. She thought the baby was his.
[Sun slaps Juliet, and turns to Jin. Jin, looking angry, turns and heads back to the beach.]

Jin knew Juliet's declaration contained an importance much greater than yet another revelation of Sun's secret life back in Korea. Something more was at play here. He needed to talk with someone. But his father was thousands of kilometres north. The best Jin could do was to occupy himself with the skill his father taught him.

BERNARD: You realize we're the only two married guys on the island?
....
JIN: Married.
BERNARD: ... It's not easy, is it? Oh, I mean, it's—it's wonderful, but... Rose ... has cancer. She's sick. Dying... She says she's better now. She says it's this place ... the island. But when the camp split up, I was sure that she'd want to go with Locke. Why would she want to leave the island, and risk getting sick again?
JIN: Then why do you stay with Jack?
BERNARD: Because it was the right thing to do. Locke ... he's a murderer. See, it's all about karma, Jin. Do you know karma?
[Jin nods]
BERNARD: You make bad choices, bad things happen to you. But you make good choices...

Bernard's life was all about Rose. She was making a decision to leave the Island, even though it meant her death. Bernard's words could only make Jin think of Sun, that her decision to stay would mean his wife's death. It was a thought unsettling in his mind. "Karma," Bernard had said. "Make good choices."

He had made all the bad choices in Korea. "You make bad choices, bad things happen to you." Jin and Bernard fished for many hours. Jin, silent, sat next to Bernard and thought about his marriage, about Sun, about her life, about her coming death.

Reconciliation

As the sun set, Jin approached their tent carrying grilled fish on a plate. Sun was inside. What followed was the most important scene of Season Four.

JIN: I made ... dinner.
SUN: I thought you had left me. Will you let me try to explain?
JIN: It won't matter.
SUN: Just listen, maybe—
JIN: I know why you did it. I know the man... I used to be. Before this island, I withheld my affections... And I know... that whatever you did... you did to that

man. His actions caused this. So I forgive you.
[Sun smiles in tears, they embrace]

Three Years and Lifetimes Apart

Jin fulfilled his promise to get Sun off the Island, but keeping the promise meant paying a steep price. Sun thought Jin was dead. When the Island's representative, Christian, showed her the "New Recruits" photograph from 1977, he told her Jin was there with them. "I'm sorry, but you have a bit of a journey ahead of you." Jin might as well have been dead. Thirty years in the past, the Purge would take him long before Sun could figure out a way to reach him.

Sun did everything in her power to get back to Jin. She took on Charles Widmore without fear. She stared down her own father and took his company away from him. She talked with Richard Alpert, and even swallowed her distaste and talked with Benjamin Linus.

Nothing could stand in her way. But when the thing claiming to be Locke offered to bring her to Jin, she knew not to trust him. It was as if she had heard Bernard's words to Jin. "Karma. You make bad choices, bad things happen to you." Even though she sought Jin above anything else in life, she somehow knew to run away from the Man in Black. She made the right choice. Short hours later, and three years after they last held each other, they were united again. "I won't leave you. I will never leave you again... I love you, Sun."

The Perfect Example

Marriage is just about the greatest state two people can share, but it is the most difficult job in the entire world. All of us wish for marriage to work when we enter into it, but half the time—in some places more than half the time—it fails. Jin and Sun had more than their fair share of marital issues, and they brought on many of these problems themselves, by falling into easy temptations. But somehow they rose above all of these most difficult challenges, achieving something that many of us would sacrifice much to emulate. Jin and Sun gave their lives to achieve it.

In their death, I think, is a strong statement about the power of love. Many question or even condemn Jin for his decision to stay with his wife to the end. But I think he had his priorities straight. He became a courageous example to all fathers.

Fatherhood, as with any responsibility of significance, is in its essence a commitment requiring action. Jin's relationship with Ji Yeon was made possible because of the strength of his relationship with Sun. By *acting* to honour his commitment to marriage and his wife, he was honouring and supporting Ji Yeon. This was nothing the girl would understand in her childhood. But as she grew older, for the rest of her life, she would know with greater certainty than most of us that her life came about because two people loved each other more than life itself. Ji Yeon's significance goes beyond even her own life, because the essence of her, what she truly is, is based in a love that is more powerful and truer than life. Perhaps she will not recognise that or understand the implications of it until well into adulthood. But as some point she will know. Jin had his priorities straight. In the decision to never again leave Sun, he became the greatest father any girl could ever have.

When we find each other, we are no longer lost. When we commit to something greater than ourselves, give everything we have, we discover that which never dies. The sideways world was LOST's statement of the reality we should be seeking here and now, before we take our final breath in this world. Sun and Jin were the perfect couple and the perfect parents because they considered nothing in this world more precious than their marriage. In their sacrifice, they became the most complete example of the perfect human relationship, and the purest example of the lesson LOST sought to teach.

Eternity

Hurley jogged off the jungle path and onto the sandy beach, heading directly for Ben. He stopped a metre from his second in command, taking rapid breaths.

"Did Rose give you the—"

Ben patted the wooden box tucked under his arm. "It's right here, Hugo."

"Is it the right one?" Hurley frowned. "It's gotta be the right one, it's just—"

"It's the right one," Ben said, an edge to his voice. "I checked just to be sure."

"Okay, dude. Cool."

Ben pointed to the outrigger canoe at the shore. A single figure in yellow rain coat sat unmoving in the middle of the boat. "Just like last year," Ben said.

"Yeah," Hurley said, frowning, but now with a slight smile. "Don't know why it's gotta be a raincoat, it's—"

"It's tradition. Nothing wrong with tradition, Hugo."

"No, I guess not." Hurley took a big breath and exhaled. He scanned the sky for a few moments and then set his eyes on the canoe. "Okay, let's do this."

Hurley and Ben took fast, purposeful strides toward the outrigger. Ben took the bow, Hurley grabbed the stern, and together they pushed the canoe into shallow water. Ben jumped into position, looked back to be sure Hurley was settled in at stern, and they began paddling.

When his arms were tired from the constant exertion, Ben looked back. The shore must have been a good two kilometres away. It seemed to Ben they had paddled far enough, but Hurley gave no sign, and he continued paddling. The water was calm today, and cooler than on the Island. The weather could not have been better.

"Okay," Hurley said. "This is the spot."

Ben dropped his paddle into the canoe and massaged his aching arm.

"You can hand back the package."

"Right." Ben picked up the bundle, turned around carefully, and stretched past the yellow-clad figure, trying to reach Hurley.

"It's for her, dude. Open it."

"Okay." Ben dropped the clasp and drew back the hinged top on the ornate wooden box. Inside was the single white orchid Rose had chosen that very morning at the Dharma Station. It was the most perfect orchid, chosen from among dozens that had been planted for this single occasion.

Ben kept his eyes on the girl, trying above all to maintain composure. He knew Number One back in the stern was already crying.

Six-year-old Ji Yeon pulled back the hood on her raincoat, took the white flower into her hand, and gazed on it for several moments. Then, leaning over the gunwale and lowering her hand, she placed the flower on the water.

"사랑해요 엄마와 아빠," she said.

I love you, mom and dad.

The Priest

CHAPTER 14: THE PRIEST

"Dude."

—Hugo ("Hurley") Reyes

(Hurley said "Dude" 347 times over the six years of LOST)

He was cursed and crazy, so out of touch with reality that an imaginary man became his best friend, and an insane man with a vocabulary of six words was his greatest intellectual inspiration. His unearned wealth could not prevent the misfortune that visited all who came into his influence. His father left him, his grandfather died at the lottery press conference, his best friend on the Island was drowned, his girlfriend was murdered. Even the woman who interviewed him was smashed to dust in a meteor strike. He was artless, witless, helpless, hopeless.

In an Island world that prized the strange symmetries of mirror reflection, he provided the most interesting and useful insights into human capacities for harmony. His mirror revealed a reality replete with good fortune, charity, and good will. "I'm the luckiest man alive," he said, a smile brightening his cheerful face.

"Oh, the 'sideways world'," some say, scoffing. "Purgatory." No. Not purgatory, but reality. In the dark days of the Smoke Monster, his golf tournament brought sunshine. In the most memorable scene of Season Three, he proved bad luck is a state of mind. And in the last minutes of the series, his humanity and clarity of vision were honoured with the Island's most sacred trust. The mirror revealed a man with greater sanity than any of us possess, a man so blessed that he was entrusted with the very future of humankind. For our sake, for our grandfathers' and girlfriends' and children's sake, we must move beyond the curses and craziness of our lives and adopt instead the peaceful ways, the sane and blessed symmetries of this gentle man, the final shepherd of the Island, Hugo Reyes.

The First Curse

Admittance to the pantheon of the Island had one strict requirement, and Hurley paid the requisite dues even before reaching his teen years. His mother could be saint or sinner, his youth could see privilege or poverty, but in order to find his way to the Island, his father had to be a scoundrel. Jack's father was an alcoholic, Kate's father was a low-life bum, and Locke's father was a swindler. Hurley, the man who would inherit the throne of Jacob, was given the worst kind of father. David Reyes said he wanted to go fishing, said he would help his son repair the Camaro, said his son mattered, but then revealed in his actions that everything he said was a lie. Hurley's only solace, when his father abandoned him, was the chocolate bar he held in his hands.

How does a boy react when the only significant person in his life tells him that he does not matter? Hurley took the words to heart. He had no value to others, to himself, to anything of importance. His only contribution to the world would be to serve as a curse. As he grew into adulthood he returned to the only sources of happiness he knew: food and friends.

His mother mattered to him. His friends were important. Since his enjoyment of life was of no consequence, having a positive influence on the happiness of others came to bear increasing degrees of significance to him. Even if he was worthless, perhaps he could leave a positive mark in the world, however slight, by making his friends' comfort and joy his primary aim. It was a laudable and charitable disposition, though thankless in many ways. While his friends benefitted immeasurably from his selfless commitment to their good cheer, he remained morose, convinced he was a blight. When a deck collapsed under his weight, killing two people, he lost any ability to deal with reality.

Six-Fold Curse

The six Valenzetti coefficients, broadcast on a continuous loop by the Dharma Initiative radio station, drove Leonard Simms insane. The reaction could have been worse; Leonard's partner at the Navy listening post, Sam Toomey, took his own life to end the curse of the numbers. When Hurley used the numbers to win the Mega Lotto Jackpot his troubles should have disappeared. Instead, he experienced even greater degrees of misery. His grandfather died, the house he purchased for his mother burned, the man cleaning his lawyer's office windows fell to his death. Misfortune followed everyone around Hurley.

The curse did not originate with Hurley. The Valenzetti Equation was a product of the Cold War between the United States and the Soviet Union. It was humankind's ultimate curse, defining the number of years until the human race annihilated itself, "whether through nuclear fire, chemical and biological warfare, conventional warfare, pandemic, overpopulation."

Valenzetti is referenced only once in LOST, in the lower left corner of the Swan Station blast door map, where a cryptic notation indicates "low relevance to Valenzetti-related research activity." But without an understanding of the Valenzetti Equation, the final hour of LOST constitutes the culmination of a simple adventure story. On the other hand, with the grand equation in view, we discover its solution, and we understand the thesis of LOST.

The numbers permeated the series, from Jack's seat number (twenty-three) in Episode 1.01 to Rousseua's map to the Swan Station serial number to Hurley's investiture as Protector. Episodes that did not feature references overt or sublime to the six famous integers were unusual. Perhaps there were a handful of such episodes in which writers absent-mindedly forgot to place at least one easily-recognised allusion. It didn't matter; bloggers and analysts made up the references if they were lacking.

The numbers surrounded Hurley, which he first understood as a curse. Whether scourge or benefit, the numbers were connected to Hurley as they were to no one else, and he would have to learn to walk his path with them or in spite of them. More than any other element of the LOST mythology, the numbers were imbued with a heavy sense of inevitability. Because the strongest mythological undercurrents of the series pointed toward the numbers, we knew subconsciously that Hurley would be involved at the highest levels of the final resolution. The fact that Jacob instructed Hurley to bring Jack to the lighthouse (Episode 6.05) was no accident, and neither was it a direct result of Hurley's ability to speak with the dead. Jacob knew he had to save Jack and Hurley from the Man in Black's ravaging of the Temple because these two Candidates were destined to become Protectors. Far from acting as a curse, the number eight carved into the cave ceiling next to Hurley's name proved to be both his salvation and his destiny.

Golf Together or...

Hurley thought himself cursed. If asked, he would almost certainly have said he was not happy. Yet he brought more happiness into the lives of his fellow survivors than anyone else on the Island. Episode Nine's golf game was certainly the most memorable diversion of Season One, organised at Hurley's insistence when he realised everyone was becoming unnecessarily stressed by the strange events in the jungle.

Whether he was dispensing smiles to cheer up depressed survivors, giving Jin a thumbs up when he rose in the morning, organising golf games, or distributing food from the Dharma pantry, Hurley was the supreme instigator of almost every movement toward what my generation called peace, love, and togetherness.

Perhaps we occasionally saw him as the comic, or the buffoon—the humorous relief in otherwise cheerless situations. Perhaps we considered the golf game and later events as merely the diversions that everyone at the time must have understood them to be. But Hurley's leadership in the social realm had far greater consequences than a mere afternoon's entertainment. Live together, die alone, Jack was wont to say. Yet Jack became a dividing point, not a centre of attraction or reconciliation. Hurley liked just about everyone, and everybody loved Hurley. Even in the most trying situation, Hurley endeavoured to bring people together. Jack had an intellectual awareness of his famous motto. Hurley carried the motto in his heart, lived by its words, and practiced them in almost every phrase he uttered and every action he took. The successful resolution of the great conflict—the battle with the Smoke Monster—was more a result of Hurley's cheerful team building than Jack's epiphany and rise to leadership.

Libby

Libby was not only Hurley's lover, but more importantly, she was antagonist to Dave, Hurley's imaginary friend. While Dave was busy trying to get Hurley to stuff food in his mouth or throw himself off a cliff, Libby urged Hurley to liberate himself from addictions, and especially his addiction to food. She never told him what to do or how to do it, but she became the most positive force in his life.

Libby and Hurley had both been treated at the Santa Rosa Mental Health Institute. They became exemplars of the topsy-turvy nature of the LOST world. We accept the notion that "crazy people" are those poor souls who are incapable of living normal, healthy lives. Yet these two former crazy people carried on a romance that was marked by greater sanity than any other relationship on the Island. While Sun and Jin were cheating on each other and Kate was trying to arrange her schedule so she could sleep with Jack one night and Sawyer the next, Libby and Hurley were just two young people in love. More than that, they appreciated each other, helped each other, and gained strength from each other.

Taken together, Libby and Hurley made an important statement about mental health. The socially accepted definition of sanity, they argued, has to change. Our attitudes about sanity and insanity need adjustment. I am among those who feel Libby and Hurley had it right. Our common need to amend the definition of sanity is something that goes far beyond the borders of a television series.

A Devout Meditation

Thomas Merton, The mid-twentieth century spiritual writer, revealed to us the insidious danger of widely-held attitudes toward sanity in his short essay "A Devout Meditation in Memory of Adolf Eichmann." Eichmann was one of the leading organisers of Hitler's "final solution"—the genocidal extermination of the Jewish race throughout the world. Psychologists examined Eichmann and found him sane, making him eligible to stand trial for his crimes. This is what Merton had to say about the determination of Eichmann's sanity:

"One of the most disturbing facts that came out in the Eichmann trial was that a psychiatrist examined him and pronounced him perfectly sane. I do not doubt it all, and that is precisely why I find it disturbing.

"If all the Nazis had been psychotics, as some of their leaders probably were, their appalling cruelty would have been in some sense easier to understand. It is much worse to consider this calm, "well-balanced," unperturbed official conscientiously going about his desk work, his administrative job which happened to be the supervision of mass murder. He was thoughtful, orderly, unimaginative. He had a profound respect for system, for law and order....

"The sanity of Eichmann is disturbing. We equate sanity with a sense of justice, with humaneness, with prudence, with the capacity to love and understand other people. We rely on the sane people of the world to preserve it from barbarism, madness, destruction. And now it begins to dawn on us that it is precisely the sane ones who are the most dangerous."

Throughout the six-year run of LOST we saw countless instances of "sane" people pointing guns at each other, even when there was no apparent reason to be pointing a gun. Jack's extreme state after having survived the opening of the hatch was illustrated perfectly during the scene in which he chased the fleeing Desmond through the jungle, finally stopping him at the point of his pistol. Desmond was no longer a threat to anyone, he merely wished to leave. Somehow the "sanity" of the moment had convinced Jack of the appropriateness of threatening to shoot an innocent, unarmed man who was fleeing a situation that frightened him.

I make no argument here regarding the merits or practicality of the application of deadly force. Certainly there were other instances of "sanity" that we ought to find objectionable and cause for re-evaluation. One such instance was the Season Three move by the Others to kidnap all the female 815 survivors of childbearing age. Hurley, never constrained to accept other people's definition of sanity, decided this demonstration of coordinated sanity could not stand. He fired up the rusting Dharma van and mowed down the men who had come to abduct his friends.

The Road to Shambala

If "Tricia Tanaka Is Dead" is not among your top ten LOST episodes I recommend you re-evaluate your ranking. This gem from the mid-point of LOST not only stands as the turning point in the show's mythology, but it contains the most delightful scene in the entire series.

Until this episode, Hurley was convinced the numbers were cursed, he was cursed, and he could never be anything more than a source of bad luck to anyone interacting with him. A three-minute ride in a twenty-year-old Dharma van turned Hurley's life around and gave every viewer-participant around the world reason to express hope for the survivors of Flight 815.

"You make your own luck" became Hurley's new watch words after this amazing ride. The attitude seems contrary to the relentless, destiny-driven atmosphere of LOST. When Hurley popped the clutch and the engine turned over we became witness not only to Hurley's makeover, but to a completely new page in the book of LOST mythology, breaking philosophical ground that had not yet been opened to our curious explorations.

Particularly in the case of the numbers and Hurley, the idea of free will seemed long buried, the decision having been reached almost with the pilot episode that free will was an illusion. Later episodes hammered away at the idea of inevitable destiny. "Dead is Dead," "What's Done Is Done," and other pronouncements were delivered episode after episode, cementing in our minds the idea that some indomitable force of nature was driving the survivors toward an event of monumental importance that could not be delayed or rerouted or denied.

Hurley's van ride was the spectacular precursor to Faraday's Boulder of Season Five and Jack's acceptance of the yoke of Protectorship at the end of Season Six. Faraday's Boulder—the idea that a big enough splash in the currents of time could actually change history—was conditional on the idea that human beings are the variables in the flow of spacetime. "What's Done Is Done" is not an absolute, Faraday said, because human beings could change their behaviours. Sawyer groaned that Faraday's plan hadn't worked, since it did not bring Juliet back to life and they were still stuck on the Island. In a certain sense, Sawyer was correct. The placement of the nuclear device atop the electromagnetic leak had not created a new stream in time as Faraday predicted. But it did work in the way circumstances required, catapulting all of them thirty years back to the future so that Jack and Kate could kill the Smoke Monster.

The tragedy of Juliet's death might have been avoided, had anyone been listening to Hurley. The survivors didn't need a Ph.D. in theoretical physics to tell them human beings have free will. "You make your own luck, dude," Hurley would have told them. They could have slain the Smoke Monster two years earlier—and all of them could have taken a Dharma van on the road to Shambala.

A Deception Regarding The Lie

Hurley could not tell a lie. Even when the stakes were high, when lives were on the line, convincing the great truthteller to collaborate in deception was all but impossible.

JACK: Hurley, what about you?
HURLEY: I don't think we should lie, dude.
JACK: We need to protect the people that we left behind, Hurley.
HURLEY: How does lying protect them?
JACK: It protects them from Charles Widmore. The guy hired a boatload of people to kill all of us. He faked a plane crash. I mean, you think telling him the truth, he's just gonna... leave them alone?
...
HURLEY: But he'll never find them. I mean, the Island disappeared. We all saw it. It's gone. Bloop!
JACK: You think anyone's gonna believe that... believe any of it? They're gonna think you're crazy.
HURLEY: Not if someone backs me up. Sayid, come on... I don't want to spend the rest of my life lying. Do you?
SAYID: No. But... I don't believe we have a better choice.

[Hurley takes Sayid's response badly.]
SAYID: Sorry, Hurley, but we have to lie.

The sequence above, from Episode 5.01, "The Lie," showed us the Hurley we came to know over the course of six years. Honest, dependable, incapable of telling a lie. These statements would mean even more to us than they do—if they were true. Hurley may not have enjoyed distributing deception and lies, but he was able to spread falsehoods as well as anyone else. The sequence below occurred in the police interrogation room in Los Angeles (Episode 4.01, "The Beginning of the End"):

DETECTIVE: I knew somebody on your plane.
HURLEY: Really?
DETECTIVE: Her name was Ana Lucia Cortez. She was my partner before I made detective. Dark hair. Gorgeous. Maybe you knew her? Maybe you met her on the plane? Before it took off?
HURLEY: Sorry, never met her.

Readers familiar with the chronology will recognise that this event in Episode 4.01 took place *after* the decision on Penny's boat in Episode 5.01. Hurley's deception with Ana-Lucia's former partner was therefore just part of the Oceanic Six's grand lie. But he lied before this occasion, too. For instance, in Episode 3.19, "The Brig," Sayid and Hurley were working on the satellite telephone Naomi had brought with her to the Island. The two of them were trying to keep Jack from finding out about Naomi's presence, because if he had found out, he might have told the newly-arrived Other, Juliet, and no one trusted her. They believed their chances of getting off the Island were greater if Juliet didn't find out about the possible rescue freighter. Kate approached, and asked Hurley what he had in his hands.

KATE: What's that? Is that a radio? Where'd you get it?
HURLEY: Uh, the luggage.

Sayid and Hurley felt it important to keep the truth of Naomi's arrival from Kate, since she was one of Jack's closest friends, and once in Jack's hands, the information would be communicated to Juliet and then Ben and his henchmen. So, Hurley lied.

Lying was not something Hurley ever felt comfortable doing, and the reticence he displayed in upholding the great lie of the Oceanic Six was well in keeping with his character. But as we discovered in the first four seasons and late in final season, Hurley was not above lying, especially if he believed a little deception would help his friends. Telling the truth was not necessarily a goal for Hurley, but it was useful to the greater objective of making good moral choices. Morality was Hurley's guiding light, and he felt uncomfortable traveling outside the straight and narrow. Even the proper treatment of a skeleton was important to Hurley:

SAWYER: [pointing at Roger] Skeletor seems to like it. [Sawyer clinks the beer can on Roger's skull] Bottoms up.
HURLEY: That's not cool, dude. That guy had a mom, a family, and friends.

The fact that Hurley was primarily driven by morality is important to keep in mind as we proceed with a consideration of Hurley's final days before returning to the Island, and his ascendency as a leader and finally as the Protector at the end of Season Six.

The Great Deceiver

When Locke asked Ben how he became Leader of the Others, he explained that he had been born on the Island. On Ajira Flight 316 back to the Island, Jack wondered how Ben could concentrate on reading.

JACK: [Sighs, to Ben] How can you read?
BEN: My mother taught me.

These were trivial matters, but even in the mundane details of his life, Ben felt it necessary to lie. He was born in Oregon, not on the Island, and his mother died giving birth to him, so she could not have taught him to read.

Deception was more useful in some cases than others. After Ben's people had infiltrated the survivors' camp and killed several of their members, Rousseau and Sayid discovered him in one of Rousseau's net traps. Not knowing who he really was, they were ready to believe the tale he concocted, that he was "Henry Gale, from Minnesota." (Although he claimed origin in Minnesota, I consider this lie part of the Canada Deception, as I discussed in *LOST Humanity*, Chapter Ten)

Ben was more comfortable lying than telling the truth, as we saw on the long Ajira flight. Yet, just as truth was not Hurley's supreme virtue, so too, deception was not the vice that ruled Ben's existence. While he did lie out of habit, and perhaps even sometimes created deceptions for the simple pleasure of doing it, more often than not there was a reason for his fabrications. Whether he was trying to save his own skin, or prevent communication with Widmore's freighter, or deter anyone from leaving the Island, Ben usually lied in service to a greater purpose.

While he sometimes had to fib extemporaneously, he also created grand deceptions with enough thought and backing to stand the prodding of the most determined sceptic. This pre-planned scheming required the careful evaluation of statements, their strengths, their causal connection to chronologies, people, and events, and their ability to prepare his victims for the manipulation he sought to perform.

The challenge that drove Ben to scheming and lies was preparedness. As he relayed to Mikhail on the walkie-talkie, "Everything I did, I did for the

Island." He had to be ready for anything, because people like Charles Widmore and Alvar Hanso would stop at nothing to control the Island's power. "This Island is under assault by forces stronger than anything it's had to deal with in many many years. And we are meant to protect it... by any means necessary." We need to keep this in mind as we examine the Hot Pocket Incident.

The Hot Pocket Incident

Episode 5.02 began with a discussion of the Lie fabricated by the Oceanic Six, and it ended with the greatest lie that anyone would ever tell during the six years of LOST. That greatest of fibs began with a confrontation between Hurley and the person who became his primary nemesis, Benjamin Linus.

[A Hot Pocket rotates inside of a microwave. Ding! The door opens, and Hurley extracts his snack... He drops the Hot Pocket onto a stack of paper napkins on the counter. A shadowy figure steps into the kitchen.]
BEN: Hello, Hugo.
HURLEY: Aah!
[Hurley flings the Hot Pocket. It strikes the door frame next to Ben, leaving a greasy mark.]
HURLEY: Get away from me. Get away!

Ben tried to talk Hurley into going with him to return to the Island, but he didn't even want to listen to Ben. "You're playing one of your mind games," Hurley said. He became so agitated, so sure that he would face the worst of any possible fates if he followed Ben, that he ran out of the house, screaming to the police waiting outside to take him into custody for murders he did not commit.

HURLEY: Hey! Hey, you got me! That's right, you got me!... I'm the killer!
DETECTIVE: Stop! Police!... Slowly drop down to your knees!
[Hurley complies. Ben stands near the house, watching.]
HURLEY: I'm the killer. I'm crazy. I'm a murderer. I killed four people... three people. However many are dead, I killed them. I killed them.
[Handcuffs click on Hurley's wrists.]
HURLEY: I killed them all. J—just—just get me away from here.

Hurley's confession to dire crimes he did not commit marks an important milestone in the story, and a turning point in the lives of both Hurley and Ben. This incident demonstrates something about LOST that makes it different from most other dramas.

Conflict in LOST is never abstract. Conflict is always personal, to the point that without a disagreement between distinct individuals, there is no dramatic action. Even something like the Smoke Monster, which at first appeared to be the most impersonal of all monsters, was personalised to a greater degree than many of the other characters in the series. In fact, one of the series' most accomplished actors was enlisted to portray the Monster for the last season of the show.

The Strange Attractor

For every conflict there was a single protagonist and a single antagonist. This unusual arrangement paralleled the designation of a "Constant" for each character, so that every main character had a single positive relationship and a single negative relationship. Every main character also had a responsibility to reconcile with a minor character in her past. Hurley's Constant was, of course, Libby, and his reconciliation relationship was with his father, David. But the most interesting of Hurley's relationships was what I call the Strange Attractor relationship (See *LOST Humanity*, Chapter 13). In Hurley's case, the Strange Attractor was Benjamin Linus.

I will not redevelop the Strange Attractor idea here. Those who wish to fully understand the idea should read Chapters 2, 3, 10, 12, and 13 of *LOST Humanity*. The basic idea of Strange Attraction is that two characters are drawn into personal opposition to each other over a shared aspect of their personalities. But the opposition is not geared exclusively toward conflict merely for the sake of drama. The true rationale for the Strange Attractor is in character growth.

So, for example, Kate was in personal opposition to (Strange Attraction with) Claire over the idea of motherhood. Recall Claire's easy acceptance of motherhood and Kate's fundamental opposition to the idea (she left her husband, Kevin, because she thought she might be pregnant). Kate came to embrace motherhood at a time when Claire was no longer capable of being a mother. The personal orientation of these two women with respect to motherhood had changed. Both of them had grown, but they remained diametrically opposed to each other around the core idea.

In the same way, Hurley and Ben were in Strange Attraction around the idea of honesty. Hurley was the best example of honesty and truth, and Ben was the supreme example of dishonesty and lies. From the moment of the Hot Pocket Incident to the very end of the series—and beyond—Hurley and Ben remained in opposition to each other.

But the purpose of the Hurley-Ben Strange Attraction was not some Gilligan's-Island amusing elaboration of cute scenarios dealing with an always-honest Hurley and an always-lying Ben. In the final days leading up to Hurley's installation as Protector, he lied frequently. At the same time, Ben was beginning to become a more reliable source of true information. They were both growing around the idea of honesty, but more serious considerations were at play, as well.

Protector and Consigliere

Honesty was their Strange Attractor, but honesty was the final objective of neither man. Hurley learned not to be "honest to a fault," and Ben learned that manipulating people was not the best solution to every problem. By the time Ben became Hurley's consigliere, they had both progressed beyond their starting positions relative to the notion of honesty, but they remained diametrically opposed, and honesty always figured as their chief point of division.

The primary objectives were different, and in the end these goals were informed to a large extent by the major personal deficits of the two men. The superficial, knee-jerk reaction had always served Hurley. If his immediate response to a situation had not always been the reaction he might have chosen on careful reflection, it always had the benefit of conforming his very well-developed sense of morality. On the other hand, Ben's careful manipulation of people and situations meant that he was hyper-aware of evaluating options on a constant basis. He lacked a moral basis for his decisions, though, and weighed everything in favour of whatever momentary objective was important to him in any situation. Hurley lacked analytical, decision-making skills, and Ben lacked a moral foundation for his analysis.

Ben was an architect, then, and Hurley was a dreamer. Ben would never have thought of a good game of golf as a means of refreshing the souls of those who were stressing over polar bears and columns of black smoke and the disappearance and death of fellow survivors. Hurley dreamed, and his dreams were full of the needs and desires of everyone around him. When there are immediate needs, there is no need for planning.

Ben was useful to Hurley because the position of Protector was not responsible only for short-term duties. Hurley was deep into his responsibilities for the long haul—potentially for many times the length of an average human life. Hurley was useful to Ben. Even though Hurley was perhaps twenty years Ben's junior, nevertheless he had spent a lifetime knowing what was right and what was wrong, and acting on that basis. Ben would possibly always suffer moral deficiency, but thanks to Hurley, the correct basis for any analysis or decision tree was never further away than a short walk through the jungle or across the warm sand of the ocean beach.

Blessed and Sane

He crashed on the Island thinking himself the most accursed man in the world. His adventure ended with his installation to the most blessed position a human being could occupy, for all eternity if he so desired. His way of doing things proved to be the most sane, based solidly on the most important elements of humanity. Hurley found his identity as the Protector, the shepherd of the Island, the priest to all humankind.

The Saint

CHAPTER 15: THE SAINT

"You'll find me in the next life, if not in this one."
—Sayid Hassan Jarrah,
translating Nadia's words on the back of a
photograph, "Solitary" (Episode 1.09)

He was the only character to die twice on the Island.

Did he deserve resurrection? His major accomplishments before death were tortures and murders. He was a respected officer in Saddam Hussein's Republican Guard, but only due to keen ability in using the implements of terror to extract confession from the most recalcitrant prisoner. So effective was he as paid assassin in Ben Linus' employ that he ran out of victims to kill. In violation of the precepts of Islam, he wore gold jewellery, drank Scotch Whisky, and engaged in fornication. By any measure, by his own admission, and most pointedly by the teachings of his faith, he was not a good man.

More than any other character, he struggled with the morality of his actions. Twice he left society, explicitly acknowledging the dark blemishes on his soul. He sought redemption with greater vigour than anyone around him. If his sins were profound, his condemnation of them was sure.

In the end, his faith teaches that he did not die. By giving up his life so his friends might live, the darkness inside him was wiped away. When his body is found, it is not to be washed, for the Quran says he is already clean, inside and out. This is the story of the last great saint of Mittelos, Sayid Hassan Jarrah.

The Struggle Begins

Sayid's father was one of the great heroes from the days of Amad asan al-Bakr, President of Iraq before Saddam Hussein. He was a man respected, not only in his village, but throughout the country. Especially during the years of terror, starting in 1979, he was a pillar of honesty and integrity. He taught his sons virtue and instilled in them the tenets of the Islamic faith. Most of all, he insisted they understand that a man must not disdain difficult tasks. One such task was the taking of life.

The Quran is very clear about the precise manner in which an animal's life is to be ended, especially if the animal is to be used for food. The killing must be done cleanly and humanely, so as to prevent the animal's suffering. If the animal is not respected, or if the killing is performed contrary to scripture, the transgressor is to be held in violation of Islamic law, and the meat from the animal is considered unclean—not suitable for consumption. Halal is more restrictive even than kosher law.

A man must understand that the taking of life—even animal life—is forbidden. An exception applies only in the case in which an animal is required for food, and even then the many rules surrounding the killing, butchering, and preparation of meat must be scrupulously obeyed, or the butcher brings contempt upon himself.

Such was the framework in effect when the great hero of Iraq came to his eldest son, Omer, and instructed him to kill a chicken for dinner. It was an honour, an acknowledgement that Omer was moving into manhood, and he would be expected to complete tasks not agreeable to women and not suited to children. The task was also a challenge, one which the great hero was expecting his son to embrace without hesitation.

Considering the enormous stakes for Omer, we cannot know the rationale for his hesitancy in killing the chicken. He may have flinched at the thought of killing an animal; after a boyhood full of the Quran's teachings on the sacredness of life he would have been more hesitant in this regard than boys from Western countries. Perhaps he knew of the difficulty of adhering to law during the disagreeable business. Maybe he was simply fearful of displeasing his father.

Regardless of the reason, Omer's younger brother, Sayid, was ready for the passage to manhood even if his brother was not. He said the requisite prayer, killed the animal humanely, and allowed Omer to take the credit. But when the father assumed Omer had done it, the older boy corrected him. So it was Sayid who received his great father's approbation and gratitude. "Well done, Sayid," he said.

Perhaps if his older brother had been more of a man Sayid would not have learned to volunteer for the assignments no one else desired. Perhaps he would not have become a perpetrator of crimes he knew to be contrary to his father's moral teachings and those of his faith. But the lessons of childhood are not easily overcome. Ten years later, serving in the Republican Guard, Sayid's superiors knew exactly the type of work he was suited to perform.

No Redemption Without Atonement

The blood of many innocents on his hands, Sayid left the Republican Guard and searched the world for Nadia. He gave up military life altogether and worked for a time as a cook in Paris. Perhaps he thought he had made amends for his crimes. Perhaps he believed by living life as "Najeev" he could begin anew, unencumbered by the heinous behaviour of a previous life.

Even if he could forgive himself, scattered around the world were the broken and suffering victims who would never forget. Someone once said all sins are social; what more social sin than torture? The Nazis branded their victims, tattooed numbers onto their arms. But neither the Nazis nor Sayid had any need to mark their interrogation targets in this manner. Victims of torture have suffered brutal attack on every aspect of their humanity. They are broken; it becomes society's task to restore those few faculties amenable to our care, and to ignore the effects that are beyond our ability to fix.

Amira reminded him he could never separate himself from his past. Her disfigured arms were the results of his expert wartime handiwork. The scars ran even deeper in her soul, to the point that she found more in common with a suffering cat than with the cruel human beings around her, of whom Sayid was the premier example of inhumanity.

Seeing the depths of the woman's pain, Sayid could no longer bear his false denials—to her or to himself—and he confessed. Amira's husband, Sami, was ready to turn Sayid into dog food. Amira was wiser than either her spouse or the torturer in chains before her. She showed greater courage, demonstrated complete fidelity to faith, when she forgave crimes that should have been unforgiveable. She pardoned Sayid, unlocked his chains, and allowed him to start his life again.

Journey of Redemption

The cause is always just, or so it seems to the one willing to help the wronged.

Shannon was not yet his lover, but when circumstance indicated Sawyer had stolen the asthmatic woman's inhaler, Sayid felt revulsion at the confidence man's inhumanity. One does not treat a suffering human being in this manner, and one especially does not disrespect a woman in this way. The others tried to reason with Sawyer, to no avail. Sayid knew what must be done, and he knew he was the only one trained in such operations.

The torture of Sawyer revealed nothing. It would be three years, plus thirty years' mileage, before Hurley discovered the inhaler at the entrances to the caves. Sawyer had never possessed the inhaler. The only result that obtained from Sayid's use of torture was a deep wedge of enmity driven between two men.

Even without evidence of the inhaler's whereabouts, Sayid knew the torture had been futile. Sawyer likely knew nothing about the device. That he was an uncultured and uncaring human being was evident in every foul utterance from between his lips, but a lack of benevolence did not confer guilt. Sayid confessed his shame to Kate, kissed her hand, and left the safety of the camp on a journey of redemption.

It must have seemed to him cosmic retribution when his sojourn brought him to a trap, the lair of the Island's most crazed inhabitant, and prolonged torture aimed at forcing from him knowledge of Alex's condition and location. The torturer, subjected to the same tools of the craft he manipulated with such ease, facing cruel demand for information he did not possess. He could only guess who Alex might be, for he had never heard the name. It was through Danielle Rousseau that the survivors obtained their first maps of the Island, and learned they were not alone. Somewhere on the Island—perhaps watching their every move—were the Others.

Ask Dr. Science

Sayid's walkabout journeys were not the only occasions during which he made important discoveries. He repaired the cockpit transceiver that first captured the French woman's recorded voice. Familiar with all manner of communications equipment, he calculated the age of the message from the esoteric iteration count alone. Sayid's expertise was not confined to the torture of prisoners; from complicated electronic devices he devised radios, transceivers, telephones—even a radar for Michael's raft. Every new improvised gadget from Sayid's beachside laboratory provided an occasion for greater insights into the Island.

Sayid understood science. He had a broader and more practical technical education than even Jack Shephard, and he profited from a lifetime of having to apply scientific knowledge and method in diverse and time-critical situations on the battlefield and in real life. When he determined a magnetic deviation of greater than twenty degrees from Locke's compass, he knew the deflection was too severe to dismiss. Months before physicist Dr. Daniel Faraday's arrival on Mittelos, and only short days after the crash, he already knew there was something strange about the Island and its electromagnetism.

Sayid was expert in all manner of technical specialties, including avionics, telecommunications, electromagnetism, and cartography. But possibly it was his understanding of human nature that proved most valuable to his fellow survivors. The scene of his final interrogation with "Henry Gale" was one of the most powerful in the six years of the series. He had just buried the woman he loved, Shannon.

SAYID: Where is she buried?
GALE: What?
SAYID: Listen to me. You said you buried your wife. Tell me where.
GALE: What are you going to...?
SAYID: Where!!
GALE: In the jungle. By the balloon, in the jungle.
SAYID: How deep? How deep did you dig the grave?

GALE: I don't—it was...
SAYID: How deep? How many shovelfuls of earth? Did you use your hands? How long did it take you?
GALE: I don't remember.
SAYID: You would remember! You would remember how deep. You would remember every shovelful, every moment. You would remember what it felt like to place her body inside. You would remember if you buried the woman you loved. You would remember—if it were true!

From the moment "Henry Gale" answered he didn't remember the number of shovelfuls of dirt he had dug for his wife's grave, Sayid knew "Henry" was an imposter, lying because he was one of Them—an Other.

This conversation, in the midst of the last torture Sayid would perform, revealed much about both master manipulator Benjamin Linus and spiritually tortured Sayid Jarrah. Whoever this "Henry Gale" person really was, he didn't care about people. He had never had a wife, maybe never had anyone close to his heart, certainly he had never had to endure a loved one's death. Sayid was a torturer, and he would soon become a professional killer, but he had a heart. He deigned to allow others into his heart, to feel their pain as his own, to feel the complete sense of devastating loss that was the only good part of death.

The Economics of Retribution

The teaching of the Holy Quran is clear. Murder is not permitted. It is an abomination before the Creator of all that is good. Exception is made for the taking of animal life, but the rules of halal are strict, and are to be scrupulously obeyed.

Human life is another matter entirely. If animal life is sacred, human life is infinitely more sacred. The most Holy Book tells us, "the taking of one innocent life is like taking all of Mankind" (5:33). To take life in the manner of an assassin, as Sayid did, is to profane the Quran. It is simply not a thinkable option to any person of faith.

Sayid knew he had placed himself in grave danger by his actions. Perhaps no earthly judge would ever know of his foul deeds, but the Judge with greatest bearing on his final disposition certainly did know. Was redemption even possible at this point?

Eternal Penance

He could have gone to a monastery. They don't ask you there what your religion is. The pay is low, but then, Sayid wasn't interested in the rate of compensation when he joined Build Our World. He was never going to leave the Dominican Republic. He would spend the remainder of his miserable life building homes for hurricane survivors, for the destitute, for the poorest of the poor. His only hope was that eternal penance would save him from the worst tortures of the next world.

We were never told of Sayid's true motivation for leaving the Dominican Republic. Neither Locke's visit nor Ben's seemed to convince him to abandon his volunteer work. But Ilana knew to find him in a bar, drinking hundred-dollar-a-shot Scotch. Apparently he had not distributed his assassin's fees to the poor.

I wonder now, in light of events that occurred in Dharmaville later (later in this case, of course, meaning thirty years *earlier!*) if Sayid didn't already have a plan. Ben was a calculating mass murderer, in Sayid's own words, "a monster responsible for nothing short of genocide." Might not the removal from this world of one as evil as Ben serve as a great work of penance, perhaps even greater than a lifetime of work for the poor?

A Second Level of Karma

The bullet from Roger Linus' rifle penetrated Sayid's abdomen in precisely the same location Sayid had shot his son, Ben. Karma, again. Both shots would have been lethal without medical attention, or a miracle. Ben was put in the care of an obstetrician. No one had taught her what to do with a bullet to the abdomen, but at least she had proper medical equipment. Sayid had the benefit of a bona fide trauma surgeon, but in a van zipping along at 80 kilometres per hour down bumpy dirt roads Jack was not going to get the opportunity to operate.

Both the twelve-year-old boy and his would-be assassin would need a miracle to survive. Lucky for Ben, the Temple was in peak condition in 1977. Not so thirty years later. Dogen's blade-across-the-palm test showed the healing waters no longer healed. Sayid would have to be left to his own devices, some other miracle, or a painful death by internal haemorrhaging and sepsis.

No one could account for Sayid's resurrection hours later and thirty years in the future, by the side of the healing waters. Miles confirmed what everyone believed, and what Dogen feared: Sayid had been dead, but now he was alive. Since the pool had not cured Sayid, Dogen believed there could be only one possibility. Somehow, perhaps through the "sickness", the Man in Black had raised Sayid from the dead. Dogen's tests only confirmed Sayid's state. He had the sickness; his full surrender to the Smoke Monster, to "evil incarnate", was inevitable.

Green Life, Green Death

Those who have read my previous essays know of my abiding fascination with the events surrounding the green pill in Episode 6.03. I've written three essays on the green pill. I recommend those who have not yet read any of the previous analyses take a look at Chapters 1, 3, and 12 of *LOST Humanity*.

Part of the fascination of these scenes, for me, centres around Jack's rejection of Dogen's assertion. But Jack takes this rejection to an entirely new, almost unthinkable level. He places his trust in Sayid, just as Sayid places his trust in Jack. The event was beyond comprehension because the evidence of Sayid's turn to evil was so strong. Dogen was a man of integrity, and he believed Sayid to have succumbed. Sayid's behaviour was not in keeping with anything we saw before his resurrection.

Subsequent events gave us no reason to believe Sayid carried within him even the smallest particle of humanity. These events appeared to make Jack's actions in Episode 6.03 all the more inscrutable. Probably the most reasonable conclusion we might have been able to offer, up until Episode 6.14, is that Jack made a very bad judgment. He was wrong about Sayid.

Think Not of Him as Slain

What Sayid did in saving everyone on the submarine was no accident. No evil thing could commit the selfless act he performed. Few righteous men can ever claim the courage and goodness that filled Sayid's heart.

[Sawyer pulls all the wires from the timer - Sun and Jack gasp - timer pauses at 1:31 and then countdown accelerates.]
SAYID [to Jack]: Listen carefully. There's a well on the main island, half mile south from the camp we just left. Desmond's inside it. Locke wants him dead, which means you're going to need him. Do you understand me?
JACK: Why are you telling me this?
SAYID: Because it's going to be you, Jack.
[Sayid grabs bomb and runs off.]

We should have known. Dogen was a good man, but he was no judge of character. Jack was right to have trusted Sayid. Sayid lived so that he might save Kate and Jack—the Dragonslayer and the Bringer of Light. He gave his life so his friends could live. No greater love has any man than this.

This is what Holy Scripture says of Sayid Jarrah: "*the saving of one life is like saving all of Mankind*" (Holy Quran, 5:33). We might argue that he saved only a handful of lives by sacrificing himself in the submarine. But those handful of lives saved the Island, and therefore saved the world. Sayid saved us all.

When his body is found, there will be great sadness for the passing of this most holy man. But the sadness will mix with joy. There will be music, and feasting, and speeches of remembrance, and the deepest fondness in human hearts, for all know of the final truth contained in his life and acts: he did not die, and all the beauty of paradise attends him.

الصـــالح الرجل ، جراح ســـعيد

The Saviour

CHAPTER 16: THE SAVIOUR

"We need to start figuring things out...Everyman for himself is not going to work. It's time to start organizing. We need to figure out how we're going to survive here...Last week most of us were strangers, but we're all here now. And god knows how long we're going to be here. But if we can't live together, we're going to die alone."

—Jack Shephard, "White Rabbit"

It was preposterous.

Push the "execute" button every 108 minutes. Why? Because Marvin Candle commands you to do so. That is, accept on faith the instructions of a man in a white lab coat—a man of science—to perform a nonsensical task on obsolete equipment in an ancient facility built by a long-dead organisation.

The orientation film's use of scientific imagery to perpetuate the charade was an assault on the very foundations of reason, logic, and science, an absurdity not worth any thinking person's indulgence, least of all that of expert spinal surgeon Jack Shephard, M.D.

Jack left the Swan Station after viewing the orientation film with Locke and arguing with him over the significance of the film. But something drove him back to the station. Was it the fact that John had saved his life a few weeks before? Or was something else in play?

LOCKE: You have to [push the button].

....

JACK: No. It's not real. Look, you want to push the button, you do it yourself.
LOCKE: If it's not real, then what are you doing here, Jack? Why did you come back? Why do you find it so hard to believe?
JACK: Why do you find it so easy?
LOCKE: It's never been easy! .... It's a leap of faith, Jack.

Jack Shephard, without a word, reached out his right index finger and depressed the execute button. He had taken the first step on an arduous, lonely, soul-shaking journey. In just over three years, Jack Shephard, man of science, would be transformed into Locke's disciple, the Island's supreme shaman, committed man of faith.

Disorientation

"Jack is here because he has to do something. He can't be told what that is. He's got to find it himself."

Jacob's words in "Lighthouse" were in full force on the afternoon of September 22, 2004, when Jack experienced the most bewildering set of conditions he had ever been forced to confront.

It took Jack only a few seconds to figure out what might have required several minutes of anyone else. But Jack had been trained in logical thinking all his life, and his nimble mind quickly strung the facts together into sequences of empirical findings that could lead to only one rational syllogism: the wreckage on the beach, the people screaming and moaning and limping, those unconscious but still alive, and those who would never again draw breath were all the aftermath of a tragedy in the air. The plane had crashed.

Jack sprang into action, calling upon every skill he had learned in medical school and in the school of hard knocks going back to the grade-school punch in the face and his father's contempt for Jack's abilities. He brought a pregnant woman to safety, freed a man pinned under wreckage, resuscitated a woman with neither pulse nor breath, saved several people from the concussive effects of explosion, gave instructions to others trying to help, organised the relief effort, and became the *de facto* leader of the forty-eight who survived.

None of it seemed to matter. Not the several lives he saved, not his leadership speech six days later, not his ability to triage actions into tasks immediate, tasks for later, and tasks not actionable. Save those close to death, treat minor wounds as time allows, and say a prayer and wrap a red tag around the toes of people whose injuries are beyond the limits of a septic and deadly environment. Federal Agent Edward Mars should have received a red tag. Anyone else would have given him morphine and a prayer. Or Sawyer's remedy. But euthanasia was not in Jack's medical playbook, and allowing anyone to die was not in Jack's personal playbook. He had to save everyone. He had to fix everyone, even if he caused them pain. He had to prove his father wrong, and the reproducible exactitudes of science and medicine provided the path toward the spiritual and professional redemption that his father had taken from him.

"You don't have what it takes, Jack." Christian's words to Jack were a gauntlet thrown to the ground, a summons to determined and sustained action to prove valour and substance. The island, this ordinary, tropical oasis in the sea, was to be Jack's operating suite, the place where he would demonstrate forever that he did have what it takes.

It was not until that evening that Jack and those who now looked to him as leader and medical saviour would realise that the crash was the least of their present concerns, and that this island was not ordinary, perhaps not even tropical, and it was definitely not an oasis. Some being or force or entity was able to fling a one-hundred kilogram man several hundred metres and spew tonnes of dirt and trees into the air in a split second. Polar bears roamed the Island, seeking human flesh for their next meal. Mysterious music and scratchy voices came from places—or times—distant. A recording in French was being broadcast every thirty seconds—for the last sixteen years.

These were phenomena beyond Jack's abilities, and therefore beyond the scope of science. Nothing in experience or training or intellect of even the most gifted scientist or accomplished physician could bring coherence to the events and conditions manifest on the Island. Charlie framed the problem:

"Guys, where are we?"

The Island was unlike any other place on earth. Science was not only useless here. It was invalid. It did not contain the assumptions, tools, or processes required to deal with any of the Island's questions.

The crash was the first step, the grand cataclysm that would reach into Jack's soul, violently loose him from the solid foundations of reason that had grounded him, oriented him, provided him with objective bases for decision and deed. It was the first punch to the gut. There would be many more, a flurry of punches over three years, not only painful, but deadly. The Island was not gentle with Jack.

Foundations

His name is Roger Bacon. Nowadays he would be addressed as "professor" or "doctor", but he conducted his experiments and gave his lectures in the early years of the University of Paris and Oxford University, starting in 1237 and ending in 1294. His title at Oxford was Master, though after his death he was known worldwide as Doctor Mirabilis ("wonderful professor").

Bacon was the first in a long line of philosophers who adhered to the intellectual rigours of empirical science. His latter-day disciples include the British philosophers John Locke and David Hume. Bacon is most often credited with the first full development of what we now understand to be the scientific method. His decree at Oxford: Accept nothing on faith. Believe only what eyes see and ears hear. For Bacon, the only legitimate route to scientific understanding was the difficult, time-consuming road of empiricism. Before Bacon, the world's most authoritative "scientist" was the ancient Greek philosopher, Aristotle.

Aristotle, if he had witnessed Bacon's slow, determined, precise placement of mirrors, lenses, and torches in his optics laboratory, would have scoffed at the medieval professor's slavish devotion to unnecessary experiments. Observation of *natural* phenomena (not laboratory creations) and armchair philosophising was all that was required to reveal the secrets of nature, even phenomena as apparently complex as the behaviour of light as it passes through lenses and bounces off mirrors. Raw syllogism and understanding of Causes were sufficient to any scientific endeavour. Bacon would have listened (he understood the Greek language, after all), but patience wearing thin, he'd probably have responded in Latin or French, chuckling to himself over the ancient philosopher's inability to understand.

Among the several areas in which Bacon faulted Aristotle for lack of rigour was the notion of Final Cause. The Final Cause was an entity's purpose. The

Final Cause of a pencil is writing. One need not have any experience to assign a Final Cause. The question of a pencil's purpose, a pencil's destiny, was not a question Bacon could address in the laboratory. He could load a sharpened pencil into a crossbow and with it pierce a man's chest. Did this mean the pencil's "Final Cause" was instrument of death? The question of purpose or destiny is not a question admissible to empirical science, and to pose it in the laboratory is to misunderstand the entire methodology and intent (purpose!) of experimental science.

Science Without Purpose

Science is confined by logic. If I expand the limits of research to any inquiry that might be included within the scope of logic, science, and mathematics, I must necessarily accept that certain limits nevertheless exist. Most importantly, I may not ever claim to investigate or to have discovered any facet of reality. The best I might hope to accomplish, even after a lifetime in the laboratory, is to establish the adherence of certain observed phenomena to MODELS of reality that I create through inference, induction, and deduction. These models are most often referred to as theories, but they can never explain the real world. We rely on assumptions that negate any possible connection with reality.

One of the most important assumptions underlying science is Ockham's Razor. In plain language, Ockham's Razor insists the scientist must accept the simplest solution to a problem as being the correct solution. If I can imagine a chemical reaction as being the result of the collision of five molecule, but I can equally imagine that the reaction is the result of the collision of just two molecules, and if every observation I have made supports either of the fruits of my imagination, I must accept as valid and correct the imagined event that includes just two molecules. The reality may be that only one molecule is required, or seven molecules are required, or the event occurs only when there are sunspots on our solar system's star, but I can never know this. Even if the model I develop happens to support a theory that is close to reality, I may not ever claim to have elucidated even the slightest aspect of reality. I am allowed to conclude only that certain behaviours seem reproducible and that they also seem to adhere to a model consistent with Ockham's Razor and the other underlying assumptions of the scientific method.

Science and logic are imperfect subsets of reality. If we rely on logic as revelation of reality we will discern only an incomplete, warped world far from true reality.

Science makes sensory observations, catalogues these data, uses the rules of mathematics and logic to create connections among the observations, and builds empirical findings into models of reality that we call hypotheses and theories. A scientist truly comfortable in her laboratory will never claim she is revealing reality, only a poor model for certain physical behaviours that seem to follow a reproducible pattern. There is no truth in science. Science is not a tool for illuminating the fulness of reality.

I pick up a pen with the five fingers of my right hand. Science notes this fact, records the observations associated with the act. And that is all science can do. Science cannot tell us my motivation for picking up the pen, cannot predict what I will do with it, how I will do it, what the future outcomes will be, or how the ramifications of the simple act will ripple through the greater world, how the act will affect others.

Science cannot place even the simplest act within the continuum of reality. Complex interactions are so far outside the realm of pure science that they virtually defy adequate description. In fact, no interaction can be fully characterised. Science and logic must be forever partial, incomplete statements of certain events, and they can never claim to explain a basis in reality.

Life With Purpose

Imagine now you are approaching Master Bacon on a cold winter day on the busy Oxford campus. You see his brown robe—the Franciscan habit—and his strange haircut, called a tonsure. The good friar is on his way from the lecture hall to mass at the basilica, where he is to be the celebrant. He carries two books in his arms: his *Opus majus V* (collected works in optics), and the Bible.

Perhaps you are Aristotelian in your outlook, but whatever your philosophy of life, you carry an ornate and very sharp pugio (Roman dagger) and when you draw close you raise it to his neck, ready to end his life.

"Renounce your belief in optics," you say, "or prepare to die."

Bacon laughs, hands over the book he laboured over for many years, and says, "Fine. I renounce my belief in optics."

Probably you are emboldened by this unexpected and easy success, for the next words out of your mouth are these: "Renounce your belief in your Deity, or prepare to die."

The response is immediate and unexpected.

"I cannot but renounce the way in which I practice my faith, for I am a weak and unworthy servant of my Master. But the One I worship as Creator I embrace as Redeemer, never to be renounced, always to be served and adored. I hope your dagger is sharp, for your path to this Bible lies over my dead body."

Roger Bacon was a practitioner of pure empirical science. He was also a priest, a friar in the Franciscan tradition. There was for him no conflict between faith and science. But if push came to shove, Bacon would sacrifice science in an instant. He would never sacrifice his faith.

Becoming Roger Bacon

One man became a persistent thorn in Jack's side. Like his father, this man was essentially telling Jack that he was not up to the tasks before him. Everything he had based his life on, according to this man, was fundamentally flawed, insufficient to the daily struggles of life in this hostile place, invalid to the enormous problems of the Island.

LOCKE: You and I don't see eye-to-eye sometimes, Jack... you're a man of science.
JACK: Yeah, and what does that make you?
LOCKE: Me, well, I'm a man of faith. Do you really think all this is an accident—that we, a group of strangers survived, many of us with just superficial injuries? Do you think we crashed on this place by coincidence—especially, this place? We were brought here for a purpose, for a reason, all of us. Each one of us was brought here for a reason.
JACK: Brought here? And who brought us here, John?
LOCKE: The Island. The Island brought us here. This is no ordinary place, you've seen that, I know you have. But the Island chose you, too, Jack. It's destiny.

This video, narrated in John Locke's own voice, is arguably the best fan-produced Lost trailer (though my favourite remains this one, also produced by SL-Lost: http://www.youtube.com/watch?v=swHST-s0s3E), and one of the reasons I decided to submit essays at SL-Lost. The video I think captures something of the essence of LOST; I find it difficult to view it now without becoming a bit misty-eyed.
http://www.youtube.com/watch?v=z-TWQV1KLsE
Locke was primary proponent of the nonsense Jack had heard on the Swan Station orientation film. By the time Locke and Jack viewed the film they were firm adversaries. I am not certain about Jack's rationale for resolving the conflict over pushing the button. As I speculated in the introduction to this chapter, he may have pushed the "execute" key out of some feeling that he "owed" Locke something for saving his life. Or perhaps he realised pushing the button was the quickest way to end a pointless argument that had already consumed precious time of far too many people.

Most likely, Jack had no rationale. No syllogism led to the conclusion that he had to press the button. Rather, I believe he had the first glimmers of a "Final Cause". He could not yet discern a purpose for pushing the button, but he was willing to admit of the possibility of a destiny not distilled from logic. He had already tasted failure, in the death of Boone on his makeshift operating table. That same night he found his advanced training of no use, and minimum medical knowledge not indispensible to the survival of his flock; Kate, with no medical training, delivered a very healthy Aaron Littleton into the world. I think that first bit of doubt regarding the universal applicability of science was what allowed him to follow another man's instinct. Locke referred to any decision to push the button as "a leap of faith". Compared to the enormous leaps that would be required of Jack in the next thirty-eight months, depressing the execute key was a small step. But it was the first movement, a significant step, toward a life of purpose.

Jack's Reality, 2004

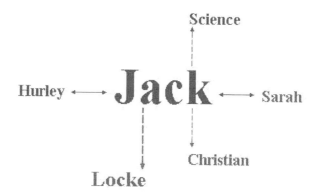

Jack enjoyed a reciprocal love relationship with Sarah for the first few years after he operated on her spine and restored her ability to walk. His higher calling at the time of the crash was Science. He enjoyed several reciprocal trusting relationships, the most visible example being the one with Hugo Reyes, though he trusted several others, among them Kate Austen, Sayid Jarrah, and later, Bernard Nadler. Hurley was always special. Even from the earliest days of the crash, Jack entrusted Hugo with essential tasks: the survivor census, the distribution of food from the Swan Station stores, the holding of survivor medical information. Hurley was Jack's first lieutenant on the Island and closest friend off the Island.

Jack presented a solid exterior persona, but he was near the end of his rope emotionally and intellectually. His closest friend, his wife, left him for another man. He had never really been attached to Sarah the woman, never allowed his spirit to touch hers. She had been a project for him, something to "fix", not a person to respect and adore and love. Science was the purpose to which he had dedicated his life, but the routines of syllogistic logic could do nothing to alleviate the fact that his father died in an alcoholic stupor and his body had somehow migrated out of its coffin to places unknown.

Jack had no soul mate, only very peripheral trust relationships with a handful of people, he was beginning to question his life's calling, and he was the victim of two individuals who seemed to torment him at every turn. Christian believed Jack continually fell short of what he ought to be. Locke told Jack that everything he believed in, the purpose to which Jack had dedicated his life, was insufficient.

Jack's reality is our reality. Who among us has committed heart, mind, and soul to a purpose greater than self? Who among us has a true soul mate? Jack's lack of clear antagonist, and the pain associated with that ambiguity, was our pain, too. Who was the true antagonist in LOST? John Locke? Christian Shephard? Benjamin Linus? Charles Widmore? Martin Keamy? Stuart

Radzinsky? A great deal of thought over several years would be required to discern the identity of the true antagonist.

Jack's Needs

Sarah Shephard was a beautiful woman. She was kind, gracious, self-sacrificing—in every way beautiful. I would imagine just about anyone looking at her would say Sarah is a pretty woman. Everyone, that is, except Dr. Jack Shephard. Jack, before 2007, would look at her and note only that Sarah had a perfectly formed spine, that he had "fixed" her. Such were the depths of his psychosis, his self-absorption.

Jack near the end of 2004 was experiencing the beginnings of a life-altering sequence of events. His conversion was accelerated by an emotionally degraded condition, but the extraordinary transformation he was to undergo would nearly destroy him. He would need something—some constant—to ensure his survival through the worst of the storms to batter his soul.

He found that Constant in a woman of extraordinary beauty. Kate Austen never told anyone that she attached the oxygen mask to Agent Ed Mars, that she ensured the survival of the man who had relentlessly hunted her across the United States. She never told anyone of her deep love for her mother, for Tom Brennan, for Claire and Aaron. Her love of others showed in her attitudes, in her actions, in her lovely smile. A fugitive, a murderer, Kate paradoxically had deep inside her an abiding respect and love for her fellow human beings. The great surgeon Dr. Jack Shephard, accomplished and admired, paragon of virtue, exemplar to all, never felt that deep love in his life before the Island. Kate possessed a beauty entirely foreign to Jack's understanding, but he needed empathy for others, had to understand and act on others' needs if he was to become the person he was destined to be. More than anyone he had ever known, Jack needed Kate Austen.

Jack's Descent

The crash of Oceanic Flight 815.
The Smoke Monster.
Charlie's hanging and almost-death.
Boone's death.
Shannon's death.
Capture and imprisonment by the Others.
Desmond's prediction of Charlie's death.
Charlie's death.
Keamy's band of Blackwater thugs.
Locke, right about everything:
> The freighter coming to kill them, not rescue them.
> Having faith strong enough to move mountains—
>> and the Island on which the mountains stood.
> Their purpose on the Island.

The resurrection of Christian Shephard.
And on top of it all, Locke's death—by suicide.

Less than two years after their rescue from the Island, Jack was at the end of his endurance. Everything he believed was proven wrong. Everything his greatest nemesis said was true, and then some. Locke had accessed some reservoir of truth that went far beyond the facts Jack had once believed were incontrovertible truth. The truths Locke put into words had nothing to do with science, were unconstrained by even the most generous allowances of logic. Locke had discovered absolutes not subject to the shifting sands of hypothesis or theory. They were true in the past, true now, would remain always true regardless of future events.

Little remained to anchor Jack in this world. His apartment full of maps and protractors and global coordinates and calculations and flight schedules, he was obsessed by a single idea: returning to the Island. It was the only place his life had any meaning, but there was no way to return. He stood on top of the bridge, looking to the bare concrete far below, ready to end his life. He was startled out of his plan by the sound of a crash behind him. He temporarily reverted to his former self, saving a woman and her child from the flames. But his final salvation was delivered by a most unlikely agent. "We have to return to the Island," Ben Linus told him, and Ben knew exactly the way it could be accomplished. Jack Shephard was ready.

Jack's Post-Enlightenment Reality

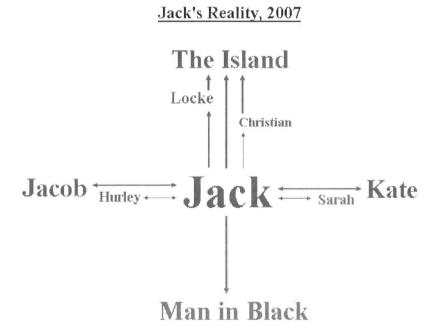

Jack's Reality, 2007

That which does not kill us makes us stronger.

Jack was no Übermensch, for belief in such a monstrosity would require a relinquishing of faith. Jack's transformation was a knock-out blow to the warped Nietzschean ideal of radical individualism and the denial of absolute truth. Jack's journey almost killed him, and did make him stronger, but his was a strength based on service to Locke's eternal truths, not a Nazi-like worship of self.

Jack became a man of faith due to the good example of John Locke. The transformation was not instantaneous, but occurred over several months. In the critical weeks leading to Jack's final purpose, he had still not formulated an understanding of his destiny. At the end of Season Five, only days after he had stopped feeding his body opiates and vodka, he remained largely incoherent. Sawyer beat a confession out of him: Jack wanted to detonate the hydrogen bomb so he could have a second chance with Kate. His mind was still foggy from the drugs, I think.

Had he forgotten Kate's words on Penny's ship? "I have always been with you," Kate told him. Kate was Jack's Constant. He didn't need to do anything, least of all risk the lives of dozens of people and the welfare of the Island, to secure his place in her heart.

Such were Jack's actions as he came out of his psychosis and began to understand his destiny. Attempting to detonate the bomb accomplished nothing that had not already been established. Everyone knew of "The Incident"; it was not until Juliet died and everyone else was transported thirty years into the future that we understood who was responsible for the catastrophic event. Perhaps history would record that Stuart Radzinsky alone was guilty of an over-exuberance that led to the uncontrolled discharge of raw electromagnetic power. But Jack's folly certainly contributed to the severity and enduring effects of the catastrophe.

Jack was stronger, not only through enlightenment, but through those who came before him, through the one who risked all and died to bring him back to the Island. The one whose body was not resurrected, and lies on Boone Hill, on the Island that was his Constant.

Compare Jack's pitiful, bottom-of-the-barrel existence in 2004 with the emotional and spiritual wealth and richness of his life in 2007. In 2004, Jack believed John Locke and his own father to be enemies. In 2007, Jack considered Locke his spiritual master. And though he did not yet know it, Christian Shephard did more than bring Jack the physical refreshment of liquid water (in "White Rabbit"). Christian also shepherded his son to the spiritual renewal that only the living water of the Island could provide. In the space of three years, Locke and Christian went from apparent enemies to the spiritual leaders of a vast cohort: Kate, Hurley, Sawyer, Ben, Richard, Miles, Frank, and the great martyrs, Charlie and Sayid. They were all conspiring to pull Jack to greatness, to fulfill his destiny, which was the destruction of evil and the salvation of the Island.

Love and Faith

There are many types of love, and many ways to express and understand faith. Romeo and Juliet expressed erotic love. Kate's love of Claire and Aaron was not erotic, but agape, or altruistic love.

Many fans of LOST consider Kate's decision to leave the Island, and Jack's decision to stay, to be unrealistic, and not in keeping with their spiritual connection. Wouldn't Kate have stayed with Jack to the bitter end? Perhaps she could have pulled him to the Temple, to heal his wounds.

No. The depiction of their parting was entirely realistic. But don't trust me on this point. Trust your grandmothers and great-grandmothers, and anyone who lived through or fought in the War.

"Casablanca" told the story of a woman and a man who truly loved each other. They went their separate ways, just as Jack and Kate did, and for essentially the same reasons. Ilsa Lund's feelings for Rick Blaine were stronger than her attachment to the freedom fighter, Victor Laszlo. But Laszlo was Europe's hope against Nazi plans to enslave the world.

Ilsa: But what about us?
Rick: We'll always have Paris. We didn't have, we, we lost it until you came to Casablanca. We got it back last night.
Ilsa: When I said I would never leave you.
Rick: And you never will. But... Where I'm going, you can't follow. Ilsa, I'm no good at being noble, but it doesn't take much to see that the problems of three little people don't amount to a hill of beans in this crazy world.

With those words, Rick forced Ilsa on the plane, to maintain her position as wife and help mate to Laszlo. Neither of them wanted to leave the other, but the salvation of Europe, the salvation of the world, literally rested on their decision. Depriving themselves, they made the only possible decision, the only human decision. A decision based in faith.

"Casablanca" was intended to be just another crank-'em-out propaganda piece, something to stir up the boys on the front and keep the fires burning back home. It became much more than that; to this day, "Casablanca" is regarded by many as the finest film of the twentieth century. The acting was first rate, but the production values, even by 1942 standards, were poor.

There can be only one solid reason for Casablanca's appeal over the decades: It describes something of the true nobility of the human spirit.

Your grandmothers and great-grandmothers know the film, feel its authenticity, because they know of real-life Rick Blaines and Ilsa Lunds. Countless thousands of men gave up family and girlfriend or wife to fight in the war. Many who might have been rejected for service falsified medical records so they could fight. The United States was a latecomer to World War II, but thousands of men in that country smuggled themselves across the Canadian border before the U.S. declared war and fought in the Canadian or British armies. John Paul Merton, U.S. citizen and brother of famed spiritual writer

Thomas Merton, died while flying for the RAF. John Gillespie Magee, Jr., author of "High Flight" (the poem that for many years was the "sign-off", in the days when television stations "went off the air" (stopped broadcasting), usually somewhere between midnight and two a.m.: http://www.youtube.com/watch?v=EzQYd_INSOg), was an American eager to fight. He slipped into Canada and died, in flight, wearing a Royal Canadian Air Force uniform.

John Paul Merton and John Gillespie Magee, Jr., and the countless thousands of others, did not leave behind friends and family, wives and girlfriends to fight for England or for Canada. They did it to fight for us, for all of us in this world. Their love for family and spouse was not weak. It was strong. They were willing to die for that love. "Greater love hath no man than this, that a man lay down his life for his friends." The sacrifice they made is not "proof" of anything, but is the surest testament to the abiding goodness of the human spirit.

Island Faith

The LOST character most closely associated with an organised religion was the Roman Catholic, Mr. Eko. It can be argued, and I think correctly, that the character most truly observant of the meaningful tenets of an organised religion was the Muslim, Sayid Jarrah. We saw Ben praying in a Christian church. Charlie crossed himself before he died (though with his left hand; perhaps a brand of Anglicanism that is not much publicised outside of the U.K.?). Kate was married in a Christian church, though she profaned the proceedings by marrying under false name and false pretense.

But adherence to organised religion is not what LOST means by the word "faith". Neither is faith on Mittelos a question of simply believing in something. One might be the most devout Muslim, the most observant Jew, the most committed disciple of Jesus, and fall far short of LOST's definition of faith.

Faith for LOST is not only an acceptance of the validity and truth of things unseen and unprovable, it is the surrender of self to the service of humanity. Kate gave up self, gave up a future with Jack, to serve Claire and Aaron. Jack gave up his self, his very life, to serve the Island, and through it, all of humanity. Faith on the Island of Mittelos is the kind of faith Rick and Ilsa expressed, the sort of faith for which John Paul Merton and John Gillespie Magee, Jr. gave their lives. It is the type of love that requires no tit-for-tat reciprocity. John Locke, at the time wheel, did not ask what was in it for him when Christian Shephard, the Island's representative, told Locke he would have to die, that he was to become the "sacrifice the Island demands". He accepted his fate, because he was the Island's truest and most humble servant. He believed in (we without his brand of faith might say he "loved") the Island.

The Final Journey

Much will be written about Jack Shephard in years to come. He was one of the most lovingly-created heroes in fiction, and the entire story of LOST will transcend time and culture. This is not "Soylent Green", a film that really should not be watched without having first consumed at least a quart of hearty ale, and definitely not viewed by anyone who did not live through the seventies. LOST is more akin to Star Trek in its universal and enduring appeal, in its courageous exploration of core human values.

Jack brought people together. They worked together, lived together. "If we can't live together, we will die alone." Jack's work save people, saved the Island society, saved the Island itself. Before Jack first woke on the Island, the shepherd who watched over Mittelos called the dog, Vincent. "Come here," Christian said. "Good boy.... I need you to go find my son. He's over there in that bamboo forest, unconscious. I need you to go wake him up.... He has work to do." Three years later (or thirty years later), Jack's work completed, the Island again summoned Vincent. The Island's saviour, the most deserving of the Island's servants, could not possibly be the one who would die alone. So Vincent, humble servant that he was, accompanied Jack on the last moments of his journey through life. It was an ending fitting to the man, fitting to his faith in things known but unseen, of things unprovable but undeniable. Jack Shephard, man of faith, died in the place for which he had given his life. It was the final *apologia pro vita fidei*, the best way to complete a story grounded in the highest ideals of our shared humanity.

The Seer

Three days before you came down here, before we met, I heard a banging on the hatch doors, shouting. But it was you John, wasn't it? You say there isn't any purpose, there's no such thing as fate. But you saved my life, brother, so that I could save yours.
— Desmond David Hume, "Live Together, Die Alone"

He was the focus of the greatest single hour of LOST.

His countenance was the most expressive of any to have occupied the small screen in six years, for he was alone in being asked to perform deeds beyond the capacities of mortal men.

Yet he failed in every occupation he attempted. He backed out of relationships, after six years with Ruth, after several years with Penny Widmore. He was not religious, and he failed as a monk. He designed sets for the Royal Shakespeare Company, and was let go. He tried the life of a soldier, but couldn't follow orders; after several months in military prison, he was dishonourably discharged from the Royal Scots Regiment. Even pushing a button every 108 minutes was beyond him; his inattention caused the crash of Flight 815.

In spite of constant failure, he was unique. A miracle. Immune to the most severe effects of electromagnetism, he traveled freely in time, in any direction. He was the only person in over two thousand years to descend to the Cave of Light and survive. It was he who rendered the Smoke Monster mortal and frail, susceptible to Kate's bullet and Jack's final push.

But his greatest accomplishments were achieved in that fifth episode of the fourth season, when the greatest secret of LOST was revealed uniquely, miraculously, by the story's most expressive character: Desmond David Hume.

A Higher Calling

Desmond Hume had the most diverse background of any of the major characters of LOST, but his life was founded on some of the most predictable patterns as well. Most of his life was spent rudderless, relying entirely on the caprices of those around him to provide the wind to fill his sails and determine his life's course. Although he was dependent on the whim of strangers, he would not commit, even to his dearest friend and soul mate.

He met Ruth during the 1980s. Though we don't know how they met, later events in life give us a solid basis for extrapolating a reasonable guess as to circumstance. She was probably performing a function beyond Desmond's skill level and far outside his normal range of interests. The most obvious possibility is set design. Perhaps she was painting a bridge three metres across that would seem twenty metres wide on stage, explaining her creation to the admiring Scotsman. "Even you could do it," she might have said. Weeks later Desmond would be painting his own bridges, building his own platforms, designing entire scenes.

The beginning of their relationship would have been innocuous enough. Probably Desmond would have had no understanding of the direction they were headed. If he knew, he would have ended things sooner than he did. He was a free spirit. Even though he loved Ruth he could never commit his life to her, or to anyone else.

"Okay, yes, I was scared about the wedding, so I had a few pints too many... I asked am I doing the right thing, and that's the last thing I remember."

He couldn't commit to Ruth. His ignorance of the responsibilities of life proved to be a blessing in his next vocation, though; if he had known of the rigours and requirements of monkhood, he never would have accepted Brother Campbell's hand.

"And when I woke up, I was lying on my back in the street, and I dunno how I got there and, there was this man standing over me, Ruth. And he reached out his hand and he said to me, can I help you, brother? And the first thing I noticed was the rope tied round his waist, and I looked at him and I knew, I knew, I was supposed to go with him... I was supposed to leave everything that mattered behind, sacrifice all of it, for a greater calling."

He had no idea of the life he was pursuing. "We dated for six years," Ruth told him, "and the closest you ever came to a religious experience was Celtic winning the cup." He endured the brief test of postulancy, somehow remembering not to speak a single word for the several weeks of the examination period, and became a novice monk. But the Abbot knew he was not called to religious life, even before Desmond sampled an entire bottle of Moriah Vineyards red one evening.

DESMOND: Are you firing me?
BR CAMPBELL: I am indeed.
DESMOND: You can't do that, I heard the call.
BR CAMPBELL: I'm sure you did hear the call, but the abbey clearly isn't where you were meant to end up. I have little doubt that God has different plans than you being a monk, Desmond. Bigger plans...

We might have taken Brother Campbell's words as the reassuring but ultimately meaningless parting words of a former employer, except for one small photograph on the Abbot's desk.

Eloise Hawking may or may not have been related to Brother Campbell, but she was surely a significant donor to the monastery. She had no interest in the monastery *per se*, however she was most interested in the impressionable man who would briefly claim a cell in its dormitory.

The issue for Eloise was Charles Widmore's penchant for high-end wine and liquor. Moriah Vineyards was the most expensive Scottish red wine, and Charles ordered several cases at a time. Eloise knew Charles sometimes dispatched Penny to pick up a few cases, and that was the nexus of the problem. Desmond could not be allowed to meet Penny.

Perhaps Brother Campbell was delinquent in notifying Eloise of the monastery's most recent postulant. Perhaps she didn't make the instructions clear enough to the good Abbot's ecclesial mind. Or possibly it was an accidental result of miscalculation. Whatever the genesis, the result was not in accord with Eloise's plans: on the morning of his first day as an ex-monk, Desmond met Penelope Widmore.

A Tear in the Fabric of Time

Desmond's character and suitability for a sexual relationship with Penny were of concern to neither Eloise Hawking nor Charles Widmore. He might have been the perfect man for Penny, or he may have been the type of man who would use her, or ruin her life. None of that mattered to Eloise, and by force of her unopposable character, none of it could matter to Charles Widmore, either.

That Desmond could not be allowed anywhere near Penny was not due to any defect of character, but entirely the result of his necessary vocation. He had to go to the Island, there to push a button every 108 minutes. So Faraday's journal said, so it had to be. Widmore took extreme measures to prevent Desmond from involving himself with his daughter.

WIDMORE: You know anything about whiskey?
DESMOND: No, I'm afraid not, sir.
WIDMORE: This is a 60 year MacCutcheon, named after Anderson MacCutcheon, esteemed Admiral from the Royal Navy.... Admiral MacCutcheon was a great man, Hume. This was his crowning achievement. [Widmore pours some into one glass.]
WIDMORE: This swallow is worth more than you could make in a month. [he drinks it down] To share it with you would be a waste, and a disgrace to the great man who made it — because you, Hume, will never be a great man.
DESMOND: Mr. Widmore, I know I'm not...

WIDMORE: What you're not, is worthy of drinking my whiskey. How could you ever be worthy of my daughter?

Eloise and Widmore's efforts paid off. Combined with Desmond's innate fear of commitment, Widmore's psychological slap in the face and Eloise's insistence that he was destined not to marry Penny all conspired to force Desmond to reject Penny's love. "It's all happening too soon—you moving in. Your painting rooms; your changing things.... Why would you leave your flat, your expensive flat... I can't look after you. I haven't got a job.... I can't even afford five quid for a bloody photograph. You deserve someone better."

Desmond's aversion to responsibility was real, but it is a common characteristic of those of us afflicted with the Y chromosome. Many of us overcome youthful stupidities; my wife and I will celebrate 18 years of marriage and 30 years of friendship this month. I was a much worse case than Desmond, and in many ways I still am. But the point I wish to make here is that settling down into a lifelong commitment is something that even the flightiest among humankind can achieve, and Desmond would have been not at all unique in turning his life around in this manner.

Whether Desmond was eternally destined to spend three years entering the same six integers into a computer every 108 minutes is open to debate. We can deliberate the failures and successes of his early life. We might even argue over the necessity of his actions at the Heart of the Island. But there is one matter to which I believe all must surrender any objection: Desmond Hume and Penelope Widmore were destined to spend their lives together.

This is no small matter. In fact, it is upon this relationship that LOST concentrated the full force of its dramatic energies.

Eloise and Widmore's actions to separate Desmond from Penny constituted a tear in the very fabric of time. They believed physical presence and action in designated locations of spacetime to have greater influence on events than the connections between people. In this false belief they erred. Neither space nor time, nor even the worst forms of psychological coercion and abuse, could prevent the inevitable union of Penny with her beloved. By attempting to pull Desmond away from Penny they were actually weakening the temporal fabric they so strenuously endeavoured to protect.

The Constancy of Time

"You are uniquely and miraculously special."

Faraday's words to Desmond in 2004 had their origin in Desmond's London flat in 1996. It was there, falling off a ladder while painting, in less than a split second, that Desmond traveled forward in time eight years.

I might have begun this section by stating that in late 2004 Desmond turned the key in the Swan Station reset box and this resetting of time was responsible for his strange spacetime epiphany in 1996. But this would be tantamount to saying the past can be changed, a statement very much in opposition to the prime rule of time travel: Whatever happened, happened.

That Desmond was the single exception, that he was able to work around this rule, should not be taken as licence for those of us endeavouring to understand to take illegal shortcuts in our pursuit of truth. We do not share Desmond's unique time travel abilities. In the end, who is to say that a fall from a ladder might be any less capable of inducing accelerated travel through time than the turning of a failsafe key at an electromagnetic research station? We are perfectly within the acceptable bounds of analysis to claim that Desmond's time travel adventures began in London in 1996 and not on an island somewhere in the Pacific in 2004.

Desmond was not able to control the flashes from one spacetime to another, but he did travel freely, in directions that we would understand as forward and backward travel in time. He predicted events, but not accurately. "I remember this night. [he sees a TV showing a soccer game] Graybridge come back from two goals down in the final two minutes and win this game. It's a bloody miracle. And after they win, Jimmy Lennon's going to come through that door and hit the bartender right in the head with a cricket bat because he owes him money." Desmond remembered the incident correctly—but he was exactly twenty-four hours off; Jimmy Lennon didn't come into the pub until the day after Desmond's prediction, but he did exactly as Desmond predicted.

Course Correction

Eloise wore an ouroboros pin during her lecture on the rules of time. Seeing the brooch made me deeply aware of what we lost on May 23, 2010. Such care was taken in enriching every scene with symbols and meaningful, multi-faceted images and dialogue. LOST had unparalleled depth and significance—to the extent that even months later we are endeavouring to unravel its meaning. LOST is a magnificent gift we can treasure, but there is a certain sadness in knowing we have only six years to examine.

According to Lostpedia, "Ancient civilizations used The Ouroboros as a symbol of Recurrence. Typically the symbol consists of a snake's body forming a circle with the head swallowing the tail." We know of several instances of time loops in LOST. I have written extensively about the compass, for example, endlessly exchanged between Locke and Richard in a continual loop between 1954 and 2007 (see Chapter 8, "The Leader"). Many such time loops were created, and in fact, the entire edifice of the series was built on the predictability and periodicity of temporal event and human behaviour. "They come, they fight, they destroy, they corrupt. It always ends the same." The Smoke Monster could never lose, because he knew the rules, and predictability, immortality, and imperviousness to any instrument of death meant he would always be several steps ahead of any challenger. The fabric of the universe was warped in his favour.

Changing a single event in the past was possible. Because Desmond floated freely between past and future, he knew the course of events, and he could take action to prevent undesired outcomes. But that was not enough, because the universe tended to correct course.

MS. HAWKING: That man over there is wearing red shoes.
DESMOND: So, what then?
MS. HAWKING: Just thought it was a bold fashion choice worth noting.
[Suddenly, there is a loud crash behind the bench Ms. Hawking and Desmond have been sitting on. Some scaffolding has fallen and killed the man with red shoes.]
DESMOND: Oh, my God. You knew that was going to happen, didn't you?
MS. HAWKING: [nods]
DESMOND: Then why didn't you stop it? Why didn't you do anything?
MS. HAWKING: Because it wouldn't matter. Had I warned him about the scaffolding tomorrow he'd be hit by a taxi. If I warned him about the taxi, he'd fall in the shower and break his neck. The universe, unfortunately, has a way of course correcting. That man was supposed to die. That was his path just as it's your path to go to the island. You don't do it because you choose to, Desmond. You do it because you're supposed to.

Charlie Pace had to die on the Island. He had been destined to die by electrocution in a lightning storm, but Desmond foresaw his death and used a golf club and wreckage wire as a lightning rod, saving Charlie's life. The universe course-corrected by planning Charlie's death by flying arrow through the neck, but Desmond saw the future, and again took steps to prevent fate from taking his friend. Finally, after preventing the musician's death by drowning, Desmond told Charlie the truth: Charlie was going to die.

An objective observer might conclude that Charlie's presence in the Looking Glass Station, and his crucial three-word warning ("Not Penny's Boat") to Desmond altered the course of time. By delaying Charlie's death until he made a substantial contribution to everyone on the Island, any "course correction" would be partial at best. Therefore, Desmond successfully broke the rules of time travel.

Many sound theories have been based on this premise, and I have to believe there is merit to such a claim. Most importantly, Charlie's warning, and his death, served to enhance Locke's position, proving his actions—even his murder of Naomi—to have been more than warranted. Many on the Island would die because of the freighter mercenaries' unholy project, and Charlie's warning undoubtedly saved many lives. There were obvious short-term effects, such as Hurley's decision to follow Locke so that Charlie's death would not have been in vain. The credibility boost that Locke received may have had long-term effects, as well. It is possible the Charlie's support of Locke's position may have helped sway Jack during his three years off the Island, possibly accelerating his movement toward life as a Man of Faith.

Sound arguments can be made against this theory, but I do not wish to debate them here. Whether Desmond's actions to save Charlie constituted a violation of the rules of time travel, he certainly achieved something of note to the story in saving Charlie's life three times, and in being present to receive Charlie's warning. I believe notable importance attaches to this fact, since part of Eloise's rationale for forcing Desmond to the Island was to ensure three years of code entry as "the only truly great thing" Desmond would ever accomplish. I disagree. I believe saving Charlie and at least three other acts were of greater moment than entering the integers every 108 minutes.

Physical Endurance

After rejecting Penny, Desmond walked by a Royal Scots Regiment recruiting office. Volunteering may have been the result of long planning and research, but this seems unlikely. Regardless of the time and care he may have taken in reaching a decision about military service, he was psychologically and physically unprepared for the rigours of life in the Royal Scots. Desmond had a strange knack for choosing vocations for which he was particularly ill-suited at the time.

But fate conspired against Desmond in ways he never could have prepared for. Even if he had been in top psychological and physical shape, he could never have steeled himself for the disorienting effects of suddenly traveling several years into the future.

He faced the deepest challenge of his life during the Christmas of 2004. He had no anchor in time, no Constant to orient him, and the result was physical trauma. The violent effects of sudden, involuntary time travel were literally ripping him apart inside, tearing him out of the fabric of time.

As his 1996 self struggled in the frightening and utterly disorienting environment of an ocean freighter in the Pacific Ocean in 2004, Desmond was in deep trouble. His nose had started to bleed. "When it happens again, Desmond, I need you to get on a train," Daniel Faraday told him. "Get on a train and go to Oxford. Oxford University. Queens College Physics Department." Daniel Faraday at that time was Professor Daniel Faraday, and he was conducting experiments in time travel. The younger Daniel Faraday was the only person in the world who could help Desmond.

Professor Faraday explained to Desmond his need for an anchor, or Constant. An anchor was "Something familiar in both times. All this, see this is all variables, it's random, it's chaotic. Every equation needs stability, something known. It's called a constant. Desmond, you have no constant. When you go to the future, nothing there is familiar. So if you want to stop this, then you need to find something there ... something that you really, really care about ... that also exists back here, in 1996."

Death in Its Many Forms

Minkowski was in the late stages of time travel-induced internal haemorrhaging. Bleeding from eyes, ears, nose, and mouth, he would be dead in hours or minutes, and no medication or surgical procedure could prevent his demise. This would be Desmond's fate as well, if he did not find a Constant.

In 2008 we didn't yet know the full ramifications of living life without a Constant. In the context of Minkowski's and Desmond's time travel it seemed the requirement of a Constant was a special case, that the majority of mortals who do not experience the frightening disorientations of time travel will never need to invest ourselves in "something that you really, really care about".

At the end of Season Six we learned one of the possible consequences of not vesting in something important outside oneself.

HURLEY: Hey, you around? Michael?
[Michael steps out of the jungle.]
HURLEY: You're stuck on the Island aren't you?
MICHAEL: [nodding] 'Cause of what I did.
HURLEY: And...there're others out here like you, aren't there? That's what the whispers are?
MICHAEL: Yeah. We're the ones who can't move on.

Michael committed horrendous deeds of murder and deception, but his acts did not compare to Sayid's multiple murders or the atrocities Ben carried out. Yet Ben was allowed into the sideways purgatory, and Sayid was allowed to "move on" in the Church of the Holy Lamp Post at the end of the story. *Michael was left behind not because of what he did, but because of what he did not do.* He did not forge an enduring relationship with his wife, and their marriage ended in divorce. He did not develop a strong relationship with his son, nor with anyone else, for that matter. Friends he might have retained he instead alienated by killing Ana Lucia and Libby, and by deceiving those he didn't hurt directly.

Michael had no Constant. It was this fact that prevented him from "moving on".

The significance of a Constant—something to which a person makes an enduring commitment that stands every test of time—is of paramount importance in the world of LOST. Without a Constant, one cannot receive a place in the pews of Our Lady of the Foucault Pendulum. Establishing a lifelong relationship is the primary message of LOST, as explained in Chapter 9 of *LOST Humanity.*

Those whose consciousnesses travel through time without a Constant will experience disorientation, internal bleeding, time seizures, and death. Those who die without a Constant will experience only whispers and shadows—the endless sadness of realising what might have been, the eternal emptiness of spiritual isolation.

Rectifying History

Eloise Hawking and Charles Widmore were not objective "time cops" selflessly devoting themselves to the maintenance of the universe's internal clock. Eloise's objective was to make amends for killing her own son. Widmore's plan was to seize control of the Island. When Eloise told Desmond that his destiny was not with Penny, she was wrong. She may have been correct that Desmond was destined to enter the Valenzetti coefficients every 108 minutes for three years until the computer was destroyed and he was forced to turn the failsafe key, but she was incorrect again in stating that "pushing that button is the only truly great thing that you will ever do."

Desmond's trans-spacetime experiences of Penny had relevance to him because of the constancy of their relationship. Regardless of any of the particulars of the reality around them, they were destined to recognise in each other something essential to their being. In the sideways reality or on the Island, they found the completion of themselves in each other.

In the world of LOST, nothing is more important than the establishment of a personal Constant. A Constant is necessary to a life well lived, and it is necessary to those who wish to "move on" from this life to the next (see *LOST Humanity*, Chapter 9). Without a Constant, one is destined to spend eternity with the whispers and regrets of a life devoid of meaning.

In contacting Penny from the freighter during Christmas, 2004, Desmond was not changing history. He was rectifying the time error that Eloise had attempted to perpetrate. Desmond needed Penny for his own survival, but he was accomplishing something much more important, for he was to become the central figure in the Island's most important event, and our story's final chapter.

The Triumph of Odysseus

Menelaus, the most powerful man in Mycenae, summoned the King of Ithaca, Odysseus, to fight a war in a foreign land to restore property rightfully his. Three thousand years ago the great adventure began with the launching of a thousand ships to recover from Troy the woman whose beauty has never been equaled. Our modern-day Menelaus, the most powerful man in England, summoned ocean-faring Odysseus to fight a war in a foreign land, to restore property he claimed as his own, a land whose power has never been equaled. Four years ago, in 2007, this final battle of the great war began with the launching of a single submarine. For the magnificence of our great Odysseus was such that he alone could usurp the power of the gods, turning their immortality to dust.

The Odyssey is the world's greatest adventure story, and Odysseus the world's greatest hero. Son of a god, Odysseus inherited deep masculinity and strength of purpose. He carried himself in the manner of all men aware of their abiding dignity; in Homer's words, he was "in bearing, like a god." The great king and hero of the Trojan War took a torturous ten years to return to Ithaca, facing every manner of physical test of his crew and himself.

But we know Odysseus not for his great physical strength, rare masculine beauty, or dignified bearing. We know Odysseus as the resourceful fighter, the cunning leader, the man who, by guile and force of character, finds a way out from seemingly impossible situations. During the war, he thought up and fashioned the Trojan Horse. To defeat the Sirens, Odysseus had his men poured wax in their ears so they could not be lured by the seductive devils' irresistible song. Captured by the giant Cyclops, facing certain death at the hands of the one-eyed cannibal, Odysseus plied the monster with wine, waited until he fell asleep, then burned out his single eye. After ten long years, he returned to his Penelope.

Desmond endured physical challenges of space and time in his quest to return to his Penelope—to his Penny. Shipwrecked, like Odysseus, spending long years on an island, like Odysseus, he never gave up hope of finding her. Most of all, like Odysseus, we know Desmond not for any physical ability, not even for the rare capacity to resist the terrible physical effects of unearthly magnetic force, but rather for his strength of character, for strength of spirit. Desmond deserved Penny not for any physical prowess or superhuman ability, but for entirely human reasons: for faith in their sharing, for hope of finding her, for love of her as soul mate, friend, wife. Most of all, for never giving up, for applying every resource he could muster to find her and keep her.

Desmond—the Island's Odysseus—is made hero because of his humanity, because of the choices he made, because of his relentless drive to share love with Penny. The awful force of the magnetic chamber—sufficient to kill ordinary mortals—was no challenge to our Odysseus. His easy triumph over the normal constraints of the physical world, and in fact his triumph over the very fabric of space and time, was not the message of the final battle. The lesson driven home is that Desmond's unrelenting focus on Penny allowed him to achieve in the spiritual realm feats that far outshine even the superhuman abilities he demonstrated with so little effort in the magnetic chamber.

Desmond's humanity is more important, and more powerful, than the greatest of superhuman abilities. This is an important revelation, and quite possible the single most critical truth of series. Desmond is the physical embodiment of the great truth of LOST:

Humanity is more important, more enduring, and stronger than anything in the physical world.

Odysseus' physical body expired thirty centuries ago. But his spirit lives on, and can never be vanquished. On the Island there is nomos (law) and physis (nature). The forces at play are stronger than anything known in the physical world. But the force above all forces is the only one that is truly irresistible and unstoppable: Pneuma (spirit). Desmond's success was inevitable, not because of Jacob's "progress", but because this is how we are made. This is who we are, as human beings, as those aware of innate, abiding dignity, carrying ourselves in calm possession of every faculty of mind and body, in bearing, like a god.

Our Necessity, Our Triumph

Favoured of the gods, Odysseus returned home to his Penelope, but only after enduring trials, torments, and tribulations. He was of all the characters of LOST the most expressive, the most adaptable, the most willing. He performed his mighty deeds and exited quietly without acknowledgment or fanfare. He saved Charlie, and by doing so enabled the musician to perform the single greatest act of his life. He defied Eloise and Widmore and restored his relationship with the only woman in the world who truly mattered. He moved a stone that no other could touch, a simple act that turned an immortal force of nature into a fragile old man, and allowed the great Man of Faith to restore peace to the Island and equilibrium to the world.

Fair Odysseus, in bearing like a god, was as human as any among us. He was our triumph, our necessity, for in every age women and men of character and will quietly perform great feats that no others dare. In a story of magnificent men who lead legions and armies, of great warriors who win against crushing odds, we remember first the quiet one. We read of wise Agamemnon, strong Ajax, good Diomedes, cunning Menelaus, kind Patroclus, incomparable Achilles. Their strategies and speeches and battles fill the pages, testament to heroism, record of brotherhood, witness to destiny. But the greatest of these is fair and strong, quiet and sure, testament of humanity, witness to civility. The greatest of these, the one we remember in our dreams, carry in our hearts, proclaim in our words, with wisdom surpassing Agamemnon, strength beyond Ajax, kindness above Patroclus, is the one beloved of Athena, beloved of Penelope: the quiet one, the good and fair Odysseus, the Scotsman, Desmond David Hume.

The Shaman

"I'm an ordinary man, Jack, meat and potatoes, I live in the real world. I'm not a big believer in magic. But this place is different. Special. The others don't want to talk about it because it scares them. But we all know it. We all feel it... I've looked into the eye of this island. And what I saw...was beautiful."

　　—John Locke, "White Rabbit"

"Psyche profiles said you would be amenable for coercion."

Deputy Sheriff Eddie Colburn was matter-of-fact in his delivery, and his words were in accord with everything we understood of the man. He trusted Anthony Cooper and lost a kidney, then his self-respect, and finally his ability to walk. He trusted Benjamin Linus, and received in payment for his good faith a brutal strangulation by electric power cable. "Amenable to coercion" was a polite way of stating the obvious: John Locke was gullible.

He cried tears of frustration and disappointment, shouted and railed against Jack, against Ben, against the Island. He had faith and courage, but at critical moments doubt and fear overwhelmed him. When the world was against him, he planned and nearly executed his own demise. He gave up.

Weakness.

In the ordinary world, John Locke was a nobody. Not a single person, other than his most vociferous enemy, grieved his passing. He was a noisy, ignorant, gullible fool. But that was the reality of the ordinary world, the fragmented, incomplete reality of a world consumed with buying and selling, wealth and power, human creations over divine beings.

The attributes we consider weaknesses were John Locke's strengths. The world's measure of John Locke was flawed, warped, inhuman and insane. The Island's measure of the man was true: Gullibility meant trust; tears meant unwillingness to accept setbacks. And his greatest failure, his inability to convince even one of the Six to return, proved instead to be his greatest strength.

LOST was about our humanity, and the story's natural narrator was its strongest and most faithful voice: Prince of the Island, Man of Faith, John Locke.

Things Known and Possessed

Richard Alpert had a deeper understanding of the Island than any single person before him, perhaps including even his boss, Jacob. The Island's leadership saw Richard as the person most suited for recruiting tasks: locating and coercing Juliet Burke, and three times over a period of eighteen years gathering intelligence on a most remarkable boy: John Locke of Tustin, California.

Richard placed six items in front of five-year-old Locke. "Which of these things belong to you *already?*" Richard asked. Locke claimed the bottle of sand, the compass, and the knife. Richard didn't like the choices. He gathered the items into his bag, stood up suddenly, and left with few words.

Eleven years later, Richard attempted to entice Locke to a summer science camp. The teenage Locke's response was inevitable: "I'm not a scientist." Richard was again disappointed in the young man he thought might one day become their leader. Six years later, in 1977, Richard confided his doubts to Jack.

RICHARD: ... John Locke... never seemed particularly special to me.
JACK: You said you had a question.
RICHARD: You know him? Locke?
JACK: [chuckles] Yeah. Yeah, I know him. And if I were you, I wouldn't give up on him.

Richard took Jack's words to heart. Seeing John Locke again on the Island in late 2004, the ageless one confided to Locke his doubts about Ben Linus' leadership, while at the same time giving his future leader a nudge toward realising his destiny.

RICHARD: ... when word got back here that there was a man with a broken spine on the plane who could suddenly walk again, well, people here began to get very excited because that, that could only happen to someone who was extremely special. But Ben doesn't want anyone to think you're special, John.
LOCKE: And why are you telling me this?
RICHARD: Ben has been wasting our time with novelties, like fertility problems. We're looking for someone to remind us that we're here for more important reasons.
LOCKE: What do you want from me?
RICHARD: I want for you to find your purpose.

Richard had the first glimmers of an understanding that science "novelties" had nothing to do with the Island's purpose, and work along those lines was pointless. Good soldier that he was, he nevertheless spent long months preparing for Juliet Burke's recruitment, creating out of nothing the shell company "Mittelos Bioscience" for that very purpose, and learning the languages of microbiology and biochemistry so his pitch would appear authentic.

He had his doubts. He finally accepted Locke as leader, but never embraced his leadership. Had the Island ever delivered a leader worthy of the title? Charles Widmore and Benjamin Linus were dire enemies, but cut from the same self-centred cloth, neither of them truly suited for leadership. Locke didn't seem to be any more capable than the two miscreants before him who had accepted (or stolen?) the mantle of Leader.

We cannot blame Richard for his lack of vision. No man of faith, Richard seemed to accept whole, without thought, Jacob's warped view of the Island (for a broader discussion of this issue, please see http://www.sl-lost.com/2010/03/27/siempre-juntos-part-ii-cultural-inversions-in-lost-609-by-pearson-moore/). This blind acceptance is not faith, for faith is never truly blind, but always grounded in critical judgment. Richard did not exercise judgment, and he was therefore perfect in the role of consigliere. With such an intellectual disposition Richard could never be leader, but his lack of vision also meant he was not adequate judge of the qualities that might be presented by a true leader.

Disorientation

The compass young John Locke picked up from among Richard's objects is usually a symbol of orientation, of finding one's way. As with many common cultural artifacts, however, the significance of this symbol was shaken, inverted, and twisted into something entirely new for the purposes of our more complete understanding of LOST.

The history of the compass began in 1954, when Locke gave the compass to Richard as proof that he was from the future. Seven years later, Richard showed the compass to five-year-old Locke. Richard carried the compass until 2007, when he presented it to Locke, who conveyed it back to 1954 so it could be handed off to Richard. Thus, the compass became the visible symbol of disorientation, of an endless time loop between 1954 and 2007. Further magnifying the disorientation around this new symbol of etiological disorder, as Lostpedia notes, "It is also something of a self-contained paradox, since the compass was never created."

Plotting a meaningful timeline for LOST is virtually impossible. As Rose said, "God only know when the hell we are now." Time paradoxes, inversions of cause and effect, and inversions of chronology were only the most obvious of LOST's assault on social, cultural, and storytelling convention. From the very beginning, LOST attacked our pre-conditioned views of reality. The person we assumed the natural leader, Jack, instead proved to be reckless, destructive, and self-absorbed. Peaches-and-cream Kate turned out to be a thief, a liar, and a murderer. And Locke, the dangerous, possibly unhinged man with a suitcase full of knives, turned out to be the person most committed to the survivors' safety and the continuity of life on the Island.

Locke's name was in itself a part of the disorientation effort. John Locke of the Island was named after the eighteenth-century English philosopher John Locke. Locke, the philosopher, is best known as the major enlightenment proponent of empirical science as the pinnacle of human understanding. LOST's position, as articulated through the foundational speeches of the Ka-bar-wielding Prince of the Island, was that empirical science is the most baseless source of human knowledge, far surpassed by faith, which imparts true wisdom.

Faith Versus Science

Faith, properly executed, is collaborative, and must serve collaborative ends. Science may be carried out by a single investigator or in collaborative teams, but it almost always serves the ends of those in power, those who would place their selfish interests above the basic needs of others, those who would gain control of the world and the people who inhabit it (for a more complete examination of this idea, please see *LOST Humanity*, Chapters 1 and 5.

Most of the world's practicing scientists, myself included, work long hours to advance the agendas of corporate entities driven not by compassion, but by greed and thirst for power. Even those who believe themselves exploring science as an end in itself, or as a means of human advancement, or as a tool of the Common Good, are the unwitting participants in the warped agendas of those in power. My colleagues and I regularly speak of exploiting an idea or phenomenon, or working around patents. Dr. Pierre Chang may have been a concerned and loving father, he may have believed he was pursuing science for the good of humankind. But he was a corporate tool, a means to the Dharma Initiative's final goal of controlling energy, time, and all of humanity.

Science is devoid of context and compassion. It is passionless, and is all too easily corrupted. In fact, as I pointed out in "Impartial Risk", science and logic are more naturally the tools of deception and perversion than they are the "impartial" tools of altruism and empathy. Humanity, at its core, is not based on science. Humanity is based on trust, on faith, on collaboration and compassion. As I noted in *LOST Humanity*, Chapter 2, "LOST tells us if we do not form bonds like those of Jack and Sayid, if we do not respect, if we do not have compassion, we will likely end up in Widmore's camp, wearing the black uniform of Stuart Radzinsky, ready at a moment's notice to enforce our desires over the needs, even over the lives of others."

Things Believed and Shared

If one is to pursue of life in science, one must, with Father Roger Bacon (see Chapter 16, "The Saviour"), assert that things believed through faith are more relevant and enduring than things known through science. Richard's compass is relevant and endures—even outside the constraints of time and place and chronology—because it is the symbol of Richard's faith in Locke, and Locke's faith in Richard, because it is something without beginning or end, because it is something *shared.* One must assert, even on pain of death, the absolute value of Roger Bacon's embrace of poverty, for it is through Franciscan poverty that true sharing, true compassion, true participation in the fullness of our humanity, becomes possible.

Such were the teachings of John Locke, even as a kindergartener. Richard asked the wrong question. He asked, "Which of these things belong to you already?" He ought have asked instead, "Which of these items do you and I share, and which do you share with the Island?" Locke, in his three choices, answered the question Richard should have known to ask. The sand—for it was from the Island Locke loved and therefore shared; the compass—for it was from Richard from Locke from Richard and therefore shared; and the knife, for it was through the Ka-bar and the Master Bowie that Locke hunted, protected the Candidates, and enforced Island law, and therefore shared. None of the items "belonged" to Locke, any more than they belonged to Mr. Friendly or Dr. Halliwax. The three items were not objects of knowledge, but articles of faith. They were not possessions—not the accoutrements of acquisition—but rather symbols of shared ideals and actions.

Richard should have known. The five-year-old Locke's drawing of a man attacked by the Smoke Monster should have been sufficient evidence of direct connection with the Island. Locke's demeanour and the way he spoke of the Island should have signaled his true standing as Leader. But we can forgive Richard. He wasn't on the beach with the survivors of Flight 815. He didn't get to hear the speeches that planted the seeds of Jack's and Hurley's ascension to leadership—the speeches of the Island's best and truest teacher and prophet.

Teacher and Prophet

The words of John Locke resonated through LOST like those of no other character. There is no better proof of this than the most heavily quoted fan-made Season Six trailers. The creative directors at SL-Lost knew Locke was dead, but they believed his words most faithfully conveyed the full message of LOST, and they used them as narrative backdrop to a most amazing soundtrack and beautifully sequenced series of images:

http://www.youtube.com/watch?v=z-TWQV1KLsE

Even at the end of the season, when it was clear to everyone (but not at all clear, for some reason, to Pearson Moore) that Locke would not return, at least not in physical form, TheBlackBox created this masterpiece of sound and imagery, choosing to make Locke Rising the final image of the trailer:

http://www.youtube.com/watch?v=Rz1yHmUW05Y

The interested LOST aficionado can revisit any of the excellent, earlier fan-made LOST trailers and again find Locke's voice giving substance to our

Island dreams. This one was created by SL-Lost in the months before Season Five, and remains my favourite fan-made trailer:

http://www.youtube.com/watch?v=swHST-s0s3E

But this one, also for Season Five from SL-Lost, is excellent, too:

http://www.youtube.com/watch?v=o3UOAcpur-4

The most famous speech is probably his first one, in the Pilot episode.

LOCKE: Backgammon is the oldest game in the world. Archeologists found sets when they excavated the ruins of ancient Mesopotamia. Five thousand years old. That's older than Jesus Christ.
WALT: Did they have dice and stuff?
LOCKE: [nods] Mhhm. But theirs weren't made of plastic. Their dice were made of bones.
WALT: Cool.
LOCKE: Two players. Two sides. One is light … one is dark.

Locke was privy to the essentials of the Island's 2000-year power struggle—even to the details of the board game that was the allegory of their life-and-death battle over the millennia.

Not long after that, in Episode Five, "White Rabbit", Locke gave perhaps the central defining speech of the entire series:

I'm an ordinary man, Jack, meat and potatoes, I live in the real world. I'm not a big believer in magic. But this place is different. It's special. The others don't want to talk about it because it scares them. But we all know it. We all feel it.... what if everything that happened here, happened for a reason?

He goes on to say "I've looked into the eye of this island, and what I saw... was beautiful." We did not learn until Season Three, in "The Cost of Living", that Locke "saw a very bright light. It was beautiful." This was the revelation that occurred when Locke first confronted the Smoke Monster, and may be why he tried, over Jack and Kate's objections, to be carried away by Smokey. Even in this instance, Locke's intuition was entirely correct, for as we now know, the Smoke Monster was prohibited from directly harming any of Jacob's Candidates. Locke, while he still lived, was Candidate #4, the first of Jacob's Candidates at the time of the crash. It is tempting now to believe that Locke was the first to be given a glimpse of the Light emanating from the Source. In fact, such a vision of the Centre of the Island may be the only means of explaining Locke's experience.

The second important speech was delivered at the end of Season One, during "Exodus":

LOCKE: ... Jack... you're a man of science.
JACK: Yeah, and what does that make you?

LOCKE: Me, well, I'm a man of faith. Do you really think all this is an accident—that we, a group of strangers survived, many of us with just superficial injuries? Do you think we crashed on this place by coincidence—especially this place? We were brought here for a purpose, for a reason, all of us. Each one of us was brought here for a reason.
JACK: Brought here? And who brought us here, John?
LOCKE: The Island. The Island brought us here. This is no ordinary place, you've seen that, I know you have. But the Island chose you, too, Jack. It's destiny.

Locke gave important instructions to Jack at the end of Season Four, minutes before he left on the helicopter that would take him off the Island and eventually to rescue by Penny's team:

LOCKE: You're gonna have to lie.
JACK: Excuse me?
LOCKE: If you have to go, then you have to lie about everything...everything that happened since we got to the island. It's the only way to protect it.
JACK: (Sighs) It's an island, John. No one needs to "protect" it.
LOCKE: It's not an island. It's a place where miracles happen. And—and—if you—if you don't believe that, Jack, if you can't believe that, just wait till you see what I'm about to do.
JACK: There's no such thing as miracles.
LOCKE: Well...we'll just have to see which one of us is right.

Even then, at the end of Season Four, Jack should have been able to distill from Locke's words the powerful wisdom of protecting the Island. He had witnessed first-hand the attempt by Widmore's goons to take control of the Island and to kill everyone there. He must have been able to surmise that Widmore's intentions were anything but altruistic, and that he intended to subsume to his desires and quest for power the full force of the Island's unearthly abilities. But Jack was nearing the bottom of his journey to spiritual freedom, and not nearly in a position to take to heart any pearls of wisdom from Locke. Was the disappearance of the Island enough of a shock to logic-bound Jack? Whatever the reason, Jack did follow Locke's instructions, informing the Six that they would have to lie. Not yet a true believer, though, Jack replaced Locke's reasoning with his own rationale: they would have to lie, not to protect the Island, but to protect those who remained on the Island.

Doubts, Fears, Frustrations

Locke was consumed by the need to uncover the full meaning of the Island, to discover his true destiny in this place of miracles. He communed with the Island as no one ever had. No one—not Ben, not Richard, not even Jacob himself—was connected to the Island with the same titanic spiritual and emotional forces connecting Locke to this place. The forces connected him to a raw power, to that "beautiful, bright light" that we now know was the Source. But the Source was the origin of all life, all death, all rebirth. It was unimaginable and untamed power, of the variety that cannot be harnessed or tapped for any purpose.

Until Desmond and Jack's descent to the Light, Locke was the person in closest spiritual proximity to the awful forces of the Heart of the Island. He enjoyed the full force of insight and intuition emanating from the Source, but he also suffered the full force of its awful and uncontrollable power.

He cried. He cried often. It was not unusual for Charlie or Jack or Boone to run into Locke in the jungle, crying bitterly into his arm or into the branch of a tree. These were not the tears of some petty disappointment. They were the tears of a man pulled to the painful raw edges of emotional existence, the laments of a man feeling not his own pain, but the pain of thousands, the pain of the Island itself.

His faith was deep, and therefore his doubts nearly consumed him. The importance of doubt in a life of faith may not make sense to the lukewarm, to those who have not experienced the highs and lows of the spiritual journey. The Dark Night of the Soul is a horrible, angst-ridden but entirely necessary component of the spiritual life, integral to any honest attempt to commune with the Creator. Mother Teresa, soon to be Saint Teresa of Calcutta, was brutally honest in letters to her spiritual advisor, Fr. Michael Van Der Peet. Daily, day after day, weeks and months turning into years and then into long, unrelieved decades of spiritual pain, Mother Teresa confided to Fr. Van Der Peet and to her journal that she doubted. She doubted that Jesus listened and heard, doubted He was with her, doubted even the very existence of God. David Van Biema of Time magazine wrote an excellent article on the subject (http://www.time.com/time/world/article/0,8599,1655415,00.html), and I encourage everyone to read this most enlightening essay.

Locke's tears were not the tears of weakness, but the tears of one whose great strength was nevertheless no match for the awesome and terrible forces of creation, the forces of life and death and rebirth that made the Island the very centre of the earth.

But Locke's pain always received a response of hope from the Island. Sawyer and Locke, time traveling in Season Five, saw the brilliant column of white light pierce the darkness. They both understood what it was. It was the night Boone died. The night Aaron was born. The night of Locke's deepest pain.

SAWYER: That light in the sky — it was from the Hatch, wasn't it?
LOCKE: The night that Boone died ... I went out there and started pounding on it as hard as I could. I was ... confused ... scared. Babbling like an idiot, asking, why was all this happening to me?
SAWYER: Did you get an answer?

LOCKE: Light came on, shot up into the sky. At the time, I thought it meant something. SAWYER: Did it?
LOCKE: No. It was just a light.
SAWYER: So why'd you turn us around then? Don't you wanna go back there?
LOCKE: Why would I wanna do that?
SAWYER: So you could tell yourself to do things different, save yourself a world of pain.
LOCKE: No, I needed that pain — to get to where I am now.

Locke recognised the necessity of that Dark Night to his journey. The path to enlightenment is not easy. We do not seek enlightenment because it is fun. We seek it because it is difficult, because those things in life that are attained only through danger, adversity, and sacrifice, are the things of greatest value to our truest selves.

Even when Locke had reached the very end of his emotional capacities and in hopeless resignation sought his own death, the Island sent an angel to save him. The suicide would not have worked, anyway. Would Locke have become even more deeply depressed at his inability to take his own life? Would he have recognised the futility of it all, and devoted himself instead to the Island's well-being? We cannot know the answer, since the angel who believed himself to be preventing Locke's suicide (the suicide would never have succeeded, since Locke was still a Candidate), only minutes after talking Locke down wrapped a power cord around his neck and choked the life out of him.

O Happy Fault

Locke's was the sacrifice truly demanded by the Island. He was the spirit closest to the Island. In many religious traditions, foremost among them Christianity, those closest to the Creator are the ones required to make the greatest sacrifice. Jesus died a criminal's death. All of His apostles were executed by the most painful means available at the time. Locke was attached to the Island unlike anyone else in history. He would suffer the most emotionally and spiritually gut-wrenching journey of any of the Island's servants.

Locke was the sacrifice demanded by the Island. His death was the final push that Jack required, finally ending the good doctor's drug-induced stupor and self-pity and redirecting him toward the final great service to the Island.

In the end, Locke's doubts, fears, and frustrations, as much as his wisdom, strength, and intuition, proved to be the necessary elements in the redemption of Katherine Anne Austen, the salvation of Dr. Jack Shephard, and the preservation of Locke's Constant, the Island.

Canton-Rainier

In Season Five Jack Shephard was portrayed as the Doubting Thomas, the disciple who required proof before he would believe the resurrection. But resurrection was not the event we were asked to dwell on. In Season Four and Season Five, a van labeled "Canton-Rainier Carpet Cleaning" became the focus of our attention. Even before any of the episodes had aired, enterprising internet analysts found the surreptitiously obtained photographs of the van and tore apart the name. Within hours we knew what "Canton-Rainier" meant: It was an anagram for "Reincarnation". I expected resurrection, but the plan was much grander than anything I could imagine prior to the last episodes of Season Six. Reincarnation means returning in a different physical form but containing the same essential spiritual substance. Resurrection means spiritual continuity into a fully reanimated formerly dead body. How could I have known that LOST would attempt a fusion of the two forms of rebirth?

SMOKEY: This remind you of anything, Jack?
JACK: What?
SMOKEY: Desmond...going down into a hole in the ground. If there was a button down there to push, we could fight about whether or not to push it. It'd be just like old times.
JACK: You're not John Locke. You disrespect his memory by wearing his face, but you're nothing like him. Turns out he was right about most everything. I just wish I could've told him that while he was still alive.

With these words Jack paid tribute to the man who, with his own blood, had paved the way for Jack's redemptive salvation of the Island. But Jack's words were a sign of something much more significant taking place.

By the end of LOST, Jack's thoughts were one with those of his master, John Locke. The prophesy of Canton-Rainier came into full reality with the breathtaking illumination of Jack Shephard. Jack, falling to the very nadir of his spiritual journey at precisely the moment of Locke's murder, became the happy recipient of all of Locke's teachings, all his prophesies, all his intuitions. Just as Boone died at precisely the moment of Aaron's entry into the world, so too Locke's death ushered into the world a new Jack Shephard.

John Locke died, but he was reincarnated into the soul of his former nemesis, now his closest disciple. The dead soul of Jack Shephard was reanimated, resurrected by the spiritual force of will of the Island's most beloved son.

Regardless of the way in which we choose to contemplate The End, there is one truth upon which all of us I think might find common ground. Locke's spirit did not die at the conclusion of "The Life and Death of Jeremy Bentham". Locke's spirit guided Jack to the Source, just as Locke guided all of us, along every one of the 121 steps to The End. "You were special, John," Ben told the man he had murdered. Long after all of them had died, Locke continued to affect Jack, Hurley, and Ben—everyone whose lives had been touched by this trusting soul, this man of faith. Locke is the soul of LOST, and just as his spirit will never die, the Island will forever remain a place to contemplate, wonder at, a place of highest joys and deepest sorrows, where human weakness and doubt become unopposable strength and unwavering faith. A place of things believed, things shared, things of our common culture and deepest humanity.

The White Rabbit

CHAPTER 19: THE WHITE RABBIT

This is a place that you... that you all made together so that you could find one another. The most important part of your life was the time that you spent with these people on that island. That's why all of you are here. Nobody does it alone, Jack. You needed all of them, and they needed you.

—Christian Shephard, "The End"

LOST was about us.

"You were all looking for something that you couldn't find out there. I chose you because you needed this place as much as it needed you."

Jacob was speaking to Kate, Jack, Hurley, and Sawyer, but he could have been speaking to all of us. We are all "metaphorically lost in our lives." It was Jack's story, but it was the story of everyone Jack met, everyone who brought him to that place, everyone Jack needed to become the person who saved the Island and saved all of humanity. "The most important part of your life was the time that you spent with these people on that island. That's why all of you are here. Nobody does it alone, Jack. You needed all of them, and they needed you."

How many people in this world have shed tears over a television program? Yet, from the dozens of real-time videos I have seen of our reactions to that final episode, very few of us around the world made it through that evening without shedding tears. The six years were powerful for us because the Island was not something distant or foreign. It lived in our hearts, because all of us were Lost. All of us were on that Island with Jack and Kate and Hurley.

I am as Lost as anyone else. Lost as a writer, Lost as a scientist. Most of all, Lost as husband to my wife and Lost as father to my children. My shortcomings are not any lesser than those of Michael Dawson, David Reyes, or Roger Linus. I most enjoyed the Kate and Locke storylines, and I suppose I'd like to believe that I most identify with Jack or Jin, but the character who consistently garnered my fascination and rapt attention was Christian Shephard.

The Father

The painful and strained relationship between father and child was the most frequently recurring motif in LOST. We learned in Season One (Episode 11) that "All the best cowboys have daddy issues." All of the final Candidates (Locke, Hurley, Sawyer, Jack, Jin, and Kate), with the exception of Sayid, experienced difficulties with fathers as a central issue in their lives. Some analysts have argued that the struggle with a father figure was the unifying theme of LOST. Certainly for Hurley, Kate, and even Jack, one could find deep support for the notion that a rift between father and child was the most important conflict in the survivors' lives.

As I made clear in *LOST Humanity*, I see the reconciliation factor (usually between father and child) as one of the three important relationship types in LOST, the other two being the Constant relationship and the Strange Attractor (struggle) relationship. Every character who wished to "move on" had to have a Constant relationship, and every character was required to develop herself through personal, one-on-one struggle (Strange Attraction) over an issue critical to the character. The informal, unifying idea expressed in these formal relationship types is the one Jack articulated at the very beginning of Season One (Episode 1.05). I will discuss the ramifications of the "Live together, die alone" thesis later in the chapter.

The critical confrontation occurred early in Jack's childhood, when a playground fight ended with Jack's life-long friend, Marc Silverman, getting beaten by bullies. Jack tried to intervene, but was knocked to the ground by the stronger boys. Christian framed the problem as being a result of Jack's inherent lack of leadership ability:

"Don't choose, Jack, don't decide. You don't want to be a hero, you don't try and save everyone because when you fail... you just don't have what it takes."

Those of us who are fathers recognise the value of instilling self-confidence in our children. Christian's words, "you just don't have what it takes," have to be understood as supremely destructive of a young child's self-image. These are precisely the kinds of words that should never be communicated to a child, even if the parent believes the instruction is warranted.

We instinctively recognise the high potential for harm in Christian's speech to Jack. The words were so out of line, in fact, that some have attempted to defend Christian. Perhaps, they say, Christian was giving Jack "tough love." Perhaps Christian was merely setting the bar high, telling his son he didn't have what is required, knowing that his son would rise to meet the challenge. The "Boy Named Sue" argument, if you will, from the famous song by Johnny Cash. Another possibility, to be discussed later in this chapter, is that Christian was preparing Jack for the challenges he would face on the Island.

Several other defences of Christian's choice of parental routines have been proposed. I find no substance to any of these arguments, and I find nothing in any of these rationalisations that brings cohesion to any other theme or to the hero's journey that Jack would have to take. Christian Shephard was just a bad father, plain and simple.

Whether Christian's "Boy Named Sue" approach to parenthood was intentional or not, we know that Jack did rise to the challenge. Like Locke, he appropriated to himself the attitude that no one could tell him what he couldn't do, because he had the right stuff. He endeavoured to prove not only that he was a leader, but that he was a better surgeon, better father—better person—than his dad had ever been. In his great professional standing and rare abilities, Christian provided Jack with a high mark to achieve. It is important to Jack's story that we understand Jack for the most part achieved that high mark, but never thought so himself. His father had given him great expectations that he would never be able to attain, at least psychologically.

Christian was no exemplar of virtue. He engaged in at least one extra-marital affair, resulting in the birth of Claire Littleton, Jack's half-sister. He drank alcohol to excess, and if Jack's testimony is correct, his addiction led to the death of at least one surgery patient on the operating table. Jack became Christian's mirror. Even if Jack wasn't drinking to excess before the crash of Flight 815, he was so committed to viewing Christian as a threat to his personal and professional advancement that he constructed in his mind evil conspiracies in which Christian was having an affair with his wife, Sarah. Jack's decision to reveal his father's impaired condition during the operation that led to the patient's death was not so much an example of doing the right thing as it was a means of getting back at his father.

Whatever else we may glean from Jack's relationship with his father, we need to take away three critical truths. First, Christian set a high standard for Jack's later life. Second, Christian's bad parenting, and especially his pronouncement that Jack didn't have what it took, formed Jack into the results-obsessed person he became; "I can fix this" became Jack's creed. Finally, Jack's need to prove his abilities had its origin in Christian's low opinion of him. Christian was the source of Jack's inner turmoil, but deep inside, Jack understood reconciliation with Christian as the only way he could ever achieve balance in his life.

The Empty Tomb

Jack felt the strong need to pursue Christian's apparition. Christian had created the turmoil in Jack's soul, and Jack needed to reconcile with him to achieve the spiritual peace he had been seeking all his life.

The empty tomb was the final, heart-rending negation of all of Jack's hopes. He would be deprived even of the ability to mutter, "I love you, Dad," to a long-dead corpse. The corpse wasn't there, and Jack would never find peace.

The empty tomb meant he had to find some other means of achieving solace. The empty tomb was the necessary impetus to Jack's three-year journey from the Mr. Fix-It Guru of Science to Locke's Disciple and mature Believer in the Island.

Christian was the Good Shepherd, leading Jack beside still waters (Episode 1.05). We know now, after Season Six, that the Island's streams provided much more than physical liquid refreshment. Water was one of the two elements necessary to the Heart of the Island. Water was, in fact, the very blood of the

Island's conscious existence. In leading Jack to the Island's flowing water, Christian was confirming Jack's leadership and his eventual status as Protector. Jack would become Messiah and sacrificial lamb, even to the point of bearing the wounds of Christ.

Most of you reading this are rebelling at this point. Christian was not leading Jack to water, he was leading Jack to his death, off the edge of the cliff into the dry ravine below. And it wasn't Christian leading him, you say: It was the Man in Black, taking on the image of Christian to mislead Jack. Not only did the Man in Black himself confirm this to Jack (Episode 6.13), Carlton Cuse confirmed the fact in his final on-screen appearance prior to the airing of "The End":

"Once [the Man in Black is] the Smoke Monster, he only can assume the form of dead people on the Island. *The Man in Black appeared as Christian Shephard.* [Emphasis is mine] He most notably takes the form of John Locke." (Carlton Cuse, "LOST: The Final Journey," May 23, 2010).

Indeed. I am now convinced that Christian's apparition in Episode 1.05 ("White Rabbit") was due to the Smoke Monster. However, I feel the true nature of the apparition goes far beyond a cursory statement of the apparition's origin. We need to consider carefully exactly what the Smoke Monster was before we can understand the meaning behind the attribution of the apparition's identity.

I, Smoke Monster

Recall from the chapter on the Man in Black that, on entering the Source, he lost his own identity and assumed, at least in part, the identity of the Island:

"The Man in Black existed as the Smoke Monster—as a human/island hybrid who was neither human nor Island. He judged not as a human, not as a non-human, but as dictated by the strictures of the Source, as executed by the Island itself. He desired in the same way he always had, but now he had absolute power to pursue his desires."

The Man in Black went into the Source as an unconscious but fully-constituted human being. When he exited the Source, his body was a dead hulk, and he was left as a being without corporeal existence. His humanity was gone, as he himself stated many times. He could acquire the appearance of a human being only by taking on the form of a dead person. At first, he preferred to take on his own form, but when it suited him, he could take the appearance of anyone who had died.

We cannot think of the Man in Black before and after contact with the Source as the same entity. He was different. In particular, the entity was subject to forces and realities outside the range of those known to the Man in

Black before the Source-induced transformation. Important aspects of the Smoke Monster's being originated outside the Man in Black.

When the Smoke Monster took on a particular human being's form, he also took on aspects of that person's personality. The Smoke Monster could not call upon certain aspects of the Man in Black's personality without taking on the Man in Black's form. So, for instance, when he took the form of John Locke, he cried out at one point (Episode 6.04), "Don't tell me what I can't do!" This was surprising because it was an emphatic recitation of John Locke's catch phrase. The Smoke Monster was exhibiting a frame of mind that the Man in Black never had, that only John Locke had shown in the past. When he took on a particular person's form, he in some ways *became* that person.

I am not convinced that the Smoke Monster always enjoyed a choice regarding the form he would project during an apparition. It seems to me certain forms would have been more advantageous to others for a particular apparition, while other forms would have worked against the Man in Black's desire to leave the Island. I think the consideration of whether or not the Smoke Monster was always able to conform himself to the Man in Black's desires is an important consideration to the elucidation of the Smoke Monster's true nature.

The Smoke Monster appeared to Mr. Eko as his brother, Yemi. He appeared to Ben as Alex and to Richard as Isabella. In general, his appearance as a victim's loved one occurred in conjunction with the judgment or coercion of the victim to perform the will of the Man in Black.

But the Smoke Monster adopted other forms. In particular, he took on the form of Christian Shephard at least once. It seems likely, in fact, that all of the appearance of Christian Shephard were due to the Smoke Monster. This choice seems to work against the interests of the Man in Black, as I will explain.

Christian Shephard appeared to Michael on the freighter, to Locke in Jacob's cabin, and to Sun at the Dharma barracks. In none of these apparitions was there any indication of judgment or coercion. One could certainly argue that if the apparition was due to the Man in Black a note of coercion could be posited. However, I find no direct evidence of any attempt to coerce in these apparitions of Christian Shephard.

The strength of the coercion attempt in apparitions to Ben, Mr. Eko, and Richard was augmented tremendously by the Smoke Monster's decision to appear as a loved one. How could Mr. Eko ever say no to his brother, who had always been there for him, and had been a true priest? How could Richard ever doubt any words that came from the mouth of his Constant, Isabella? In fact, given a choice, why would the Smoke Monster ever choose to appear as anyone other than a person dear to the victim he wished to mislead or seduce into an action benefitting the Man in Black?

In the case of his apparitions to Michael, Locke, and Sun, he chose a form that was unknown to all of them.

[Episode 4.11, in Jacob's cabin]
Locke: Who are you?
Man: I'm Christian.

[Episode 4.14. On the freighter, after Michael runs out of coolant to inhibit C4 explosion, a man appears behind the table of C4]
CHRISTIAN: You can go now, Michael.
MICHAEL: Who are you?
[Loud explosion]

[Episode 5.09, at the Dharma barracks, a door creaks]
MAN: Hello.
LAPIDUS: Who the hell are you?
MAN: My name's Christian.

If the Smoke Monster's intention had been coercion, why did he not appear to Locke as Helen, or as Anthony Cooper? If he had wished to influence Michael, why didn't he appear as Walter, or as Michael's deceased ex-wife, Susan?

Clearly, Christian Shephard's apparition to Michael had nothing to do with any type of coercive activity. Michael was a split-second away from dying, yet whatever entity appeared to Michael in Christian Shephard's form thought it essential to inform Michael that his work was done, that he could go. Michael could not perform any physical activity in the split-second of life remaining to him. Why was it important for Christian Shephard's apparition to interact with Michael?

I cannot think of a single reason the Man in Black would have had to appear in such a way to Michael. In fact, the presence of the Smoke Monster in an enclosed location just before an explosion would seem to violate one of the best-understood rules of Smoke Monster navigation: He couldn't deal with high-energy sound. Whether it was the sound energy of the sonic fence or the sound of exploding dynamite, the Smoke Monster had an extreme aversion or complete inability to deal with it.

If Christian's apparition was not due to the Smoke Monster, who would have caused it? Apparently it was a person carrying some authority, or believed himself to bear unusual authority, since he elevated himself to the position of judging whether or not Michael had completed his task.

Michael tried to kill himself in New York—twice. Both suicide attempts failed. Tom Friendly explained it to him:

MICHAEL: Go away!
[Michael turns to walk away.]

TOM: I got some bad news for you, amigo. You can't kill yourself. The Island won't let you!
MICHAEL: (Panting) What'd you say?
TOM: No matter how bad you want to, no matter how many different ways you try, it won't happen.

It was the Island that decided Michael had to return, to redeem himself. He accomplished that redemption by killing Widmore's mercenaries on the freighter. If the Island was the entity that forced him back to complete his work, it only makes sense that it was the Island that decided he had accomplished that task. "You can go now, Michael," was the Island informing Michael that he had completed his work.

The entity that appeared to Michael on the freighter, a split-second before the boat was blown to bits, was not the Man in Black. It was not Jacob. The entity that appeared to Michael was the Island.

The Island took the form of Christian Shephard on the freighter.

The entity that appeared to Sun and Lapidus at the Dharma barracks likewise was not in the employ of the Man in Black. The being that helped Sun reunite with Jin was neither the Man in Black nor Jacob. It was the Island.

The entity that appeared to Locke, both in Jacob's cabin and under the Orchid Station was not coercing Locke into any action that could have helped the Man in Black. Rather, the being was helping Locke to bring back Jack, which would mean the end of the Man in Black. The entity sitting in Jacob's cabin and holding the lantern at the time wheel was, again, the Island.

The Messenger

[In the Sideways World]
KATE: Who died?
DESMOND: A man named Christian Shephard.
KATE [chuckling]: Christian Shephard? Seriously?
DESMOND: Seriously.

Kate's reaction to the name "Christian Shephard" is telling. It's the reaction we should have had. Were the writers serious? Did they intend for us to understand Christian Shephard as a divine messenger? As a pastor or priest? As a symbolic representation of the Good Shepherd? There is really no good way of stating Christian Shephard's exact role. As Desmond was wont to say in the Sideways World, "Something like that."

The Smoke Monster appropriated Christian's form, but on those occasions when this occurred, the Man in Black had no say in the proceedings. The

Island was broken, and one of the ways in which it was broken was in being unable to adopt human form without the Man in Black having some type of presence, perhaps as the entity that allowed the appropriation of a form. "Help me," the Island said the first time Locke visited Jacob's cabin. The Island was begging for help because the presence of the Man in Black at the Source had profaned the water and the Light, and created a human/Island hybrid entity that we perceived as a moving column of black smoke. The Island was connected to a dark entity that prevented the Island from carrying out its true purpose, which was the guarding of humanity.

Sometimes the hybrid didn't even have a will of its own. It was regularly summoned by people like Ben, for instance, to destroy or judge. The strange human/Island hybrid judged according to Island rules, but it did so in a form foreign to the Island's inner constituency.

The appearance on the Island of a figure key to the emotional/psychological/spiritual development of a potential man of faith was key. In the precious moments after the crash of Flight 815, the Island took on Christian's form and called out to Christian's agent, Vincent.

CHRISTIAN: Good boy. Yes. [He leans down and pets him.] I need you to go find my son. He's over there in that bamboo forest, unconscious. I need you to go wake him up. Okay? Go on.
[Vincent whines and runs off.]
CHRISTIAN: He has work to do.

Only the Island could assign work, or decide an agent's work (like Michael's) was done. The Island knew that Jack's assignment was the most difficult of all, and would require years of preparation. Jack would need help, and he would have to be disposed toward accepting that help. As Christian said, "Nobody does it alone, Jack. You needed all of them, and they needed you." Perhaps the Island played a role in bringing about the critical sequence of events that led to Jack's declaration on the sixth day of their Island odyssey:

"It's been six days and we're all still waiting. Waiting for someone to come. But what if they don't? We have to stop waiting. We need to start figuring things out... Every man for himself is not going to work. It's time to start organizing. We need to figure out how we're going to survive here... Last week most of us were strangers, but we're all here now. And God knows how long we're going to be here. But if we can't live together, we're going to die alone."

With nudges from John Locke and Christian, Jack was on his way. At critical times over the next three years, the Island took the form of Christian, acting as messenger in one instance, as guide in another, assisting everyone who needed help so that Jack's work could be completed.

In the end, Jack was correct in believing that Christian was the key to his life's struggles. It was with Christian, his father, he would have to reconcile before he could move on. It was with Christian, the Island's messenger, he would have to interact in order to free the Island from its connection to the Man in Black. It was Christian, finally, who opened for Jack and his friends the grand portals to the Light that would allow them to move on.

The very first mystery posed by LOST was the identity of Christian Shephard. We should have known that it would be the final mystery to be resolved. When Jack moved his hands along the closed casket inside the church, we knew he would open it. We also knew what he would find inside: nothing. His father was not dead, because his father was carrier of the faith and hope and love that were always the key to finding oneself together with others. Live together, in the end, meant that Christian would never be found to have died alone. He was the Good Shepherd to Jack and everyone else in his flock. He was the Island's representative, the representative of everything that is good, everything that allows good people to bring an end to the state of being Lost.

"And once they are able to metaphorically find themselves in their lives again, they will be able to physically find themselves in the world again." And so they did. They left the Island and found themselves by finding each other.

Christian left us with two important thoughts that I carry with me now that the series has ended. We need to move on, but we do so in a place that is without time. We also need to do something very much connected with time, something that places dreams and memories in their proper context, anchors us in our present reality, and makes every experience alive with meaning and fresh with excitement and relevance to us, our struggles, and our loves. Above all else, he said, we need "to remember."

Here then, in volumes lovingly crafted from my memory of the best series ever produced for television, my contribution to Christian's call. When I find myself in a place without time, I too will move on. But until then, I will follow Christian Shephard, and I will remember.

Pearson Moore
June 2011

Other Works by Pearson Moore

Cartier's Ring: A Novel of Canada

Direwolves and Dragons

Intolerable Loyalty: The Invasion of Canada, 1775

LOST Humanity: The Mythology and Themes of LOST

About the novel:

She is healer, hunter, warrior. Her strength will inspire generations. Her
courage will found a nation. Experience history as never before. See the birth of
Canada through the eyes of the woman who lived and breathed it: Myeerah of
Hawk Clan, Matriarch to a nation.

"Only men have dreams such as this, not girls. Not the daughter of a slave." So
begins an adventure that will span eight decades across two continents. From
swashbuckling pirates on the high seas to the slave traders of Mexico, to the
genocidal wars of North America, Pearson Moore engages from the very first
page, using a vibrant prose style that captivates the imagination, and the heart.

Twelve years of intensive research went into building the rich historical
background for Cartier's Ring, including dozens of trips to Québec, Montréal,
Upstate New York, and Midland, Ontario. But it is the emotional depth of
Myeerah's story that brings the novel to life. You will feel her pain as she is
beaten and enslaved, touch her tear-streaked face as she witnesses the ritual
torture and execution of her brother, share in her joy as she overcomes
deprivation and starvation, and cheer when she vanquishes her enemies.

Cartier's Ring

A NOVEL OF CANADA

Pearson Moore

Cartier's Ring is available now at major bookstores.

The only Game of Thrones companion book you'll ever need.

GAME OF THRONES
Season One Essays

Pearson Moore

COMING SOON!

Honour. Freedom. Loyalty.
Yearnings of the heart, defined in the crucible of war.

Intolerable Loyalty: The Invasion of Canada, 1775

COMING SOON!

About LOST Humanity

This is LOST as you've never experienced it before. Pearson Moore goes to the heart of LOST, uncovering and explaining the fascinating core concepts: Faith versus Science, the Numbers, the nature of good and evil, and the struggle between free will and destiny. He will lead you to ideas and conclusions you never imagined, opening the world of LOST in fresh and exciting ways.

Whether you understood LOST or were completely baffled, whether you loved it or hated it, Moore will show you concepts and ways of thinking about LOST you will find nowhere else.

Moore's innovative thoughts and vibrant prose will keep you engaged as he explores the Island and its characters. He approaches LOST from four "nonlinear" points of view: Disorientation, Metadrama, Literary Analysis, and Chaos Theory. This is in-depth analysis that never lets go, keeping you immersed in the LOST world from cover to cover.

There's no filler here. No interviews with stars about the cars they drive or the planes they fly. No weird theories. Just solid, thoroughly-researched, rapid-fire analysis from one of the most cited LOST authorities on the Internet. You may feel exhausted after a chapter. You may be shocked. You may become upset. But you will never be bored.

The heart of the book begins with Chapter Ten. It is here that Moore unleashes the four "nonlinear" concepts to reveal the hidden meanings of LOST. He discusses the need for disorientation, and how this is essential to understanding LOST. He proposes the idea that LOST is metadrama, and he explains how understanding LOST in this way is useful to unraveling its secrets. He makes fresh use of literary theory, in ways never before applied to LOST.

Finally, Moore brings an astounding, completely new perspective on television analysis with his concept of the Strange Attractor, an idea borrowed from chaos theory. It is here that Moore's analysis shines, allowing a depth of understanding never before achieved.

For less than the cost of a cup of coffee, you can explore the stimulating world of LOST with an animated, engaging, thought-provoking guide. The Island awaits. Prepare to get LOST.

LOST Humanity is available in major bookstores.

Made in the USA
Lexington, KY
12 October 2012